RENEWALS 458-4574

WITHDRAWN
UTSA LIBRARIES

International Political Economy Series

General Editor: **Timothy M. Shaw**, Professor of Commonwealth Governance and Development, and Director of the Institute of Commonwealth Studies, School of Advanced Study, University of London

Titles include:

Hans Abrahamsson
UNDERSTANDING WORLD ORDER AND STRUCTURAL CHANGE
Poverty, Conflict and the Global Arena

Sandra Braman (*editor*)
THE EMERGENT GLOBAL INFORMATION POLICY REGIME

James Busumtwi-Sam and Laurent Dobuzinskis
TURBULENCE AND NEW DIRECTION IN GLOBAL POLITICAL ECONOMY

Elizabeth De Boer-Ashworth
THE GLOBAL POLITICAL ECONOMY AND POST-1989 CHANGE
The Place of the Central European Transition

Bill Dunn
GLOBAL RESTRUCTURING AND THE POWER OF LABOUR

Myron J. Frankman
WORLD DEMOCRATIC FEDERALISM
Peace and Justice Indivisible

Helen A. Garten
US FINANCIAL REGULATION AND THE LEVEL PLAYING FIELD

Barry K. Gills (*editor*)
GLOBALIZATION AND THE POLITICS OF RESISTANCE

Richard Grant and John Rennie Short (*editors*)
GLOBALIZATION AND THE MARGINS

Graham Harrison (*editor*)
GLOBAL ENCOUNTERS
International Political Economy, Development and Globalization

Patrick Hayden and Chamsy el-Ojeili (*editors*)
CONFRONTING GLOBALIZATION
Humanity, Justice and the Renewal of Politics

Axel Hülsemeyer (*editor*)
GLOBALIZATION IN THE TWENTY-FIRST CENTURY
Convergence or Divergence?

Helge Hveem and Kristen Nordhaug (*editors*)
PUBLIC POLICY IN THE AGE OF GLOBALIZATION
Responses to Environmental and Economic Crises

Takashi Inoguchi
GLOBAL CHANGE
A Japanese Perspective

Jomo K.S. and Shyamala Nagaraj (*editors*)
GLOBALIZATION VERSUS DEVELOPMENT

Dominic Kelly and Wyn Grant (*editors*)
THE POLITICS OF INTERNATIONAL TRADE IN THE 21st CENTURY
Actors, Issues and Regional Dynamics

Craig N. Murphy (*editor*)
EGALITARIAN POLITICS IN THE AGE OF GLOBALIZATION

George Myconos
THE GLOBALIZATIONS OF ORGANIZED LABOUR
1945–2005

John Nauright and Kimberly S. Schimmel (*editors*)
THE POLITICAL ECONOMY OF SPORT

Michael Niemann
A SPATIAL APPROACH TO REGIONALISM IN THE GLOBAL ECONOMY

Morten Ougaard
THE GLOBALIZATION OF POLITICS
Power, Social Forces and Governance

Markus Perkmann and Ngai-Ling Sum
GLOBALIZATION, REGIONALIZATION AND CROSS–BORDER REGIONS

Leonard Seabrooke
US POWER IN INTERNATIONAL FINANCE
The Victory of Dividends

Timothy J. Sinclair and Kenneth P. Thomas (*editors*)
STRUCTURE AND AGENCY IN INTERNATIONAL CAPITAL MOBILITY

Fredrik Söderbaum and Timothy M. Shaw (*editors*)
THEORIES OF NEW REGIONALISM
A Palgrave Reader

Amy Verdun
EUROPEAN RESPONSES TO GLOBALIZATION AND FINANCIAL
MARKET INTEGRATION

International Political Economy Series
Series Standing Order ISBN 0–333–71708–2 hardcover
Series Standing Order ISBN 0–333–71110–6 paperback
(*outside North America only*)

You can receive future titles in this series as they are published by placing a standing order. Please contact your bookseller or, in case of difficulty, write to us at the address below with your name and address, the title of the series and one of the ISBNs quoted above.

Customer Services Department, Macmillan Distribution Ltd, Houndmills, Basingstoke, Hampshire RG21 6XS, England

© George Myconos, 2005

All rights reserved. No reproduction, copy or transmission of this publication may be made without written permission.

No paragraph of this publication may be reproduced, copied or transmitted save with written permission or in accordance with the provisions of the Copyright, Designs and Patents Act 1988, or under the terms of any licence permitting limited copying issued by the Copyright Licensing Agency, 90 Tottenham Court Road, London W1T 4LP.

Any person who does any unauthorized act in relation to this publication may be liable to criminal prosecution and civil claims for damages.

The author has asserted his right to be identified as the author of this work in accordance with the Copyright, Designs and Patents Act 1988.

First published in 2005 by
PALGRAVE MACMILLAN
Houndmills, Basingstoke, Hampshire RG21 6XS and
175 Fifth Avenue, New York, N.Y. 10010
Companies and representatives throughout the world.

PALGRAVE MACMILLAN is the global academic imprint of the Palgrave Macmillan division of St. Martin's Press, LLC and of Palgrave Macmillan Ltd. Macmillan® is a registered trademark in the United States, United Kingdom and other countries. Palgrave is a registered trademark in the European Union and other countries.

ISBN-13: 978–1–4039–9338–0 hardback
ISBN-10: 1–4039–9338–6 hardback

This book is printed on paper suitable for recycling and made from fully managed and sustained forest sources.

A catalogue record for this book is available from the British Library.

Library of Congress Cataloging-in-Publication Data

Myconos, George, 1959–
   The globalizations of organized labour : 1945–2005 /
George Myconos.
     p. cm.—(International political economy series)
   Includes bibliographical references and index.
   ISBN 1–4039–9338–6 (cloth)
    1. Labor unions. 2. International labor activities. 3. Globalization. I. Title.
  II. International political economy series (Palgrave Macmillan (Firm))
HD6483.M897 2005
331.88′091—dc22   2005043426

10 9 8 7 6 5 4 3 2
14 13 12 11 10 09 08 07 06

Printed and bound in Great Britain by
Antony Rowe Ltd, Chippenham and Eastbourne

The Globalizations of Organized Labour
1945–2005

George Myconos

Contents

Acknowledgements vi

List of Abbreviations vii

Introduction 1

Part I – 1945–72 19
Prevailing structural imperatives 19

1 1945–72 – Internal Change: Antagonism and
   Shallow Integration 25

2 1945–72 – External Change: Incorporation and
   Statist Internationalism 47

Part II – 1972–89 67
Prevailing structural imperatives 67

3 1972–89 – Internal Change: Expansion and Uneasy
   Integration 74

4 1972–89 – External Change: From Incorporation
   to Partial Disengagement 95

Part III – 1989–2005 117
Prevailing structural imperatives 117

5 1989–2005 – Internal Change: Consolidation
   and Integration 123

6 1989–2005 – External Change: Eviction and Insinuation 140

Conclusion: The Past and Future Globalizations of
Organized Labour 149

Notes 158

Bibliography 189

Index 202

Acknowledgements

My heartfelt thanks go to Professor Paul James, of the Globalism Institute, RMIT University, Melbourne. I am privileged to have received guidance from this remarkable man, and to have benefited from his generosity and insight. This book would be much diminished without Paul's assistance.

Professor Joe Camilleri, of LaTrobe University, Melbourne, also warrants special mention. As an irrepressible activist thinker, intellectual, and teacher, Joe continues to inspire and amaze.

I am also deeply indebted to my *companēra*, Lesley Walker. Her humour, patience, affection – not to mention her no-nonsense feedback – has been invaluable. My mother, Fanny, provided unwavering and much needed support over the years taken to produce this book, as did my special friend and brother, Jim.

Finally, I would like to express my appreciation to Mieke Ijzermans from the International Institute of Social History, Amsterdam. The hospitality and assistance provided by her and the Institute staff made my visit to that glorious city a memorable one.

List of Abbreviations

AFL-CIO   American Federation of Labor-Congress of Industrial Organizations. This is the principal national trade union organization in the United States.
AFRO   African Regional Organization. This is the African regional body of the International Confederation of Free Trade Unions.
AIFLD   American Institute for Free Labor Development. This is one of the offshoot bodies of the American Federation of Labor-Congress of Industrial Organizations.
APRO   Asian and Pacific Regional Organization. This is the Asia-Pacific regional body of the International Confederation of Free Trade Unions.
ARO   Asian Regional Organization. This is the first incarnation of the ICFTU's Asian and Pacific Regional Organization.
AUCCTU   All Union Central Council of Trade Unions. This was the principal national trade union organization of the Soviet Union.
CGIL   Confederazione Generale Italiana del Lavoro, or General Confederation of Italian Labour.
CGT   Confédération Générale du Travail, or General Federation of Labour (France).
COSATU   Congress of South African Trade Unions.
CTM   Confederación de Trabajordores de Mexico.
DGB   Deutscher Gewerkschaftsbund, or German Confederation of Trade Unions.
ETUC   European Trade Union Confederation.
EWC   European Works Councils. Products of the 1993 Maastricht Treaty, these are worker–business consultative bodies that multinationals are obligated to maintain in their European operations.
ICFTU   International Confederation of Free Trade Unions.
ITS   International Trade Secretariats – industry-specific transnational confederations. They are now known as the 'Global Union Federations'.

LO — Landsorganisationen i Sverige, or Swedish Confederation of Trade Union.
ORIT — Organizacion Regional Interamericana de Trabajadores, or Inter-American Regional Organization of Workers. This is the Latin American regional offshoot of the International Confederation of Free Trade Unions.
RENGO — Confederation of Public Sector Trade Unions. The principal national body of Japan.
TUAC — Trade Union Advisory Committee. This is an intermediary body representing trade union interests within the Organization for Economic Cooperation and Development.
TUC — Trades Union Congress. This is the principal national trade union organization in the United Kingdom.
WCL — World Confederation of Labour.
WFTU — World Federation of Trade Unions. This had two incarnations with the first lasting until 1949, and the second to the present (now moribund).

Introduction

This book explores the labyrinthine world of trade union relations and assesses the significance of change in the configuration and disposition of those bodies that form, collectively, organized labour's transnational advocacy network. More specifically, we address the following question: *how, and to what extent, has the transnational network of labour organizations globalized since 1945?* While elaboration of this question and the assumptions that underpin it will follow, it is enough to say here that this exercise entails an analysis of how this dispersed political community is integrated across national borders, and how its relationship to the state is changing.

The most important finding to emerge from this exploration is that even though this network has grown more integrated and globally oriented by the decade, it has remained in many ways wedded to forms of political organization premised upon the authority of the state. Expressed differently, the globalization of organized labour has not entailed an estrangement from the state. Indeed, organized labour remains preoccupied with what will be referred to as the 'state-mediated political realm'. The transnational network, I will suggest, simultaneously looks to expand and integrate across national boundaries, while striving to insinuate itself within established locales of authority. But I am aware that such notions, phrased as they are, remain somewhat vague and are in need of clarification. To this end, we digress for a moment and engage with two related narratives: what might be termed the *labourist* and the *globalization* narratives. This will help set the scene for the study and also provide an understanding of the theoretical and empirical dimensions of the research that follows. Our detour commences with an overview of the labourist narrative.

For some years, trade unionism has been considered by many to be synonymous with atrophy, reformism, and complicity. Writing in 1986, Alain Touraine proposed that 'movements such as unionism have a life history: infancy, youth, maturity, old age and death', and he implied then that trade unionism was indeed nearing its twilight years. Elsewhere, Touraine suggested that while 'trade unionism was, at a given time, a social movement; it is now a political force that is necessarily subordinated to political parties and to governments'.[1] To a great extent, such jaundiced views assumed common sense status; so much so that for a time 'trade unions' all but disappeared from the index pages of publications across the social sciences, especially – and most bizarrely – from disciplines dedicated to the study of social movements. In recent years, however, trade union politics – especially as it is manifest in cross-border activism – is once again generating interest. Many labourist accounts are now contemplating the ways in which organized labour has responded to the forces of 'globalization'. In their own ways labour-oriented scholars from across disciplinary divides, as well as practitioners, are addressing the themes evoked by the title of a recent publication, *Rising From the Ashes?: Labor in the Age of 'Global' Capitalism.*[2] Some would say that we are witnessing a transformation wherein labour organizations are increasingly seen to be 'going global'. At first glance this is a curious notion because the trade union movement has always been global. Since the 1860s it has sustained a network of confederations – purporting to represent millions of trade unionists – that have traditionally extended their reach across continents, state boundaries, and industrial sectors. In this sense the movement was 'globalized' well before the term became fashionable. Thus, when commentators contemplate a possible sea-change in the movement's orientation, they are pointing towards something more than organizational change.

As well as reflecting on the prevailing theories and strategies underpinning new forms of cross-border activism, many writers are considering the obstacles to contemporary forms of labour internationalism, and why some elements within the transnational network are more amenable to change than are others.[3] Some also contemplate the role of organized labour in emerging forms of regional and global governance, and the extent to which labour continues to rely upon the state to mediate relations with corporate actors, and those within the world of commerce in general.[4] Other research analyses the ways in which trade unions, at all levels, are increasingly engaged in 'organizing the landscape'.[5] This refers to the ways in which organized labour is able to shape the social, economic, and political settings it inhabits.

Implicit in most of this research is an acknowledgment that organized labour constitutes a transnational political community, albeit one that is extremely nebulous. And yet throughout these analyses it also becomes apparent that the language needed to understand change in all aspects of the network's existence seems to be lacking. While the above analyses are evocative, they only give partial and fragmented insights into this community's various layers of existence and interactions. They provide specialized, yet limited, understanding of how this transnational community is constituted, what holds it together, and in what ways it has changed orientation over an extended period of time. Where, then, might we find a language that is able to identify the deeper currents and trajectories at work in this area of politics? For further guidance, we might look to the burgeoning literature on globalization.

A great deal of this writing can be regarded as structure-focused. By this I mean that writing on the subject is concerned with the dramatic change wrought on contemporary life by economic, technological, political, and ideological imperatives over which agents have little control. In this sense, writing on globalization often refers to the maelstrom of influences, pressures, and images that are imposed from without, and that must somehow be endured, accommodated, or resisted. Central to all this is the notion of immediacy; that is, of the compression of time and space as it pertains to interaction and engagement with the distant. Opinions here are often divided over whether such structural imperatives are epoch-changing (for better or worse) or whether their effects are exaggerated. Irrespective of opinions, such writing invariably focuses attention on changes that are forced on traditional centers of authority, as well as on established societal forms. This tendency is manifest, for instance, in the ever-expanding literature focusing on the fate of the state, and the tenuous nature of its conceptual bedrock, sovereignty.[6]

Of central importance to what might be regarded as agency-focused globalization analyses is how agents' relationships with these centres of authority are changing given the prevailing structural imperatives. Often identifiable by phrases such as 'globalization-from-below', agency-focused approaches usually entail analysis of the ways in which the most vulnerable actors react to – indeed, resist – economic, technological, political, and ideological forces bearing down upon them.[7] In essence, a correspondence is established in such writing between agents and structures. Such theorizing is increasingly evident in the discipline of *international relations* and its related fields. It is also featuring as a common theme in some of the more recent contributions to the labourist theorizing mentioned earlier. Agency-focused globalization analyses are relevant to studies of class conflict, and of resistance to structural violence in general. They are especially interesting because they often focus on the ways in which agents – in times of upheaval – manoeuvre in the face of established or emerging centers of power, authority, and control. They also prompt us to contemplate the ways in which agents re-orient themselves in relation to the particular – whether manifest in the locale of the state, or in the more abstract form of the nation – as well as to how they interact with the distant and the unfamiliar. Moreover, agency-focused analyses provide a convenient link to research that explores the emergence of what has come to be known as the *global civil society*.

Of what relevance are these labourist and globalization narratives, and how can they be used to clarify earlier comments made in relation to the globalization of organized labour? Derived from these narratives are a number of theoretical assumptions that will underpin this study. Without pre-empting the material laid out in the methodology section that follows, it is important to now explain the nature of these assumptions, and how they relate to the question and proposition featured at the outset of this introductory section.

First, these narratives show that, notwithstanding quite profound internal heterogeneity, the transnational network of labour organizations can indeed be regarded as a distinct political community, and one that has been in a state of flux for many decades. Second, these narratives suggest that a key to understanding the ways in which actors of this sort react to structural imperatives is to understand how their relationships with traditional centers of authority have been affected. Finally, these narratives show that the malleability of the concept of 'globalization' opens up interesting possibilities for studies of this kind. Specifically, I believe they show that it is legitimate to employ the term 'globalize' as a verb; that is, as a *practice* engaged in by actors. In other words, globalization can be used, on the one hand, to refer to the ways and extent to which agents become globally integrated; and on the other, to their relative estrangement from traditional centres of authority. By incorporating these important assumptions it is then possible to speak plausibly of change throughout a diverse and extended political community across time and space. Such an approach enables the research to focus on what Walker refers to as the 'politics of connection' and the 'politics of movement'.[8] The former refers to the significance of both internal and external interactions, while the latter is concerned with the fluid nature of such relations and practices. Both, according to Walker, relate to change as it occurs across the political and civil divide.

With all this in mind, we can now return to the question posed at the outset – *how, and to what extent, has the transnational network of labour organizations globalized?* As already noted, this question turns on the notions of integration across national boundaries, and of changing relations with established forms of political authority. Throughout this study we will reflect on these notions by focusing on indicators such as organizational configuration, prevailing interests and ideologies and, most importantly, on the network's disposition towards the state.

The preceding reflections also allow for greater elaboration of the proposition made at the outset. What this proposition contends, in essence, is that the vast transnational constellation of trade union organizations has, in certain ways, become more integrated and outward-looking; an orientation founded on a growing consensus over a range of interests and ideologies. Yet somewhat paradoxically, the globalization of organized labour has not necessarily undermined the network's fixation with forms of governance and political organization premised upon the authority of the state. This, as I will point out in concluding reflections, may not in itself and in all instances be detrimental for advocates of labour rights worldwide. Indeed, we will see that labour's preoccupation with national, regional, and international regimes founded upon the authority of states will in all probability open new terrains of engagement. Interactions here will invariably entail forms of cross-border mobilizations involving alliances struck between labour organizations on the one hand, and on the other, oppositional civil realm actors that are less enamoured of the state.

The method outlined

This project requires a methodology that can shed light on the network's internal and external relations as they have evolved within distinct historical periods. This means, initially, being able to identify change within various ontological dimensions intrinsic to the political community in question. It means having the ability to give definition to the organizational configuration of the network, as well as to internal relationships, interests, and ideological dispositions. Much – though not all – of what we learn about the network's integration would be gained through these insights. The method must also enable us to map change in the network's external relations. This means being able to map the historical evolution of a movement that – notwithstanding its organizational looseness – straddles the national and global, as well as the political and civil realms. In this instance, the method must enable us to plot the intensity of engagement with actors of the political realm; that is, with states and their collective manifestations, on both the national and global planes. From this we would learn much about the network's propensity to bypass traditional centers of authority. Such a method will help identify changes in the ways in which the transnational labour movement has integrated, and the ways in which it has asserted its autonomy in relation to the state. In short, it will identify the ways in which organized labour has globalized over a period spanning almost 60 years.

Outlined next is the methodological framework that will guide the study through to its conclusion. (Figure I.1 is designed to assist the reader through this introduction to the method).[9] In addition, this guide introduces the reader to the categories of existence and interaction that will be explored in due course. In essence this will involve an examination of what will be referred to as the movement's internal and external *dimensions of change*. These dimensions will themselves be partitioned in ways that allow for a still more comprehensive analysis. Thus, the internal dimension of change will comprise organizational and integrative subcategories; while the external dimension of change will focus on the state-mediated political realm, itself divided into national and global subcategories. The following elaborates on these dimensions and categories.

The internal organizational dimension of change

The research on internal organizational change entails a relatively straight forward narrative, not unlike conventional accounts of organized labour's historical evolution. It initially focuses on the institutional configuration of the peak confederations. Analysis on this 'horizontal' plane of organizational change gauges the extent to which organized labour has over the decades attained an institutional presence beyond the European setting. Here we examine the organizational shape of the network of labour bodies that purport to represent trade unionists of all cultures and continents. This stage of the analysis also entails an examination of organizational change as it has evolved on a 'vertical' plane. This means giving definition to the regional and national bodies that – ostensibly – link peak confederations to nationally bound trade unions. This analysis of the organizational form of labour worldwide – on both horizontal and vertical planes – will help us understand the ways, and extent to which, the movement has expanded since the mid-twentieth century. In sum, change in this internal organizational dimension will represent one of a number of indicators of organized labour's globalization.

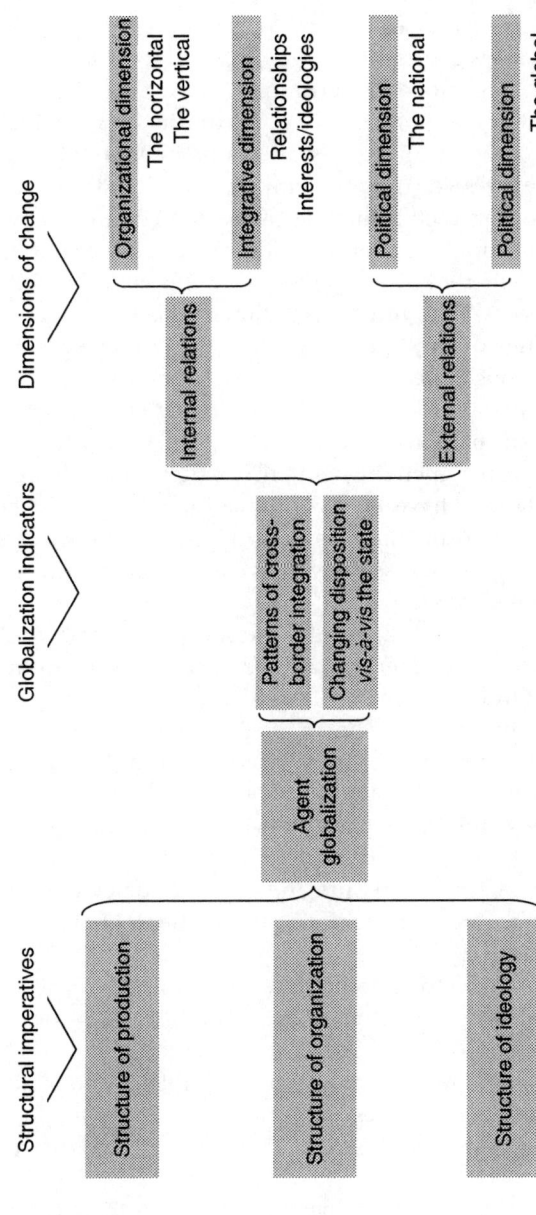

Figure I.1 A thematic guide to the globalizations of organized labour

The internal-integrative dimension of change: relationships, interests, and ideology

The notion of *integration* is used here to convey the ways in which the network is bound together. Once again we will need to rely on subcategories of this integrative dimension. The first of these will be the *relational* aspect of integration. This refers to the ways in which relationships between leadership figures and constituents are mediated, experienced, and expressed. Here the emphasis is placed on degrees of intimacy, the extent to which relationships are filtered through evolving forms of communication, and the growing reliance on electronic and symbolic forms of representation. As this study engages more fully with this relational aspect of the integrative dimension, the reader will be introduced to a range of concepts designed to better convey the nature of the transformations noted. For now it is enough to say that this aspect of the internal aims to assess change in the ways in which the network's constituent parts correspond and relate. Here the objective is to highlight the ways in which the network has been integrated, and the ways in which relations have been sustained across national borders over an extended period of time. Such an approach can also assist in gauging what Scholte refers to as the 'relative uncoupling of ... relations from territorial frameworks'.[10]

Another subcategory of the internal dimension of integrative change will be concerned with the *interests* and *ideologies* that underpin intra-network relations. Interests are considered to be those issues that are given highest priority at any given time. They are important because they give some indication of whether, for instance, the movement is orientated towards the particularistic needs of nation-based constituents, or whether greater emphasis is placed on universalizing, rights-based, advocacy. Expressed differently, intra-network tensions and discord can be assessed by considering the nature and extent of divergent interests. This is important if we are to make plausible judgments about the extent of intra-network integration.

Mapping change within the internal-integrative dimension also entails assessing the role of ideology. The aim here is to give definition to the ideological complexion of the movement. A method will be employed that identifies the relative importance and interplay of four ideological ensembles or tendencies. These are categorized using the following umbrella terms: *conservative, instrumental, developmental,* and *emancipatory* worldviews.

The conservative category encompasses worldviews that are committed to the defence of traditional centers of authority: for example, the government, the state, or the church. Essentially, ideologies falling within the rubric of conservatism have in common a system maintaining orientation. The instrumentalist category consists of those ideologies committed to calculating as well as technocratic programmes designed to attain economic and political power. More often, the term 'instrumentalism' will be used in reference to worldviews that embrace radical forms of economic liberalism, ideas promoting limitless economic expansion, and productivism. Closely related to this category is developmentalism. It encompasses such notions as modernization, Keynesianism, corporatism, the commitment to progress and, more broadly, a growth orientated consensus. By contrast, the emancipatory category of ideas includes such radical class-based doctrines as anarchism, syndicalism, socialism, anti-imperialism, and communism. We also include here ameliorative forms of reformist collectivism such as social-democracy and Fabianism. Non-class-based worldviews that oppose oppression – most notably, feminism, environmentalism, and anti-colonialism – are also considered here to belong to the emancipatory ensemble of ideas. In short, the distinguishing characteristic of this category is its emphasis on collectivist approaches that are sustained by a liberatory ethos.

In general, this approach to mapping ideological trends proceeds under the assumption that adherents to all the worldviews mentioned see them as 'universals'; that is, as ideological systems and programs that ought to apply across time and space, irrespective of context. This approach also assumes that while such layers of ideas are ever-present, they combine in different measure and are never in a static relationship to each other. Nor are these layers fixed in a hierarchical relationship; rather, they are woven together and often bear traces and residues of each others' inner logics.[11] And, of course, there often also exists great tension between and within these layers. Overall, the object of this exercise is to consider the combinations of ideas that hold sway at any given time. Coupled with the previous reflections on interests, this will provide invaluable insights into the nature of network integration within a given period.

External dimension of change

The second broad sphere of interaction to be explored is that relating to the *external-political* dimension of change. This is an important exercise because by mapping such engagement we can further assess the ways in which the aforementioned aspects of internal organization and internal integration manifest themselves in a wider context. The principal characteristic of this dimension is that it is premised upon the authority of the state. Looking at organized labour's engagement within this dimension highlights the extent to which it assumes a statist orientation.

This immediately begs clarification. The term 'statism' carries with it a great many negative connotations. For instance, when used by those of the libertarian right it refers to a pernicious intrusion of the state, and a concomitant negation of the individual's freedom. Similarly, in the parlance of the anarchist left, statism is synonymous with a self-serving concentration and corruption of power through the organs of the state, such that it destroys the emancipatory impulse inherent in class struggle. From an altogether different vantage point – from the perspective of some social scientists – statism represents both an ontological and epistemological impediment. Here 'statist analyses' can only lead to a highly distorted reading of social, economic, and political relations.

As far as it is possible, throughout this book we will rely on an understanding of labour's (fluctuating) commitment to the state that bears few of the value judgements inherent in these interpretations. Hence, the subsequent analysis of this external political dimension entails looking at the extent to which organized labour displays – to *varying* levels of intensity – the following inclinations: a disposition that privileges order – as defined by governments – over transformative structural change; a deference to the needs of the state as these pertain to matters of instrumental and strategic interests; and a disposition that buttresses the authority and integrity of the state. Moreover, such an approach requires that we contemplate dispositions that hold to the belief that most – if not all – social, economic, and political needs can be attained through a certain deference to the authority of government. Here the idea of the state dominates the imagination, and determines conceptions of what is possible.

In more concrete terms, the external-political dimension encompasses individual states as well as those intergovernmental organizations and assemblies that are invested with the legal-rational authority of the community of states.[12] A distinction will be made between the *national* plane – that which is bounded by the state – and the *global* plane; the latter representing the site of intergovernmental organization activity and of geopolitics in general. Such a schema is appropriate because it provides a framework with which to assess labour–state relations. On the national level these range from legal and quasi-legal corporatist arrangements, to those symbiotic and functional partnerships that seek to enhance the strategic interests of the state. On the global level they include interaction through the consultative mechanisms made available by a plethora of intergovernmental organizations. In sum, by viewing organized labour from this vantage point we can ascertain whether its centre of gravity in relation to the state has shifted during the period under review.

Prevailing structural imperatives

Finally, a plausible account of globalizing practices – and the complexities inherent – must take into account structural imperatives shaping the landscape inhabited by all agents within a given period. Such imperatives may derive from cultural, ideological, technological, economic, political, and environmental sources, and result in the deeply embedded patterns of behaviour and institutional forms that often act as determinants across all spheres of human interaction. To acknowledge the most important of these – at least for trade unions – we will review changes in the prevailing structural imperatives related to *production, organization*, and *ideology*.

The *structure of production* refers to the processes used to produce and distribute goods and services in a given period. An account of this structural imperative highlights changes to production processes that affect all actors in a historical epoch marked by integration within a capitalist world economy. Of relevance here, for example, is the growth of offshore production, capital mobility, the shift in the West from labour-intensive to capital-intensive production methods, and the emergence of finance and service sectors. Of concern also in such analysis is the shift in the developing world from subsistence agricultural production to urbanized labour-intensive manufacturing and assembly processes. More broadly, a focus on this structural imperative draws our attention to the nature of societal forms and communicative relationships that come to the fore, given these methods of production. This, in turn, provides insights into the ways in which actors are likely to perceive the distant, as well as the ways in which social formations are constituted and sustained on a symbolic level.

The focus on the *structure of organization* seeks to identify the prevailing administrative and authoritative forms through which power is exercised, and through which relationships are mediated. This category seeks to identify the main locales of authority, as well as the prevailing forms of governance, as they are manifest in national, regional, and intergovernmental settings. Here we also seek to give definition to the dynamics of interstate rivalry specific to the time. In practice this entails discussion of the impact of the Cold War, of decolonization, of the rise of the welfare state, and of the proliferation of intergovernmental organizations under the auspices of the United Nations and beyond. This category is of crucial importance to a study of organized labour because it gives definition to those aspects of governance that more often determine labour's political horizons.

The final structural imperative to be acknowledged will be referred to as the *structure of ideology*. Here definition is given to the ideological complexion of the period under review by reference to the interplay of the four ideological ensembles mentioned earlier. To recapitulate, these will be referred to as *conservative, instrumental, developmental,* and *emancipatory*. The aim here is to ascertain which of these groupings is more structurally determinant in any given period.

In sum, by delineating the structural imperatives at play we seek to gain a better understanding of forces shaping labour's landscape and, in turn, the constraints and opportunities open to that movement across the national and global realms. Moreover, in relating change within the movement to a broader environment, we can venture more credible assessments about the nature of network integration, and of relations with the state. These broad-brush accounts of structural imperatives will precede analysis of the aforementioned categories of network existence and interaction.

Clearly, the categories and dimensions outlined here are not completely distinct. Notwithstanding such definitional questions, the methodological framework they constitute enables us to conceive of the transnational network of labour organizations in its totality – as a political community in its own right. It will help us view this community not only as a conglomeration of organizations, but also as a unique set of relationships, interests, and political practices. Ultimately, the use of this framework will enable the research to shed light on the question at the heart of this project: how, and to what extent, has the world's loose ensemble of trade union organizations globalized?

Before proceeding a few qualifications need to be stated in relation to this method. The first relates to the culturally specific nature of the literature upon which the research is based. Given the origins of the trade union movement, it should not surprise that the bulk of the material at one's disposal derives from 'First World' sources. This poses obvious problems for a study aiming to identify 'global' trends, as reliance on this material leads to a higher degree of extrapolation than is desirable. I can see no real solution to this problem, and am left only to make clear my unease at the outset, and to stress to the reader that my observations and conclusions are presented with these considerations in mind.

The second qualification concerns a matter of style. Researchers in this field are confronted with a dizzying array of acronyms commonly used to refer to trade union organizations. To assist the reader in this respect I have included a list of common abbreviations (this appears on p. vii). Throughout the text I have tried to minimize the number of acronyms, opting instead for truncated versions of organizations' names. However, I have made three exceptions to this rule. The most important players in this research are the International Confederation of Free Trade Unions and the World Federation of Trade Unions. Because these organizations dominate much of the narrative I have, more often than not, employed their acronyms – the ICFTU and the WFTU. In addition, I have chosen to refer, where possible, to the International Labour Organization by its acronym, the ILO. While the ILO is not a central player in the research that follows, it is a ubiquitous presence and thus warrants such treatment.

The final task of this introductory section is to outline the book's structure. The study involves a review of changes that have impacted the transnational network of labour organizations from 1945 to 2005. It will be divided into three parts, each containing two chapters. The parts will focus on the periods 1945–72, 1972–89, and 1989–2005. This periodization acknowledges watershed developments that influenced trade union affairs within and across national borders. For example, the 1945–72 period was notable for the frenetic post-war reconstruction, for the use of Fordist production methods, and for the gradual integration of world markets under the auspices of a number of intergovernmental organizations. The period that followed – 1972–89 – was marked not only by a series of economic downturns, but by the unravelling of the Soviet empire, the gradual demise of the welfare state, and the rise to prominence of the highly dynamic and integrated multinational corporation. It was also marked by the rise of neoliberal free-market ideology and post-Fordist production methods. The final period – 1989–2005 – provides insights into labour affairs in a post-Cold War, post-Fordist, world marked by the phenomenon of turbo-capitalism. Preceding Part I, 1945–72 – is a brief overview of organized labour's configuration and 'globalizing' disposition prior to the periods in question.

Background: transnational labour's pre-1939 disposition

The first manifestations of a transnational network of organizations that were concerned exclusively with trade union matters appeared in 1889 with the formation of International Trade Secretariats. These confederations were distinctive because they facilitated cross-border links between workers in specific crafts or industries. The first trade secretariat to appear represented printing workers. The miners were to follow in May of 1890, forming the International Miners' Federation in London. The main trade union protagonists here were from England, France, Germany, and Austria. Other trade secretariats to emerge in this period included those representing boot and shoe workers (1889), clothing and metal workers (1893), textile workers (1894), and transport workers (1897). By 1900 there were 17 secretariats, and this was to increase to 27 by 1914.[13]

There also came into being in 1903 the International Secretariat of National Trade Union Centers, a transnational body seeking to represent the principal domestic federations of each country. By 1913 the Europe based Secretariat represented approximately 7.7 million workers of its 19 national affiliates.[14] It also had the support of the powerful American trade union movement, and was communicating with trade union federations in Argentina, South Africa, and Australia. Its last conference before the First World War, held in Zurich in 1913, saw the adoption of a proposal to change the name of the organization to the International Federation of Trade Unions. There also emerged a body serving the interests of Christian workers. In 1908 trade unionists from Germany, Italy, Holland, Belgium, Austria, Switzerland, and Sweden formed the International Secretariat of Christian Trade Unions. To 1914 this confederation boasted a membership of some 540,000 workers.[15] Thus, at the outbreak of the First World War the constellation of transnational labour organizations comprised a small number of International Trade Secretariats, the International Federation of Trade Unions, and the International Secretariat of Christian Trade Unions.[16]

In the aftermath of the First World War trade unions once more gravitated towards these confederations (now reconstituted). There also emerged at this time the Profintern,[17] the trade union wing of the Soviet Union-backed Comintern. A creation of the Bolshevik leadership, this confederation was designed to represent trade unions worldwide that were opposed to Western-style parliamentarianism. At its peak in 1929 it boasted a membership of some 17 million workers from 50 countries. In addition, there emerged after the war the International Federation of Christian Trade Unions, a reconstituted version of the pre-war International Secretariat of Christian Trade Unions. This was an overwhelmingly Catholic organization, with Protestants representing the most significant minority constituency. Its membership – peaking at three million, from approximately ten countries – consisted mainly of trade unionists from Germany, the Netherlands, and Belgium. This membership was concentrated within continental Europe and, to some extent, countries of South America, where Catholicism was ingrained.[18]

Also to appear in the interwar years was the second incarnation of the International Workingmen's Association (often referred to as the 'Syndicalist International'). This syndicalist international is here granted a more prominent place than other class-based internationals because it was more organically tied to the everyday world of trade unions than those concerned with universalizing programmes. It comprised the largest revolutionary syndicalist movements of the day, with a combined membership reaching 162,000 in 1929.[19] Consequently, on the eve of the Second World War the transnational network of labour organizations – on this horizontal plane – comprised the International Federation of Trade Unions, some 30 International Trade Secretariats, the Profintern, the International Federation of Christian Trade Unions, and the syndicalist International Workingmen's Association.

On a vertical plane, the most important national actors prior to the First World War were the American Federation of Labor, Britain's General Federation of Trade Unions – and later its successor, the Trade Union Congress – and those German trade unions linked to that country's Social Democratic Party. Also of importance to the foundation of this transnational network were France's Confédération Générale de Travail, Spain's Unión General de Trabajadores, and its successor, the Confederación Nacional del Trabajo. Similarly, the national trade union bodies of the Scandinavian countries, the Netherlands, and Belgium all played key roles in constituting transnational confederations with globalizing pretensions. Up to 1913, the International Federation of Trade Unions[20] was sustained mainly by the German, British, American, and French labour movements. In the years following the war this support fluctuated wildly as each affiliate navigated deeper political currents. The much weakened German trade union affiliates could no longer play a significant role, while the American Federation of Labor withdrew its support because of the International Federation of Trade Union's accommodation of socialistic tendencies, and for its criticisms of the League of Nations. The effect of all this was a reduction in membership for the peak body from some 23 million in 1919, to approximately 8 million in 1934. The eventual return of the American federation was the principal factor in this figure doubling towards the end of the 1930s.[21]

The importance of national players was also apparent in the constitution of the Profintern in the early 1920s. It was comprised of a peculiar mix of affiliates. These included some national trade union organizations – notably from Norway, Finland, France, and Czechoslovakia – as well as independent trade unions: organizations such as the National Minority Movement from England, and the Trade Union Educational League of America. At various times a range of what were referred to as 'revolutionary minorities'[22] gravitated towards the Profintern, though the connection between them was often informal and tenuous. We might add to this list of important national actors those that sustained the syndicalist incarnation of the International Workingmen's Association up to its demise in 1929. Among these were the Spanish Confederación Nacional del Trabajo, France's Confédération Générale de Travail, the American-based Industrial Workers of the World, and Argentina's Federación Obrera Regional Argentina. Another body with global aspirations – the International Federation of Christian Trade Unions – was sustained by a relatively small cluster of Northern European affiliates. The peak confederations within this loose ensemble of ostensibly like-minded actors were very weak and beholden to national trade union bodies concentrated mainly within Europe and North America. In every respect nationally bound actors were the more established and coherent entities than the peak bodies then in existence. This reliance on national labour bodies meant that the wider network, such as it was, could make only very limited claims to having a global identity, even in an organizational sense.

For trade unions at the national level these decades were notable for a rejection of what remained of class-based internationals – the International Workingmen's Association (and then later its second incarnation, the Syndicalist International), the Second International, and the Comintern – and for a shift towards labourist internationalism *via* the expanding network of cross-border trade union organizations mentioned above. Concurrently, these decades witnessed what might be regarded as a statist turn on the part of labour. This manifested itself in various ways. Republicanism and the right to self-determination – that is, statehood – had long been a preoccupation for labour movements of all persuasion. This commitment to the particularity of the state sat well with labour's celebration of progress and modernization, and initially found expression through a closer association with social democrat parties proliferating throughout Europe at that time.[23] The commitment was to manifest itself in support for state sponsored corporatism, Fordism, 'business unionism', managerialism and, ultimately, for statist pragmatism. A preoccupation with the integrity of the state gradually intensified as leaders throughout Europe in particular were laying the foundations for what came to be known as the welfare state. Eventually this involved the emergence of state sanctioned collective agreements, systems for conciliation and arbitration, and domestic labour laws that went some way to accommodating the concerns of organized labour. This meant that trade unions began to have a real stake in preserving the existing industrial relations systems, and in abandoning what seemed increasingly to be fanciful revolutionary political programs espoused by syndicalist, Marxist, and anarchist tendencies.

Some of the most important such developments were played out against a background of the 1914–18 conflagration, worldwide economic depression, and the looming confrontation between the anti-communist American labour movement and their counterparts within the fledgling Soviet state. That confrontation was just one indicator of an increasingly divided movement, wherein rival peak confederations vied for the allegiances of national trade union bodies across the globe. Significantly, this was an era, according to Drainville, that witnessed the transformation of

> various moments of internationalist solidarity into various terrains of programmatic struggle and left little room for an internationalist movement not identified in terms of party or state allegiances ... turning internationalism into an interstate affair, in which international solidarity was measured by state-bound allegiances.[24]

Each of the main players within the fractious transnational network of labour organizations were to be subsumed by states that were championing various ideological tendencies. For example, leaders of the British Trade Union Congress worked closely with the Labour governments of 1924 and 1929–31 to maintain their country's colonialist policies;[25] the American Federation of Labor became a more active supporter of its governments' strident anti-communist, imperialist, and productivist worldviews; the Russian labour movement – through the agency of its major national affiliate, the Russian All Union Central Council of Trade Unions, and then the Profintern – became an instrumental part of the Soviet Union's Comintern.

For their part the German, Italian, and Spanish trade union movements were enduring savage assaults by fascist regimes, with these conflicts in turn fuelling internecine struggles within the world labour movement itself. In sum, throughout this period, relations with the state became the over-riding imperative for most of the constituent parts of the loose network of cross-border labour confederations.

The absence of integration across national boundaries, as well as the lack of autonomy *vis-à-vis* the state, meant that organized labour's globalization was only of a very superficial kind, in spite of the existence of a network that by the Second World War extended well beyond the European setting.

Part I
1945–72

Prevailing structural imperatives

Our survey of the pre-war disposition of organized labour identified the emergence of a transnational network of labour organizations riven by divisions that stemmed, in a large part, from the commitment to the interests of the state. On the strength of this broad-brush account it would appear that the only aspect of a globalizing process evident at this time lay in the spread of often antagonistic peak bodies.

We now delve deeper in order to view change at various layers of the network's relationships and interactions from 1945 to the early 1970s. To re-capitulate, this involves a focus, initially, on the internal dimensions of change in the transnational labour movement. Here the nature of the network's organizational structure, its integrative relationships, and ideological disposition are considered. We then focus on external dimensions of change in an attempt to understand labour's engagement with the state-mediated political realm.

There emerges, ultimately, a network that continues to consolidate and expand – at least in an organizational sense – across continents. By the 1970s this network had managed to assert an identity distinct from the various class-based internationals that were such a feature of the pre-1939 period. Notwithstanding this continuing expansion, it becomes apparent that the network was neither integrated, nor was it inclined to disassociate itself from the state, whether thought of as individual entities or when manifest in intergovernmental organizations. While the reasons for this varied, a dogged commitment to the strategic interests of the state, as well as to growth-oriented developmentalism, stand out as important characteristics in this superficially globalized condition.

Before elaborating on this claim – and as a prelude to a study of the network's internal and external dimensions of change – it is necessary to familiarize ourselves with the broad structural imperatives bearing down upon organized labour during this period. This outline is intended to help make sense of the maelstrom of political, economic, and social events of the day. It will provide a context that will help us gauge more accurately the nature of change affecting the emerging transnational network of labour organizations. We commence by examining the prevailing structure of production. Following this is an outline of the structure of organization, and then a characterization of the structure of ideology that also pertained to this period.

The structure of production

In the period 1945–72, organized labour confronted a form of production that was, at least initially, determined by post-war reconstruction. The Marshall Plan assistance in Europe soon triggered high levels of manufacturing, consumption, and prosperity in what came to be known as the 'developed world'. This would soon include the states of Eastern Europe and China as more governments embraced modernization programmes. Beyond the world of the more affluent, food production increased markedly, as did life expectancy and, not surprisingly, population levels. Reconstruction also brought with it dramatic changes in the scale and intensity of economic activity, as well as in the methods and systems upon which production was based. Fordism and systems of 'scientific management' that had emerged towards the end of the nineteenth century now attained unprecedented levels of sophistication and reach. Nowhere was this method of planned mobilization and control of labour as entrenched as in the Eastern European states.

Initially, the re-industrialization of Europe resulted in widespread shortages of labour and led in turn to a dramatic increase in immigration from Africa, Asia, the Middle East, and the Caribbean. High employment rates, however, did not last long. Throughout the 1960s the fixation on unsustainable growth rates served to intensify competition for markets among America, Japan, and the re-emerging European powers. This competition, coupled with a slackening of growth, resulted in dramatic increases in unemployment, especially within the most affluent of countries.[26] Throughout these decades there also appeared the first symptoms of the demise of Fordism, as enterprises began to privilege greater mobility and diversification. This represented an ominous sign for organized labour, as enterprises opted for offshore production strategies ahead of those premised on export from a national centre. While the multinationals remained headquartered primarily within the industrialized countries, activity in developing regions gradually began to increase throughout the 1960s. This activity was dominated by American corporations. America's foreign direct investment *via* multinationals accounted for around half of all such activity, and was concentrated in industries such as mining, agriculture, and manufacturing.[27] On another level, the rise of the multinational corporation was to a large extent made possible by the spread of technology and innovation, especially in the fields of transport and communications systems. Mobile and flexible production systems that were emerging were particularly reliant on changes in the field of communication technology. The range and sophistication of the communications media improved markedly in the wake of the Second World War. Benefits from the advent of satellites, transatlantic and transpacific telephone cabling, advances in aerospace technology and electronics in general at first accrued to the military, and later also to the business and wider communities. The introduction of television supplemented the ever-improving systems of telegraphy and radio transmission, as well as the more sophisticated methods for producing printed material. All of these innovations were to change profoundly aspects of socialization, debate, education, resource distribution, entertainment, and the integration of systems of power and organization – all fundamental to the evolution of political communities such as labour.

The structure of organization

In this period the main organizational features with which labour leaders had to contend were the Cold War alliance systems that had emerged in the early 1950s. The alliance systems put in place by the respective antagonists – the United States and the Soviet Union – were all-pervasive, reaching across all continents. The web of diplomatic and military systems of control that developed throughout the 1950s and 1960s represented the principal locales of power and authority in world politics. Moreover, the majority of conflicts – and, indeed, international relations more broadly – came to be mediated and controlled by functionaries of the superpower antagonists. As will become apparent, this was to have a profound impact on organized labour's ability to establish an integrated and unified cross-border network.

The influence of the Cold War was such that the process of tense integration it generated continued in spite of rapid decolonization and the success of numerous movements of national liberation. Indeed, few if any of the newly independent states from East Asia and the Pacific,

South Asia, the Middle East, Africa, and the Americas could remain, as one author put it, 'outside the orbit of the superpowers'.[28] Decolonization nevertheless caused a sea change in international relations, not least because it ushered on to the stage states that would come to play significant parts in the shaping of world affairs.

In spite of the hostilities between the superpowers, and the growing intra-alliance economic tension in the West, the post-war period was marked by organizational integration. This integration occurred on many levels, but it was most evident in the formation of the Bretton Woods institutions. These were designed to regulate global finance and trade, and included the International Monetary Fund, the General Agreement on Tariffs and Trade, and the World Bank (then known as the International Bank for Reconstruction and Development). This integration also began to feature on a regional plane, with the establishment of the European Economic Community in 1957 serving as one of many examples.[29]

In the context of a study of transnational labour the most important characteristic of such interconnectedness was what might be termed 'managerial internationalism'. Aside from the Bretton Woods institutions and United Nations special bodies, there was a staggering proliferation of 'global public utilit[ies]'[30] in the post-Second World War period. In essence, this period saw significant change in the organization of regional and worldwide governance institutions, while at the same time witnessing the concentration of power within two superpowers camps.

Labour leaders during this period also saw the transformation of states themselves, with high levels of state intervention in economic affairs becoming the norm. This manifested itself into centralized command economies, or into what we now refer to as the 'welfare state'. The notion that government ought to assert its influence over the economic sphere was made acceptable, on the one hand, by state socialism and, on the other, by Keynesianism. The provision of social welfare programmes also became a core function of the state. In addition, many came to view the early 1970s in particular as the prelude to the age of corporatism, wherein select civil society actors – trade unions among them – were incorporated into the decision-making processes of state.[31]

The structure of ideology

The final structural imperative identified is that pertaining to the ideological tendencies of the time – worldviews that are here classified under the aforementioned categories: conservative, instrumental, developmental, and emancipatory. To a great extent the 1950s and 1960s witnessed a confluence of all these ideas. The ideal of national autonomy and statehood provided the lightning rod for this convergence. For instance, while conservative worldviews – in the form of nativism and insular statism – were again prevalent following the war, they were expressed in terms of national regeneration and reconstruction. In addition, developmentalism became wedded to the notion of state-building, particularly through the implementation of modernizing, growth-oriented, Keynesian forms of economic planning.

Oppositional movements also became preoccupied with the state, as the ideal of national liberation and state autonomy came to be conflated with emancipation. Many advocates of the ideological tendencies within the emancipatory category – namely, the anti-colonial, anti-imperialist, socialist, and even communist – saw the struggle for national independence by those of the Third World in particular as vital in the struggle against the established global order. Liberation in this sense came to represent for many a central plank in the programmes of the movements participating in the upheavals of the late 1960s. Here the struggles for independence by the likes of Algeria, Cuba, Vietnam, and the Congo were vital ingredients in any emancipatory worldview. Closely linked to the ideal of independence was the notion of progress, usually expressed in terms of national development. The connection between the two became more important throughout the 1960s.

And what of the ideological dynamics associated with the Cold War? Clearly, this conflict entailed an ideological battle between class-based internationalism and free-market capitalism. But the conflict was also about the respective superpowers' determination to maintain and enhance not only the integrity and authority of the state, but also their spheres of influence. Both antagonists sought to achieve this through alliance networks premised upon political, military, economic, and cultural systems of control. In addition, each antagonist's worldview embodied notions of progress, modernity, development, and productivism; all deemed to be universals that were inextricably tied to the idea of statehood. The common ideological tendency, in essence, might thus be characterized as a form of statist-developmentalism.

1945–72: prevailing structural imperatives – conclusion

This rather sweeping account of prevailing structural imperatives in the 1945–72 period serves an important function in our consideration of the changes in the world of organized labour. These imperatives left their mark in a number of ways. Of great importance was the implementation of frenetic programmes of post-war reconstruction and modernization, and the emergence of a political and economic orthodoxy premised upon management of the economy and the incorporation of labour. Organized labour's landscape was also marked by the emergence of the welfare state, the growth of the multinational corporation, and the quantum leap forward in communications technology. And finally, the structural imperatives bearing down upon organized labour resulted in greater regional and global integration through the agency of intergovernmental bodies, as well as a confluence of ideological tendencies that found common ground in notions of statism and developmentalism.

For organized labour there were dangers inherent in this new landscape. The most obvious of these was the political and social polarization engendered by the Cold War. Less obvious was the fact that organized labour had to contend with the fallout from the steadily intensifying economic tensions. These arose from states' desperate attempts to maintain productivity and growth rates needed to overcome competitors in what was becoming a highly integrated global market.

1
1945–72 – Internal Change: Antagonism and Shallow Integration

The organizational dimension – introduction

With this context in mind we can turn our attention to the world of labour politics and begin to explore the transformation of the network of transnational labour organizations. The task now is to assess the degree to which the network's globalized disposition was premised upon intra-network cohesion and integration, as well as on estrangement from the state. Initially, this entails focusing on changes in the network's internal organizational dimension of change. We then consider the factors that influence levels of network integration. These include the nature of intra-network relationships, as well as the interests and ideologies that prevailed. For now, the focus is on changes in organizational form.

The organizational dimension – the horizontal

In this period there continued a shift in emphasis away from radical class-based internationals, and towards an ever-decreasing number of trade union-specific confederations with transnational, globalizing pretensions. At the same time the geographic reach of the peak labour confederations increased markedly. And yet in spite of their impressive reach the peak confederations continued to serve more or less symbolic functions. This organizational expansion, in other words, had little to do with a globalization premised upon integration and estrangement from the state.

The principal pre-war confederation, the International Federation of Trade Unions, was dissolved in December 1945. Its place was taken by a new confederation, the World Federation of Trade Unions (WFTU). The formation of the WFTU, in October 1945, was initiated mainly by the

British Trade Union Congress. The emergence of this globally oriented confederation was a cause for concern for those within the ranks of the American Federation of Labor. These misgivings stemmed from the decision by the British to extend membership to the more radical organizations; those that had earlier been excluded from participation in the International Federation of Trade Unions.[32]

Even though the WFTU claimed to represent a membership of some 67 million – far exceeding the total represented by its predecessor, the International Federation of Trade Unions – it failed to live up to expectation. Deeply ingrained tensions within the world of organized labour came to the surface. These tensions will be dealt with in greater detail in subsequent discussion. They are important to mention in passing because they helped give rise to a confederation that from this point on will largely dominate the narrative. In addition to ongoing antagonism with the American Federation of Labor, the WFTU lacked the support of the Christian trade unions. They had insisted they be permitted to form their own confederation while simultaneously participating in the WFTU. This proposal was rejected and led to the Christian labour movement abandoning support for the new confederation. The fledgling WFTU also had strained relationships with the International Trade Secretariats. The latter had objected to the proposal that they be incorporated into the overall structure of the WFTU.

With the Cold War looming the British Trade Union Congress, along with the one-time radical Congress of Industrial Organizations of America, assumed strident anti-communist positions and led the majority of Western trade union affiliates out of the WFTU. What remained of the WFTU consisted of a number of affiliates from developing countries, and those from within the Soviet bloc. In December 1949 disaffected trade union leaders in the West formed the International Confederation of Free Trade Unions (ICFTU). This confederation's charter emphasized the need to preserve trade unions' autonomy from states, parties, the church, and employers. Indeed, this professed autonomy was regarded as the ICFTU's defining characteristic. Prominent among its affiliates were reformist and anti-communist elements, with the latter reflecting the influence of the American participants. The European affiliates' unease with anti-communism was to some extent ameliorated by a compromise, whereby the Confederation would have a European General Secretary and President, as well as its headquarters situated in Europe.[33]

However, the existence of other labour confederations should be noted. The International Trade Secretariats continued to operate as industry-specific advocacy organizations independent of their nation-oriented counterparts. They did, however, have a strong political and institutional affinity with the ICFTU. There were two main reasons for this affinity. First, they were able to reach a formal agreement with the ICFTU guaranteeing respect for the secretariats' autonomy. Such a formalized acknowledgement of trade secretariat autonomy was not forthcoming from the WFTU, which proceeded to form its own versions of trade secretariats known as International Trade Departments.[34] Relations were also close between the trade secretariats and the ICFTU because many of the secretariats' affiliates were also represented by the same national federations that constituted the ICFTU.[35]

Few would suggest that the trade secretariats were pivotal players in the world of transnational labour politics during this period. They are noteworthy, however, because they engaged in a form of advocacy that focused more on the organic relationship with their constituent members than on the politics of government *per se*.[36] The trade secretariats numbered 25 in 1946, but gradually consolidated their ranks to around 15 by the early 1970s.

Another constituent part of the transnational network of labour organizations up to 1972 was the peak Christian trade union confederation. Even though the International Federation of Christian Trade Unions was reconstituted in 1949, it was by then in a much-weakened condition. This was because many of its former affiliates – for example, those from Germany, Austria, and Italy – had gravitated towards the ICFTU. Though it managed to rebuild on the foundations of its affiliates in France, Belgium, and the Netherlands, overall, the International Federation of Christian Trade Unions remained a marginal player. Its political disposition can be characterized as being relatively neutral – in relation to the larger confederations – with a residual anti-communist sentiment also apparent.

A watershed year for the Christian labour movement was 1968. It was in that year that the Federation was transformed into the World Confederation of Labour. This transformation was prompted by changes in the organization's constituent base. Throughout the 1950s and 1960s the leaders of the Christian labour movement had shifted their attention to the trade unions of Africa, Asia, and Latin America. This had two consequences: first, it meant that as economic development spread in these regions membership to trade unions grew accordingly;[37] and second, that the identification with Christianity had to be reconsidered if the organization was to attract new members from the developing world. To this end, the movement adopted the name, World Confederation of Labour, and carefully removed all references to God and

Christianity from its Declaration of Principles. This secularization of the movement also coincided with a shift in political doctrine, wherein the World Confederation of Labour now openly denounced capitalism and called for the socialization of the means of production.

This overview of the organizational configuration of transnational labour between 1945 and 1972 reveals an expanding constellation of peak organizations, but one comprising fewer actors overall. Among those that had disappeared from view were the Profintern, the International Federation of Trade Unions, and the (syndicalist) International Workingmen's Association. As of 1972, the constellation was made up of the pro-Soviet World Federation of Trade Unions, the West's International Confederation of Free Trade Unions, the World Confederation of Labour, and approximately 15 trade secretariats. This re-configuration can be understood as just one in a series of changes experienced by organized labour that were triggered by the structural imperatives outlined at the beginning of this section. Important factors here were the expansion of markets and of industry, the mobility of capital, the rise in the number of independent states, and the potential for advocacy through the medium of the intergovernmental organizations. The result was that peak labour confederations gained footholds in previously unchartered territory beyond the confines of continental Europe.

However, the network's consolidation and geographical spread should not be interpreted as a sign of greater intra-network integration, and nor should it be read as signalling an estrangement from the state. Even though the remaining peak confederations attracted a greater number of affiliates from further afield, this had less to do with organized labour's globalization than it did with accommodation of the structural imperatives outlined earlier. Thus, in an organizational sense, labour remained fragmented and dependent – indeed, this lack of integrity and autonomy continued to mitigate a more profound process of globalization for labour.

The organizational dimension – the vertical

The utility of this horizontal view of labour's organizational configuration is somewhat limited as it only reveals the contours of the network relative to its peak confederations. This perspective gives us little sense of the network's depth, or of the nature of the connections between its constituent parts. For a better understanding of the organizational form of the transnational labour movement, it is necessary to also identify those intermediate actors that connected the peak confederations to their constituents throughout this period.

By 1972 the ICFTU had established a network of affiliates across the globe. The ranks of ICFTU affiliates were thinnest in Africa, where labour actors in countries that had recently achieved independence shied away from what many considered to be an international of the First World. The vertical reach of the ICFTU was improved through a system of mutual representation put in place to facilitate cooperation with the International Trade Secretariats. This provided national trade unions with a second avenue – the first being their own national federation – through which views might be expressed in the ICFTU. Up to 1972, the ICFTU had also established three permanent regional organizations as well as offices that were situated in Tokyo, Nairobi, Geneva, Jakarta, and New York. The regional organizations were better known by the acronyms ORIT (Organizacion Regional Interamericana de Trabajadores, situated in Mexico City), ARO (the Asian Regional Organization, located in New Delhi), and AFRO (the African Regional Organization). It was envisaged that these organizations, as well as the permanent offices, would enable the ICFTU to more effectively respond to problems unique to specific regions, and to also limit the centralization of power within the headquarters in Brussels.

This second tier of representation was also the site of much intra-network tension and intrigue, especially in the regions that were strategically important in the context of the Cold War. While these tensions will be explored later, it is important to flag them here because this cautions against mistaking organizational expansion for network integration. Thus, even though the ICFTU was structured in a way that enabled it to reach out (beyond Europe) and down (closer to its national constituents), its influence away from its centre was marginal. Indeed, what vertical reach and influence it did enjoy was only made possible by virtue of its association with the International Trade Secretariats, as well as with its larger nationally bound affiliates.[38] Put differently, the ICFTU remained 'a labor bureaucracy three times removed ... a [con]federation of federations, which themselves [were] organizations of top-level officials ...'.[39] To this extent it represented a microcosm of a network that had deep roots in the national – state bound – realm, in spite of an ever-expanding, transnational, organizational structure.

The other main pillar of the transnational network of labour organizations at this time was the second incarnation of the WFTU. Following the withdrawal of most of its Western European affiliates, the WFTU came to represent the labour movements situated mainly within the Soviet bloc. While it boasted a membership of approximately 150 million up to 1970, these figures aroused scepticism, as up to two-thirds of this membership derived from the affiliation of the Soviet Union's All Union Central Council of Trade Unions. Domestic trade unions' membership of this national affiliate entailed a degree of compulsion not evident in the Western context. The number of members, therefore, was much less an indication of the WFTU's legitimacy, than testimony to the extent to which it was reliant upon a specific understanding of unionism, a subject to which we shall also return in subsequent discussion. Another important distinction is that unlike the ICFTU, the WFTU did not establish permanent intermediary organizations in the regions beyond Europe. Rather, it chose to court autonomous regional and national trade union organizations, mainly from the developing world.

The outward appearance of the WFTU was one that suggested the existence of a diverse constituency. Its principal governing body, the World Trade Union Congress consisted of representatives of all affiliates – their size determining their voting rights – as well as representatives from a plethora of non-affiliated organizations. However, this apparent eclecticism masked what was in reality a highly centralized and rigidly imposed structure. Aside from its regional affiliates, the WFTU had in place a number of industry-specific confederations. Known as Trade Union Internationals, these to a large extent mirrored the International Trade Secretariats, and comprised trade unions whose national representatives were affiliated to the WFTU. The Trade Union Internationals achieved moderate success in so far as they established cordial relationships with some trade secretariats. However, they too were beholden to the central authority of the WFTU and its Soviet patron.

It remains to identify some of the more prominent intermediary labour actors that emerged in the developing world in the immediate post-war years. Some of these were to play important roles in regional and national politics throughout the period of European reconstruction and then decolonization. They are included here in order to emphasize, first, the depth and complexity of the transnational network of labour organizations and, second, the nature of the institutional representation existing between the national, state bound, constituents, and the peak confederations.

Perhaps the most important player of this sort to emerge in the immediate post-war period was the Trade Union Advisory Committee. Formed in 1948, the Committee was recognized as the representative body for labour in what came to be known as the Organization for Economic Co-operation and Development (hereafter referred to as the OECD). Although the Committee was not in any sense tied to a geographical region, it did play an important part in generating support for the

Marshall Plan, and then in the ICFTU's campaign to marginalize communist-leaning labour movements throughout Europe in the 1950s. In the subsequent decades the Committee served as an intermediary between governments and national labour federations of OECD member states.

The Committee's counterpart in Latin America was formed in 1969. Known as the Trade Union Technical Advisory Council, it was established to advise ministers of government – those that were members of the Organization of American States – of labour's position on national and regional level policy. Most of the Council's affiliates were members of the ICFTU's regional organization, the Organizacion Regional Interamericana de Trabajadores. The Council was beholden to the Organization of American States for its funding. Other Latin American organizations worthy of note from this period were the WFTU-aligned Confederación de Trabajordores de América Latina,[40] and its regional rival, the Confederación Interamericana de Trabajadores. The latter came about largely as an initiative of the American Federation of Labor, and was designed to counter the WFTU presence in the region.

The European setting was, of course, the epicentre of both national and cross-border labour activity throughout this time. In the immediate post-war period the transnational alliances that emerged reflected the changing relationships between states. The formation of the European Economic Community was the most significant event in this regard. In the years immediately preceding, and then following, its creation (in 1957) a number of European labour organizations emerged and vied for influence. The Committee of Twenty-One, formed in 1952, included national trade union bodies, as well as industry-specific labour organizations. It aimed to assert organized labour's influence in the European coal industry. A period of division followed between those labour bodies representing members whose countries had joined the European Economic Community and those whose countries favoured a free trade region. The latter category was represented by the European Free Trade Association–Trade Union Committee, an organization formed some years later in 1968.

In addition there existed the proxy organizations of those transnational confederations mentioned earlier. The World Federation of Trade Unions had a presence in Europe through the Co-ordination and Action Committee, while the Christian World Confederation of Labour established its European Organization. The International Confederation of Free Trade Unions had held sway for some time, with its European Regional Organization, but it could not maintain unity between those of its affiliates that were participating in the European Economic Community and those that were not. Of all of these, the European Trade Unions Secretariat came to be the most influential. This influence was enhanced as the European Economic Community itself expanded, thus providing the Secretariat with a growing number of prominent national trade union affiliates. Ultimately, the rival confederations resigned themselves to the pre-eminent role of the European Trade Unions Secretariat. In the years to come, this regional actor would incorporate most of Europe's trade union bodies, whether affiliates of the transnational ICFTU, WFTU, or that of the Christian World Confederation of Labour.

1945–72: The organizational dimension – conclusion

All this gives organizational shape to the transnational labour network as it existed up to 1972. What can be gleaned from this about the nature of network integration, and of relations with the state? In the post-war years a transnational network of labour organizations began to once more emerge. And within this network, greater organizational consolidation was taking place, especially among the industry-specific trade secretariats. It was also apparent that labour had throughout this period continued to extend its organizational reach to all continents. On a vertical plane, it was apparent that a system of regional and other intermediary organizations was also emerging. Ostensibly, these intermediaries served to link the peak confederations with nationally anchored affiliates. And yet the spread of these regional organizations had as much to do with the dynamics of interstate politics as it did with the emergence of a more integrated network. We refer here to the trade union organizations that emerged in response to larger structural imperatives: symptoms of which included Cold War enmity, the emergence of a non-aligned movement, as well as the formation of the European Economic Community. Put differently, a snapshot of the network's organizational configuration seems to leave much unsaid about wider processes. It tells us little about the true nature of the network's globalization, understood in terms of network integration and of change in orientation in relation to the state. The following section seeks to add colour to this still incomplete sketch.

1945–72: The integrative dimension – introduction

It is necessary to move beyond contemplation of the network's organizational form to an account of relationships internal to the movement throughout the 1945–72 period. This entails an analysis of the ways in which these relationships were mediated and constituted. Specifically, this requires a review of the forms of communication that facilitated relations, and then of the interests and ideologies that gave shape to this internal integrative dimension of change. A review of this sort makes it possible to assess more accurately the nature of the integration pertaining within the transnational network of labour organizations.

The integrative dimension – relationships

In spite of the advances in communications technology in this period, intra-network relations continued to be predicated on the slower, more detached, forms of printed media. Though telex, telegraph, and the telephone came to play an increasingly important role in administration for each of the network's parts, these technologies did not play a significant role in integrating the network as a whole. Indeed, the deeper and more broad-ranging relations with constituents – meant here to denote the members of the trade unions affiliated to peak confederations – remained heavily reliant on the older media. To this extent network integration – at least in terms of communication – remained a fraught and problematic process.

These older, printed, media came in the form of periodicals, newsletters, and pamphlets. They were especially important for those peak confederations attempting to establish themselves in regions and 'colonies' beyond the European setting. The most important of these were the Latin American, South East Asian, and African regions. At a time when the peak labour confederations were vying for new affiliates – and seeking to build alliances within a context of Cold War tension – such rudimentary forms of communications proved to be relatively successful.

For instance, the International Confederation of Free Trade Unions devoted considerable energy to distributing pamphlets and newsletters through its regional body in Latin America – the Organizacion Regional Interamericana de Trabajadores, or ORIT. This was at a time when domestic labour movements were shifting alignments among reformist, Left-nationalist, revolutionary, and even reactionary forces.

In the immediate post-war years, each of the (re)emerging peak confederations produced their own periodicals: *Free Labour World* represented the International Confederation of Free Trade Unions, and *World Trade Union Movement* the World Federation of Trade Unions. These were to be the mainstay media linking these peak bodies with their constituent affiliates, and were the principal means by which executive resolutions, declarations, reports, conference outcomes, and news items of labour affairs from abroad were disseminated throughout the 1945–72 period.

At first glance, these monthly periodicals were very similar. This was certainly the case in regard to their design and layout. However, they presented quite different perspectives. *Free Labour World* railed against what it considered to be the oppressive dictatorships of the communist bloc. For its part, *World Trade Union Movement* strove – at least on a rhetorical level – for unity and reconciliation between trade union movements of the East and West. More often, its editorials read as rallying cries calling for class-based solidarity across national boundaries.

Though print was the main communication form used throughout the 1950s and the 1960s, elements within these 'globalizing' confederations were beginning to utilize the electronic media. The use of such media was becoming routine for intra-confederation administration. This was especially so in the case of telegraphy. Beyond these bureaucratic functions the use of electronic media was limited, but not unknown. The International Confederation of Free Trade Unions, for instance, commenced weekly radio broadcasts into Eastern Europe in 1953. Through its programme, *The Voice of Free Trade Unions*, it attempted to counter what were considered to be the propaganda gains made by communist governments in the region. At the same time its regional offshoot in Latin America also employed radio in its attempts to garner support in Argentina and Costa Rica. But in spite of these experiments, it was generally agreed – at least by the ICFTU leadership of the 1950s – that print was preferable, and a far more effective means of disseminating information to constituents.[41]

As one would expect, face-to-face interaction throughout the growing network of cross-border labour organizations was limited. This was especially so in relationships between members of rival confederations, and in spite of the increasing number of conferences being held. Indeed, the level of intra-network tension was such that these assemblies functioned merely as platforms from which broadsides could be launched at rivals. Far from functioning as integrating fora they provided settings at which each confederation would proclaim their latest triumphs, usually in relation to the recruitment of new regional affiliates.[42]

Internal to each confederation, however, a degree of face-to-face engagement was facilitated by the steady increase in the number of gatherings convened to bring together delegations from a range of national settings. As transcontinental travel became more accessible towards the end of the

1960s, this form of interaction gradually assumed a more important role in the overall network's communications regime. For the International Confederation of Free Trade Unions, the most important conference was its World Congress, held at two or three year intervals throughout this period. And for the World Federation of Trade Unions, the World Trade Union Congress served as the principal site for such face-to-face interaction. In addition to these, there were a growing number of regionally focused gatherings organized by peak confederations' offshoot bodies.

Increasingly throughout the 1950s and 1960s, face-to-face engagement was also facilitated through conferences held under the auspices of the United Nations. For the International Confederation of Free Trade Unions and the trade secretariats, in particular, United Nations conferences enabled interaction between actors who were normally at very far remove. Indeed, as the years passed these fora became even more important, with proceedings reported back to affiliate bodies *via* the printed material mentioned earlier.

Ultimately, while the internal communication media employed may have enabled the various peak confederations to expand their organizational presence across national borders, they had limited effect on network integration *per se*. Though the tentative embrace of some forms of advanced communications technology would have no doubt facilitated greater bureaucratic cohesion *within* the various confederations – and, hence, the ability to grow organizationally on a global plane – the network as a whole remained highly fragmented.

And even within the various camps, confederate relationships between affiliates and peak bodies remained extremely distant and tenuous. This meant that authority within the network remained in the hands of the nationally bound, constituent parts. The communications regimes then in place did little to further integrate – in any profound sense – these highly extended and very detached relationships. While it was the case that the emergence of regional and other intermediary organizations had the potential to provide for greater interconnectedness and, hence, integration on a vertical plane, their effectiveness in this regard was negligible throughout this period. To this extent, the integrative dimension of network globalization remained underdeveloped throughout this period. To better understand the reasons for the lack of network integration – even at a time of organizational expansion on the part of trade union organizations – we must look to the political interests and ideological tendencies evident in labour circles during this 1945–72 period.

The integrative dimension – interests, ideologies

The interests that were crucial to determining the extent of integration and, hence, globalization in this period were largely shaped by the structural imperatives confronting labour leaders of the time. The structures of production and organization were particularly important. Post-war reconstruction, Keynesian economic development, and modernization programmes were characteristic of the period's structure of production, as was the increasing levels of capital mobility and the gradual emergence of the multinational corporation. The structure of organization was one in which Cold War antagonisms gradually came to determine the nature of interstate relations. The prevailing structure of organization was also characterized by an increasing number of states – resulting from decolonization and struggles for national liberation – as well as the emergence of what came to be known as the welfare state. But of all these symptoms of structural imperatives, it was the Cold War and great power conflict in general that cast the largest shadow over organized labour. This conflict had a profound effect on the interests and motivations of the major players within the transnational network of labour organizations, mitigated network integration and autonomy in relation to the state and, ultimately, retarded network globalization.

We saw earlier how the post-war community of trade union organizations – then embodied within the first incarnation of the World Federation of Trade Unions – was torn apart by these pressures. Communist and non-communist trade union organizations had existed in an uneasy coexistence under this umbrella body for four years (1945–49). However, Cold War tensions intensified following the announcement of the Marshall Plan, an initiative then considered within WFTU circles to be 'the weapon [of] the transatlantic republic of the dollar and the atom bomb ... to split Europe'. To others, the plan was a 'democratic "people's programme" for economic recovery'.[43] This polarization of communist and non-communist WFTU affiliates finally resulted in a schism, out of which emerged the International Confederation of Free Trade Unions.

While the newly established ICFTU and the second incarnation of the WFTU may not have been representative of all trade union actors in the 1950s and 1960s, their contrasting positions reflected the contending interests throughout the transnational network of labour organizations. Inevitably, these peak confederations continued to reflect the interests of the emerging superpowers. A major preoccupation of the ICFTU was the authoritarian nature of governments in the communist states of Eastern Europe and Asia. The ICFTU's reports and publications throughout this period are replete with condemnations of these regimes and what was considered to be trade union compliance therein. In reality, this meant condemnation of the WFTU, as the latter's affiliates were drawn predominantly from the communist world. Editorial headlines within the ICFTU journal *Free Labour World* were typically blunt: 'The WFTU in the Service of the Kremlin's Foreign Policy', 'Moscow's Agents [that is, the WFTU] in the Tribune of the Free World', and then, as the 1970s approached, '[the Soviet Union] Where "unions" stay silent'.[44]

This last statement was indicative of the ICFTU's antipathy towards the WFTU affiliates and the role they played domestically. Editorials focusing on what was regarded as endemic repression in East Germany, Poland, Hungary, and Czechoslovakia throughout the 1960s were illustrative. One editorial put the ICFTU's position thus: 'what interests us is the failure of the "official trade unions" [in the communist countries] to do anything for the workers in this or any other crisis'.[45] Indeed, the WFTU's tendency to highlight industrial dispute and social decay in the West, while remaining silent about such problems in the communist world, was often met with contempt from the trade union leaders of the West.

Looked at from yet another vantage point, we see profound philosophical differences between the peak confederations over the very role of trade unions. In the ICFTU worldview the 'trade union' essentially served a defensive and ameliorative function. In contrast, most of the Eastern European affiliates within the WFTU cast themselves as indispensable parts of a greater modernizing and emancipatory project. Comments by Karel Hoffmann – a Vice-President of the WFTU – shed light on how this functional role was perceived by leaders of his federation.

> The working class ... is creating even now its trade union organization as a weapon of its class struggle. This implies unequivocally that the trade unions which want to accomplish this task cannot be independent from or non-committal to the working class and its interests.[46]

Given that in this scheme of things the 'revolutionary party is the vanguard and instrument of the working-class in its efforts for imposing its basic class interests', then the trade unions' interests are necessarily subordinated to those of the party and state.[47]

The WFTU was far less strident in its criticisms of the ICFTU. Indeed, the notion of 'unity' among confederations became a mantra of sorts, appearing constantly in WFTU declarations during this period. WFTU leaders were concerned here with the need to reconcile differences between the various peak confederations, and to build close ties between workers of the West and East. In a 1972 speech to the WFTU General Council, the then General Secretary, Pierre Gensous, reflected this low-key approach. Of the ICFTU, he stated only that 'We are very conscious that there are divergences of appreciation ... [and that] The ICFTU remains fundamentally attached to reformist conceptions in its approach to problems'. The closest this leader comes to reproaching his rival confederation is in a tactful reference to the latter's tacit support for American foreign policy, '... their [the ICFTU's] Congress are strangely discreet on the painful conflicts which are going on in Indochina and the Middle East'.[48]

Yet, even though the WFTU did not overtly criticize the ICFTU, it was vocal in its attacks on the imperialist and colonialist adventures of the major Western powers, be they in the Suez, Iran, Algeria, Venezuela, Cuba, or in 'the "dirty war" which American imperialism [waged] in Vietnam'.[49] In taking such a stance, the WFTU set itself against the most important of the Western trade union bodies; most notably, the ICFTU's regional body in Latin America, the American Federation of Labor-Congress of Industrial Organizations, and the British Trade Union Congress – trade union organizations that were highly attuned to the interests of their patron governments at this time.

These differences translated into fierce competition for affiliates in the regions beyond Europe. The major confederations were eager to establish close ties with those national trade union organizations of the newly independent and non-aligned states throughout Asia, Latin America, Africa, and the Middle East. For the ICFTU of the early 1950s, Asia was of particular importance and it strove to negate the WFTU's efforts to 'spread' communism in the region. Part of this strategy was the formation of its Asian Regional Organization, and the establishment in 1952 of its ARO Training College in Calcutta. Throughout the region the ICFTU attempted to assert itself and promote the virtues of Western-style 'free' trade unionism. This was not an easy message to impart, however, because the communist/anti-communist dichotomy represented just one aspect of the complex national and regional trade union politics in these regions.[50]

Unlike the ICFTU, the WFTU did not attempt to establish an organizational base in the Asian region. Rather, it sought to exploit the anti-colonialist sentiments shared by most established labour organizations in the regions. While looking, ostensibly, to create a non-aligned trade union movement the WFTU sought to undermine the ICFTU's influence and gain advantage for its patron superpower. Tensions of this sort were replicated – in varying degrees – wherever these major peak bodies sought to establish affiliate networks in the period under review. In Latin America these peak confederations manoeuvred in a political landscape marked by fierce interstate and Cold War conflicts involving actors of all persuasion, be they left-nationalist, centrist, or right-wing dictatorships sustained by American governments. Typically, the ICFTU would attempt to insinuate itself into the region's trade union politics through its regional organization, and the WFTU would then counter by cultivating relations with the more radicalized labour actors of the region.[51]

These confederations also vied for the affiliation of the emerging trade union actors of the Middle East and of Africa. This rivalry was played out not only against a background of Cold War antagonism, but also of colonial and post-colonial tensions, with the latter counting against important European affiliates of the peak bodies.[52] The ICFTU, in particular, looked to downplay its association with former colonialist powers and to deflect accusations of paternalism. These tensions greatly hindered the formation of the ICFTU's regional body, the African Regional Organization, in 1959. At the same time, the WFTU presented itself as the champion of African and Arab nationalism, and concentrated on establishing close relations with emerging regional bodies such as the All-African Trade Union Federation, and the International Confederation of Arab Trade Unions.

Even though all this might imply that there existed a harmony of interests among each peak confederation's respective affiliates, this was not the case. Within the ICFTU affiliates were often split over the issues mentioned earlier. Interestingly, throughout these years a great deal of tension existed between the British Trade Union Congress and its American counterpart, the American Federation of Labor-Congress of Industrial Organizations. The former reflected its government's disposition by adopting a sanguine view of communism, while at the same time holding to Britain's colonialist pretensions. In contrast, the American labour body's anti-communism was so virulent that anti-colonial movements were cast in a relatively favourable light. Intra-confederation tensions of this kind were central to the American federation's decision to withdraw completely from the ICFTU in 1969. The withdrawal was, in part, a reaction to what the Americans perceived to be the ICFTU's complacency in negating communist sympathizers among its affiliates.

Internal tensions were also commonplace within the ranks of the WFTU affiliates throughout this period. These often involved the WFTU's principal affiliates from Italy and France, the Confederazione Generale Italiana del Lavoro and the Confédération Générale du Travail. From the early 1960s, these organizations railed against the conventional wisdom requiring trade union affiliates within the WFTU to act as agents of communist parties. The comments of one leader of the Confederazione Generale Italiana del Lavoro typified the resistance to such attitudes: 'The Italians hope that the WFTU Congress would abolish 'Stalinism' in relations between trade unions'.[53]

There was hardly what one could describe to be a harmony of interests even among the Eastern bloc affiliates of the WFTU. The Soviet invasions in Eastern Europe in the 1950s and 1960s created great tension among the WFTU's member organizations. These episodes will be discussed later. Suffice to say that the Soviet invasions of Hungary (1956) and Czechoslovakia (1968) placed senior non-Russian WFTU officials under intense pressure. Many openly condemned these political and military interventions, only to be marginalized and have the day-to-day administration of the Federation taken away from their control.[54]

All this has focused attention on the major peak bodies and has neglected other players, most notably the Christian-based World Confederation of Labour and the International Trade Secretariats. Neither of these were removed from the tensions that were generated by interstate conflicts. The World Confederation of Labour laid itself open to criticisms of paternalism and neocolonialism by emphasizing a 'middle-way' – characterized by a *Third Worldist* socialism – and by repackaging itself as the confederation of the developing world. And even though the trade secretariats were quite diverse in terms of political orientation, they too, were embroiled in tensions of the sort that preoccupied the major peak bodies. Indeed, some trade secretariats – like the International Metal Workers' Federation – played pivotal roles in the reconfiguration of the network in the immediate post-Cold War years. They were instrumental in ensuring that the trade secretariats were not incorporated into the first incarnation of the World Federation of Trade Unions, an organization that was then considered by many to be prone to communist domination.[55]

Although these contending interests resulted in discord among labour leaders, there was consensus of sorts on a number of very important issues. The most important of these was the need to promote an economic prosperity through growth-orientated modernization. The major confederations advocated policies that would result in increased prosperity, access to markets, and the funding of projects that promised to increase employment. It is, of course, to be expected that trade union organizations of all ideological and political dispositions would seek to promote economic development. But this tendency was especially pronounced in the post-war years – when reconstruction was most needed – and through the 1960s. Such consensus is relevant because it is premised – indeed, reliant upon – the intervention of the state. It represents yet another form of dependence mitigating greater movement autonomy and bears closer examination.

From the early 1950s, the ICFTU advocated free trade and urged governments to dismantle international tariff walls. Indeed, since its formation the ICFTU was a keen advocate of economic integration, especially within the European setting. Initially, the ICFTU worked to implement the Marshall Plan through a conservative labour body, the European Regional Organization. The ICFTU was also a consistent advocate of economic growth on a global scale, exhorting governments to create 'a dynamic world economy in the fight against poverty'. In fact, the ICFTU stressed the need to make free trade an integral part of assistance programmes for the Third World. Thus, calls for 'The decolonization of trade', and the acceptance of 'Labour's plan for trade and aid', were indicative of this confederation's emphasis on market-based economic expansion in general. In reference to affiliates among Third World unions, ICFTU leaders claimed that these also had a role to play by 'bringing the working masses into the development process'.[56]

Economic development was also important to the leaders of the WFTU, though they were less concerned with trade than with the growth of the economy, modernization, technical and scientific advancement, and fulfilling the economic demands of underdeveloped societies. All this was encapsulated in the frequently invoked notion of 'social progress'. Here economic demands and political intervention were inextricably linked. Thus, the aim was

> to ensure that in the long term, the planned balanced development of the economy will be dynamically stimulated and complemented by the development of the socialist market, consumer demand being called on to influence the short term plans of socialist enterprises ... so as to promote an even larger range of products.[57]

Even though the WFTU's approach to development contrasted with the ICFTU's – lacking the latter's enthusiasm for the free market – it nevertheless celebrated economic expansion and progress of the sort outlined earlier. Indeed, its publications throughout this period can in some ways be viewed as photo-galleries celebrating the wonders of science and economic progress. These, more often, were images of ultra-modern hydro-electric power turbines and power stations, atomic reactors, giant semi-conductors, oil refineries, manufacturing plants mass-producing tractors, and newly erected housing estates.[58]

Throughout the 1950s and 1960s a convergence of interests also emerged on a range of other issues. Though the level of commitment did not always match rhetoric, most of the major actors shared a consensus on the dangers inherent in increased Cold War militarism, the need to oppose apartheid, the importance of improving the rights of female workers worldwide, and the need to utilize the growing number of intergovernmental organizations. Also of increasing importance as the 1960s came to an end was the realization that the rising power and influence of the multinational corporations had to somehow be curtailed. This issue became a preoccupation with leaders of all the major peak bodies and represented common ground at virtually all levels of the network.

In a more abstract sense there also existed a convergence of interests on the status and centrality of the state itself. This growing fixation with the state was due in large part to the focus in the West on welfarism – facilitated by Keynesianism – and in the Eastern bloc on modernization. Both of these can be interpreted as forms of developmentalism. In addition, post-war reconstruction, decolonization, and empire rivalry between the United States and the Soviet Union were also powerful factors shaping labour leaders' commitment to governments of all types. The result was labour's enlistment – be it forced or voluntary – into serving projects of nation-building. This enlistment was facilitated not only by a commitment to state, but by what Mark Rupert refers to as the internationalization of ideas promoting a 'productivity-oriented consensus' on the questions of 'mass production and mass consumption'.[59] Importantly, this commitment was also becoming apparent on regional and global planes, a subject to which we shall return.

These interests cannot be understood in isolation from ideological tendencies at play throughout the network during this period. A focus on the ideational ties that bind the transnational network of labour organizations highlights the relative significance of the four ideological ensembles identified earlier: conservatism, developmentalism, instrumentalism, and emancipatory worldviews. This will provide yet another vantage point from which to assess the extent to which the network as a whole was becoming more integrated and autonomous – indeed, the extent to which it was becoming more globally oriented.

Certainly, the research to this point has indicated a very strong tendency on the part of labour leaders to embrace aspects of conservative worldviews that reinforced the connection to the state. However, to focus only on the relationship with the state leaves much unsaid about the evolution of the transnational network of labour organizations during this period. We have already established that many emancipatory worldviews lost resonance for many, if not most, of the actors within this network, leaving aspects of conservatism – especially the deference to the authority of the state – as the predominant ideological tendencies. While this is true, it should also be noted that alongside the ensemble of conservative ideologies there emerged a growing commitment to ideologies associated with instrumentalism and developmentalism.

This was a coupling of ideological systems that were committed, in the case of instrumentalism, to growth-oriented mass production and, in the case of developmentalism, to modernization. These ideologies combined in the post-war years and took root throughout the entire network of labour organizations. This instrumental developmentalism permeated labour movements beyond the Western setting. This was so because inherent notions – such as Taylorism and 'scientific management' – were also important features of the mass production processes being utilized within the Eastern bloc countries and beyond at the time. In his research Ozay Mehmet shows how well instrumental and developmental ideologies travelled. He traces the evolution of neoclassical economic theories and, more specifically, the emergence in the 1940s of what he calls *big push industrialization* theory. As one of the antecedents to neoliberalism, big push theory flowed from the United States to Europe via Marshall Plan re-construction, and then beyond to the Third World. Premised on a faith in mass production, industrialization, and mega projects, this worldview relied upon economies of scale and advanced technology to achieve modernization. This combination of instrumental and developmental ideologies shaped mainstream economic thinking in the immediate post-war years.

This trend towards instrumental and developmental creeds also changed the very nature of organized labour, as well as the nature of engagement with the external. The inculcation of these ideologies meant that the transnational network of labour organizations – at all levels – was more willing to embrace corporatist modes of engagement. The effect of this was a gradual dilution of the class-based emancipatory worldviews still in evidence, to the point where only the most ameliorative aspects of reformist collectivism were evident. Even where emancipatory creeds survived within the transnational network of labour organizations they were increasingly taking the form of rhetoric and exhortation. The approach to feminism was illustrative. Even though feminist principles were enunciated in intra-network declarations at peak, regional, and national levels of the world labour movement, this emancipatory creed had little substantive impact on the labourist cultures of the time. This was in spite of the fact that women were beginning to insinuate themselves into the trade union movement structures in ever greater numbers throughout the growth decades of the 1950s and 1960s.[60]

There was – especially among the peak confederations – a very real decline of worldviews that encompassed such emancipatory ideologies as radical collectivism, whether in the form of class-based anarcho-syndicalism, Marxism, socialism, or those promoting struggles for national liberation. This was in spite of the rhetoric of the 'anti-imperialist' WFTU, whose main constituents remained wedded to the conservative notion of statism. This connection to statist ideas was maintained through their anti-Western struggles for national liberation, and/or the statist forms of corporatism imposed upon them. Importantly, the tenuous nature of the commitment to emancipatory worldviews was most apparent among the peak confederations, where a broader constellation of conservative, instrumental and developmentalist worldviews became the consensus.

Among many national constituents of the transnational network of labour organizations there remained a relatively strong association with class-based emancipatory ideologies, even though a drift towards reformist collectivism was apparent. Even though organized labour had long since ceased to be a catalyst for change within the national realm, a clear break from emancipatory worldviews was not yet apparent. It should also be noted that conservative ideologies – those committed to the defence of the state, and church – also retained deep roots in the national realm.

To a great extent, many ideologies – especially the emancipatory and conservative creeds – were shaped by traditional connections to region and culture. For example, Catholic-based trade unionism was, until the 1950s and 1960s, an important feature of the trade union landscape in Germany, Austria, Italy, France, and the Netherlands. Likewise, communist and syndicalist worldviews were deeply entrenched within the Spanish, Italian, and French settings. To this extent one can refer to conservative and many emancipatory ideologies at the time as being locally embedded.

In identifying those emancipatory worldviews that endured up to 1972, it seems that only a reformist collectivism – still manifesting itself in various forms of corporatist arrangements – was well entrenched. As reformist collectivism lay very much at the intersection of emancipatory, developmental, and conservative worldviews, it is clear that emancipatory creeds were losing ground in this period. Ultimately, if one sets aside the exhortations and rhetoric of the peak confederations, there was little in the ideologies espoused by organized labour – at all levels – that was anti-statist in orientation.

It is also worth pointing out in these concluding reflections some of the ways in which the various ensembles of ideas interacted. Here the tensions, conflicts, and contradictions among and *within* ideological groupings should be noted. Throughout the post-war years the tensions existing within the ensemble of emancipatory worldviews came to the fore. In spite of the proclaimed common goals of the liberation of the working class and the opposition to capital, the rivalry between followers of the Marxist, socialist, and anarcho-syndicalist ideologies had a debilitating effect on organized labour.

Yet tensions were also evident between the conservative notion of statism, and the ascendant instrumental and developmental worldviews. For example, the conservative commitment to the authority of the church – evident at this time among many of the trade union organizations of northern Europe and Latin America – would seem to be at odds with the dynamism of instrumental and developmentalist ideologies.[61] Up to the early 1970s, the ideological systems of conservatism, instrumentalism, and developmentalism could accommodate such tensions because the most radical form of instrumentalism buttressed the principal centre of authority – the state. And of course opposition to communism, however defined, provided a very important lightning-rod for all those ascribing to the conservative-instrumental ideologies in the post-war years. This was especially so at a time when the American labour movement wielded considerable influence beyond its own continent.

Importantly, neither of these trends weakened in any profound way the connection to, and investment in, the authority of the state. Organized labour's commitment to developmentalism, for example, underscored the importance of the state. This was because the state was seen as the principal vehicle for realizing such progress, as well as for ameliorating the worst effects of changing structures of production and organization. By 1972 it was evident that while organized labour's deep commitment to conservative ideologies had situated it in close proximity to the state, it was also taking on an ideological disposition that accommodated instrumentalist and developmentalist worldviews.

1945–72: The integrative dimension – conclusion

We have shed light here on the dynamics that are internal to the transnational network of labour organizations, and where these might relate to movement integration and autonomy. It has become apparent that intra-network relations throughout this period were characterized by divisiveness and polarization. In spite of access to modern means of communication, actors within the network remained relatively detached. Authority, such as it was, lay with the nationally anchored constituent parts of the network. This reflected the growing commitment to, and importance of, the role of the state in the world of cross-border trade union politics. The interests and ideologies at play throughout the network reflected this tendency, as they did also the commitment to a modernizing developmentalism. These tendencies were deeply rooted and endured in spite of a range of countervailing pressures that operated on a more immediate level.

If we recall the earlier findings relating to the network's organizational form, we once more see a disjuncture between organizational change and levels of integration and autonomy. While the organizational configuration of the network at this time showed distinct signs of consolidation and expansion, this did not coincide with greater levels of integration, or of a disassociation from the state. The principal inhibiting factors here remained the aforementioned commitment to the strategic interests of the state, as well as the commitment to progress and development. Clearly, important exogenous factors played a very important role here: for a better understanding of how organized labour responded to such external forces we now turn to an analysis of external dimensions of change.

2
1945–72 – External Change: Incorporation and Statist Internationalism

The political dimension – the national

While organized labour engaged with the state on both national and global planes, by far the most important of these was the national. This realm represented the hub of trade union politics throughout the postwar years. This meant that even though the organizational form of the cross-border network of labour organizations was global in scope, its roots remained firmly planted within the national realm. For labour leaders this realm was the principal focus of attention for two main reasons. The first was the emergence of corporatist, Keynesian, and social-democratic forms of governance. The second, closely related, reason was the imperative to defend the interests of the state, whether this meant committing to nation-building agendas, or to government policies aimed at securing geostrategic advantage within a context of interstate relations. These factors were alluded to earlier, but are worthy of greater attention here.

The first, and most important, aspect of organized labour's engagement with the national level of the political sphere was its growing connection to government through corporatist relationships. A distinction should be made at this point between the forms of corporatism that existed in various spheres. Here Littler and Palmer provide a useful guide. They differentiate between *voluntarist/bargained*, and *statist/coercive* corporatism.[62] The voluntarist model was most prevalent in the European, social-democratic, and pro-Western group of states; while the statist model was that pertaining throughout the Eastern bloc and communist states more broadly. As the two labels suggest, there were regions in which trade unions committed themselves more or less willingly to partnership with government, and those where industrial relations regimes were imposed upon organized labour. We deal with both in turn, starting with the voluntarist form of corporatism.

The growing influence of Keynes' ideas – based on limited macro-economic management – created the political conditions in which social-democratic parties throughout the world became far more influential. Where they formed government they were instrumental in giving shape to the welfare state throughout the 1950s and 1960s. Proximity to power, through their association with social-democratic parties, consequently became a real prospect for many national trade union actors. Eliassen's reflections of the time are illustrative:

> Corporatist representation is an important strategy of all contemporary European trade unions. The number of government commissions and state offices in which the unions are represented increased steadily. In the last two decades, all European trade-union movements have tended in this direction.[63]

And from scholars focusing on corporatism in the Latin American setting – in this case, in Mexico – came similar assessments:

> This corporatism implied that unions were conceived as public and political organisms which had co-responsibility for the state's stability and the continuity of the socio-economic system. This function was put into practice through informal and formal mechanisms ... This ... has in all likelihood contributed to the construction of a particular kind of union tradition which is characterized by patrimonial relationships [and] statism.[64]

Many prominent players within the transnational network of labour organizations embraced such corporatist integration.[65] Entering into these government–party alliances meant that national trade union leaders were often obliged to forego many political aims in return for increased economic leverage. The compromise often manifested itself in trade union leaderships foregoing wage increases in return for concessions on other economic demands.

The extent of corporatist integration varied from one national context to the other. Some relationships were quite informal, such as that existing between British governments – both Labour and Conservative – and trade unions throughout the late-1940s and 1950s.[66] In addition, incorporation was not always facilitated by social-democrat parties. A case in point was the relationship between the then American Federation of

Labor and successive American governments and business elite. Though organized labour was at the time supportive of the Democratic Party, relationships with all governments were close. These relationships were founded on a shared commitment to a modernizing-productivist philosophy, as well as to a strong current of nationalistic, anti-communist solidarity with business and government.[67]

This is not to suggest that all relationships between trade union movements and centres of state power during this period were harmonious and premised upon cooperation and compliance. Indeed, as Dubois, Koscielski, Arrighi, and others remind us, the 1960s in particular were years of considerable civil and political unrest.[68] Trade union movements were often important players during such upheavals. Some labour organizations attempted to disengage from both social-democrat parties and governments. It was certainly the case that the rank-and-file of many national trade union organizations attempted to re-orientate their leaderships towards oppositional rather than instrumental goals.[69] Such tensions – between organized labour, parties, and the state; as well as between labour leadership and the rank-and-file – were especially evident within the Italian and French contexts. Yet, as Crouch argues, it was this militancy that prompted governments to redouble efforts to entice labour into corporatist arrangements.

> The period that began to gather momentum in the late 1960s was one both of increased labour militancy and of increased attempts by the state to secure order. The two processes frequently coalesced ... in such devices as national tripartite negotiations.[70]

In addition to this *voluntarist* model of corporatism, there also existed the *statist* form of political and economic integration. Such incorporation existed within communist states and affected the largest trade union affiliates of the WFTU. This form of corporatism was premised on the Leninist *dualist* model of trade unionism. This reflected an ambivalence towards unions: on the one hand the state – as represented by the ruling party – acknowledged the need for workers to be protected from harsh management practices; while on the other hand it maintained that organized labour's *raison d'être* was to serve the state and to achieve the productivity goals set for it.[71] It followed, ultimately, that trade union organizations enjoyed very little autonomy, especially during the post-war years when reconstruction, modernization, and high levels of mass production were such powerful motivating factors for Eastern European countries. Hence, communist states' trade unions 'functioned basically as transmission belts with de facto compulsory membership'.[72]

And yet here too we must differentiate between the types of labour–state relationships existing in then communist countries immediately following the Second World War. Indeed, there were periods and settings in which the degree of state control varied according to socio-political factors. While trade unions were always subordinate to government, they were under some circumstances provided with greater scope to voice concerns. There were times when a greater degree of freedom was permitted in order to reduce social tension arising from dramatic political and social change. Usually, however, those national trade union organizations subjected to statist corporatist regimes deferred to the interests of state.[73] This was most evident, of course, within the Soviet setting. To get a sense of the extent to which this was so, it is worth quoting Osakwe at length here:

> The Soviet trade unions conduct all their activities under the guidance of the Communist Party of the Soviet Union, the organizing and directing force of Soviet society ... the Soviet trade union is so involved in the day-to-day government of the society that one can hardly conceive of any measure of political independence of the former from the actual government itself. However, this is not the same thing as saying that the trade unions are an integral part of the Soviet government. The actual situation today is that the trade union organization of the Soviet Union stands between the Party and the government.[74]

In addition to these corporatist tendencies, there existed certain strategic and functional imperatives committing organized labour to the defence of state. These also served to underscore labour's fixation on the state-mediated realm. In the 1945–72 era, a nationalistic-statist turn was especially evident among trade union leaders of the colonized world. This was especially so in the years leading up to independence. Forman's phrase, 'between cosmopolitan intent and self-determination', captures the tensions inherent in these conflicting attachments.[75] In many colonized countries – and especially throughout Africa and Asia – trade union leaders often lacked the opportunities and/or the inclination to negotiate on behalf of their constituents through local processes of arbitration or negotiation. More often, the politics of anti-colonialism and national self-determination subsumed all else. The stakes were high in the struggle against the colonial powers, with political activists subject to frequent intimidation. Those that were not imprisoned or exiled were often those who continued in their semi-legitimized roles as trade union leaders. In this context, trade union leaders of the colonized world were very much embroiled in their own country's political affairs. Unlike many of their Western counterparts, their identification with a trade or to a class was not as strong as their commitment to attaining independence through statehood.

Socio-economic factors also blurred the lines between labour activists and governments within newly independent countries. These factors served to promote young politically active elite to positions of leadership within trade unions, and then on to similar roles within government. The politicized elite often gravitated to trade union ranks by virtue of their access to Western education. Such education instilled in these people the type of organizational skills needed to administer bureaucracies of all types. Having reached the level of trade union leader, many graduated smoothly into government, professional, or bureaucratic domains. In this context, the transition from union leader to government official was also more likely because the strongholds of union activity – the state utilities – were by definition connected to government. These included the instrumentalities of railways, ports, and other government services. Close relationships between government and labour officials were inevitable at a time when trade union representation consisted mainly of approaches to government employers.

A functional and strategic commitment to the state manifested itself most strikingly among the labour leaders of the most powerful states of the post-war era. These states enlisted various actors from within the transnational network of labour organizations to act as their proxies. Some of the most prominent organs within this network engaged in activities – usually of a clandestine nature – that were designed to enhance ideological, economic, and security interests of both state and business. This form of engagement in many regards straddled the two levels outlined earlier – the national and global – as the commitment to such interests usually necessitated cross-border activities in strategically important regions. This was not an arms-length engagement with the government; rather, it entailed serving the state in its dealings with other actors in world politics. Direct and indirect patronage was often extensive, with some labour organizations owing their existence to governments.[76]

The most transparent of all relationships existed between American government–business elite, and the American Federation of Labor-Congress of Industrial Organizations. The latter served its government directly or by proxy through its offshoot organizations. These included the Asian-American Free Labor Institute, the African-American Labor Center, the pre-war American Alliance for Labor Development, as well as the American Institute for Free Labor Development. These offshoots were, in effect, products of a state–business–labour alliance that worked under the auspices of the Federation. Against a background of Cold War tension these puppet organizations operated throughout Europe, Africa, Southeast Asia, Central and Latin America. Though they did provide some genuine assistance to non-American trade unions, these organizations more often aimed to pacify and/or divide elements of the indigenous labour movements that remained enamoured of communist, socialist, Left nationalist, or syndicalist ideas.[77] For example, these proxy organizations were to play key roles in the undermining – and eventual downfall – of social-democrat governments in Guatemala (1954), the Dominican Republic (1965), and Chile (1973).[78]

American interests – and those of its business community – were also pursued through other organs of the transnational network of labour organizations. Indeed, the then American Federation of Labor initially joined the International Confederation of Free Trade Unions for the most cynical of reasons. As the biographer of the AFL's then leader, George Meany, made clear:

> The AFL wanted to give legitimacy to the trade unions it was underwriting in Europe and elsewhere. The AFL wanted protective international coloration for some of the solely American activities it was conducting abroad. Finally, the AFL wanted a worldwide labor group with which to wage a propaganda battle with the now-avowedly Communist WFTU.[79]

Leaders of the American labour movement conducted an ongoing campaign throughout the 1960s and 1970s to infiltrate and co-opt the ICFTU. In addition, the ICFTU's Latin American regional body – the Organizacion Regional Interamericana de Trabajadores – was itself used as a vehicle for American anti-communist activity, as were some International Trade Secretariats. Some of the latter were swayed by their large American trade union affiliates; those that had also benefited from government largesse.[80] Overall, perhaps Robert Cox's observations provide the best summation of the political disposition of American labour at this time:

> American organized labor has, indeed, since World War II, behaved abroad as an integral element in the global expansion of American

capitalism. Whether consciously or unconsciously, its relationship to labor in other countries has been subordinated to this goal. American labor's foreign policy has stressed American interests first, international labor solidarity second – and indeed the second has been so far behind as hardly to count at all.[81]

This form of labour subordination was not limited to the American context. We can also refer to Britain's Colonial Labour Advisory Committee, whose creation in 1942, according to one scholar, marked 'the final and formal integration of the TUC [Trades Union Congress] into the British system of colonial rule'. Here the functional

> relationship, at least in the foreign and colonial sphere, began at the behest of the TUC. Initially, the state was reluctant to accept closer ties, and ... it was primarily the rise of the Labour Party to power in the wartime Coalition government that marked the decisive point.[82]

Through this medium, successive British governments sought to create stable, compliant, and apolitical labour movements throughout Britain's colonies and spheres of influence. Since the 1930s, the Trade Union Congress had played an important role in quelling labour unrest in Britain's colonies throughout Africa and the West Indies. But it was in post-war Greece that it played its most significant role on behalf of the state. Here British labour officials worked hand-in-glove with their government, instigating purges of those sympathetic to the Greek Communist Party from the public services, as well as from the domestic labour movement itself. Beyond this, cooperation with the British Foreign Office also involved using funds provided by the Confederation of British Industry to facilitate business interests abroad throughout the Cold War era.[83]

It must be stressed that in the cases cited, both American and British labour leaderships worked surreptitiously with government. There was little or no effort made to consult or gain the consent of their trade union constituents for the activities undertaken. This was not evidence simply of a marriage of convenience brought about by peculiar circumstances, but of a very profound alignment and a deeply rooted harmony of interests between labour leaders and state elites during this period.

The relationship between the leaders of the World Federation of Trade Unions and their patron, the Soviet Union, was far more overt. This was evident in the relationship with its principal affiliate, the Soviet Union's All Union Central Council of Trade Unions. In the domestic setting, this national organization had virtually no bargaining function, though it was responsible for administering systems of social insurance, welfare, rest and recreation schemes. In this sense there existed an organic – though all but compulsory – connection between organized labour and state. This, in turn, coloured the relationship between the WFTU and the Soviet Union. Indeed, even though the WFTU claimed to champion working-class internationalism, peace, and the defeat of colonialism and fascism, its actions betrayed a commitment to the geostrategic interests of its patron state.

Moreover, the WFTU's pronounced hostility to Western capitalism did not entail fighting for the rights of trade unionists in the Eastern bloc. The events of 1968 illustrate the extent of this strategic allegiance. It was then that the WFTU's Soviet-dominated leadership rounded on dissident members of its own governing Secretariat. Initially headquartered in Prague, the Secretariat of the WFTU found itself in the eye of a storm when the Soviet Union invaded Czechoslovakia. This was the latest in series of events that saw the Soviet Union come into conflict with other communist states.[84] Significantly, many highly placed WFTU officials – most of whom were nationals of non-Soviet states – expressed their opposition to this latest instance of Soviet military intervention in the region. This act of defiance resulted in the Kremlin tightening the reins within its trade union international. This it did by asserting greater control over the WFTU's governing organs, by relocating the administrative headquarters from Prague to Moscow, by denying the Secretariat any role in policy-making, and by concentrating power within the Executive Bureau.[85]

This concentration of power belied what at first glance seemed to be an organization that extended far and wide. During this period the WFTU had a presence in Asia, Africa, the Middle East, and Latin America. However, unlike the ICFTU, the WFTU did not establish a network of its own regional offshoots. It chose instead to develop relationships with autonomous regional organizations such as Italy's Confederazione Generale Italiana del Lavoro, France's Confédération Générale de Travail, Latin America's Confederación de Trabajordores de América Latina and, for a time, the International Confederation of Arab Trade Unions. The politics of state determined the nature of these regional connections. Nowhere was this more evident than in the competition between the Soviet and Chinese-leaderships to secure trade union allies throughout Asia. Competition was especially intense following the Sino-Soviet split. This rivalry severely compromised Asian trade union movements that had hitherto played vital roles in anti-colonial struggles. They were now forced to engage in a form of state politics that was scripted by those in

Beijing or Moscow.[86] Moreover, the labour movements throughout the region became important 'front organizations' that played crucial supplementary roles to the normal diplomatic machinery of state. Gary Busch's summation of labour relations in this realm is illustrative: '... for both communist and non-communist states it was much easier to use the front organizations to engage in conflict with their rivals than to engage in government-to-government confrontation'.[87] Front organizations of another sort were incorporated within the WFTU's system of *ad hoc* committees. These were bodies concerned with a range of issues relating to young workers, women, and multinationals. While not all such committees can be dismissed as instruments of state, they all remained highly attuned to the interests of the WFTU's superpower patron.

The connection to the state was also manifest in organized labour's commitment to national independence. While regional labour organizations throughout Latin America were compelled, or at least pressured, into playing the role of superpower proxies, the investment in the state throughout Africa and the Middle East often assumed an altogether different form. Here labour leaders frequently deferred to governments in order to preserve the autonomy of states that had recently achieved independence. Governments of these new republics demanded loyalty from national and regional labour organizations. The latter often chose alignment to patron states that were fiercely opposed to connections with former colonialist powers. Organizations such as the General Union of Workers of Black Africa (1957–59), the All-African Trade Union Federation (1959–60), and the African Trade Union Confederation (1962–73) were manifestations of this non-aligned statism.[88]

Another regional organization that was beholden to the state was the International Confederation of Arab Trade Unions (formed in 1956). While ostensibly an independent trade union actor, this organization played an important role in the Pan-Arabist movement headed by Nasser of Egypt. In fact, it was funded by, and headquartered in, Egypt. Its policies were determined by the Egyptian government, and were carefully tailored to suit that state's interests. Moreover, its affinity with the WFTU was due in no small measure to the latter's opposition to the state of Israel, and the fact that the rival ICFTU counted as one of its major affiliates the Israeli national labour centre, Histadrut.

The point to be emphasized here is that throughout this period the national realm represented the epicentre of labour politics. This bears directly on the question of globalization as it relates to labour because it underscores, first, the extent to which movement integration was undermined and, second, the extent to which the network remained beholden to the state. Because their political worldview(s) were fashioned by a statist mindset, leaders of the constituent parts of the network of transnational labour confederations – at virtually all levels – remained preoccupied with this realm. This resulted in a transnational network of labour organizations that comprised very ineffectual peak confederations, and one that was sustained only by the presence of its national constituents. Moreover, the only real legitimacy the various parts of the network could claim was that bestowed upon them by patron states. Indeed, throughout this period it was impossible to separate the internal dynamics of transnational labour politics from the politics of state. In one way or another the priorities, interests, and actions of the constituent parts of the network were determined not only by changes in the structure of production, but also by the organizational relationships pertaining between and within states.

This manifested itself in national and regional trade union bodies aligning with forces of national liberation and anti-colonialism, with superpower and colonialist patrons, or with nation-(re)building corporatist regimes. It is little wonder then that the peak confederations that purported to represent labour across borders invested a great deal in accommodating the interests of those powers who themselves shaped interstate relations. Leaders of these confederations looked to accommodate the interests of state and premised their representation of their constituents upon distanced and symbolic proclamations which served to obscure such overt and covert alignments. Thus, the overall complexion of this 'global' ensemble of labour movements remained one characterized by a preoccupation with the state. Such conditions limited integration and autonomy – indeed, they retarded the globalization of labour – in spite of the spread of an organizational network that spanned continents.

To recapitulate, this is not to suggest that trade unions, or their transnational confederations, were universally compliant or conformist. What is significant, however, is that the pressure on organized labour to comply, in one way or another, to the imperatives of state was overwhelming. And whether this labour–state nexus[89] was sought after by labour leaders or, alternatively, foisted upon them – through forced and unavoidable incorporation – is a moot point.

The political dimension – the global

The foregoing showed how the constituent parts of the transnational network of labour organizations were fixated on the national-political realm. In order to further gauge the extent to which organized labour was contained within the political realm in general, it is necessary to also assess the nature and intensity of the engagement on a global plane. It will become apparent that there was indeed a trend towards engagement with the intergovernmental organizations on this level. However, while one reading might suggest that this trend marks a disengagement from the politics of state – demonstrating an autonomy symptomatic of a globalizing network – I suggest rather that it simply enabled the hitherto 'free-floating' peak confederations to engage with states in a different realm of state-mediated politics.

The period 1945–72 was notable for the economic, social, and political changes associated with post-war reconstruction. We have seen how this process of reconstruction at once spawned – and was dependent upon – a large number of intergovernmental organizations. These were to become the successors to the pre-war 'Public International Unions' that were concerned with fostering industry, managing conflict, securing the system of states, and formulating transnational social and humanitarian policy. The proliferation of these intergovernmental organizations after the Second World War was quite remarkable. Leaving aside for a moment the specific organs and programmes of the United Nations, there was a proliferation of such organizations in economic, social, and political spheres.[90] These came to represent the transnational embodiments of the community of states. Given that intergovernmental organizations were borne of state initiatives – with executive bodies answerable to governments and constituents primarily made up of states – it should not surprise that they became instruments of state. While they frequently accommodated the views of non-state actors, they were primarily concerned in this period with giving voice to the state, and with achieving ends that were in harmony with states' interests.

Importantly, many such intergovernmental organizations had the potential to act as intermediaries on behalf of the various organs of the transnational labour movement. Through these, labour leaders had an opportunity to engage with the community of states. Among the most relevant organizations were the International Labour Organization (ILO), the United Nations Economic and Social Council, the United Nations Educational, Scientific and Cultural Organization, the World Health Organization, the General Agreement on Tariffs and Trade, and the Food and Agriculture Organization. While various constituent parts of the transnational labour movement also engaged with regional or group-specific intergovernmental organizations – the Trade Union Advisory Committee's organic connection to the OECD, and the European Trade

Unions Secretariat's relationship with the EEC, are cases in point – the focus here will be on the extent to which labour engaged with the specialized bodies of the United Nations. This is because all states were associated with the United Nations, and it is therefore most representative of the global-political sphere in question. In an attempt to gauge the nature and intensity of engagement by organized labour in this sphere, we focus also on the activities of the more prominent peak confederations. Beginning with the International Confederation of Free Trade Unions, we look at the nature and significance of the engagement with the agencies of the United Nations – with particular emphasis on the ILO – throughout the post-war years up to 1972.

With a declared policy emphasis on social justice within a framework of economic development, progress, and free trade, the ICFTU took seriously the work of United Nations agencies. It invested a great deal of time and energy in ensuring that such agencies were cognizant of its constituents' needs. The ICFTU's involvement with the Food and Agriculture Organization was illustrative. Granted observer status within the Organization in 1954, the ICFTU exerted whatever pressure it could in that forum with the aim of alleviating the dire food shortages existing in regions as diverse as Southern Europe, Africa, and the Americas. As well as providing a platform from which to condemn rival confederations, the United Nations through the 1950s and 1960s also provided a forum in which the ICFTU could denounce communist dictatorships – or 'Lands Without Liberty'.[91] During the 1960s – the United Nations Decade of Development – the ICFTU gradually shifted its emphasis away from communist and dictatorial regimes, and concentrated instead on promoting economic growth, especially in the developing world.[92]

Of all peak labour confederations, in this period, the ICFTU was the most active participant within the United Nations and the ILO. Though the other confederations had a presence, the ICFTU leadership held most of the seats set aside for the representatives of labour on the ILO's Governing Body.[93] An important factor in the ICFTU maintaining this privileged position was the backing it received from the United Nations Economic and Social Council, one of the six principal organs of the United Nations. Such recognition was much valued, for it also bestowed upon the ICFTU a legitimacy that extended beyond this immediate setting and into the realm of world politics more generally.

Not only did the ICFTU's Executive Board express its views through the ILO's Governing Body, it was also able to have them echoed by its national affiliates attending the annual International Labour Conference.

Moreover, because the ICFTU represented the same constituents as most International Trade Secretariats, the same viewpoints were expressed through trade secretariat participation in the various organs of the ILO and the United Nations. More specifically, the ICFTU sought to have its affiliates' views incorporated into the motions, resolutions, and declarations of all such agencies. It employed various mechanisms in these fora in order to bring pressure to bear on member governments. It issued publicity, lobbied, mobilized support, prepared briefs, held meetings, produced information, and issued condemnations against offending governments.

All this would suggest that the ICFTU – the principal organ of the transnational labour movement – had at its disposal an ideal platform from which it could develop an integrated and cohesive transnational labour movement. Furthermore, this regime seemed to also offer an important *entrée* into the world of international politics, as well as a mechanism for leverage in relation to the community of states. The reality was that the nature of the ICFTU's engagement with these intergovernmental organizations was always determined by the forces of national politics that impinged upon its own affiliates. The politics of the domestic was inescapable. The sensibilities of the various protagonist states often determined the fate of various initiatives; and so the issues the ICFTU's Executive Board deemed worthy of pursuit were not necessarily those that were canvassed within the ILO.[94]

The relationship between the ICFTU, the ILO, and the American labour–government leaderships is illustrative of the extent to which the national impinged on to the global. The nexus between the American labour movement and its government was as evident at the level of intergovernmental organizations as it was on the national plane. The strength of this American alliance was exemplified by two important episodes. These entailed the orchestrated withdrawal of the American Federation of Labor-Congress of Industrial Organizations from the ICFTU in 1969; and then, in the following year, of the American government from the ILO itself.

Robert Cox provides a useful interpretation of these events. He contends that the tensions evident between the American labour–government alliance and other actors within intergovernmental organizations stemmed from a fundamental disagreement about the purpose of such organizations. According to Cox, for example, the tripartite system of representation upon which the ILO was founded was understood by the Americans to represent corporatism writ large. The assumption on the part of the Americans was that corporatism – whether national or global in scope – was premised upon an uncritical acceptance of a liberal internationalist order. From this perspective corporatism was not expected to accommodate competing interests, especially when such interests ran counter to the preferred order. From the perspective of American labour leaders and their governments, a high degree of acquiescence within both the ICFTU and the ILO was expected. When it was not forthcoming, withdrawal from these bodies was inevitable.

This is indicative of the extent to which organized labour remained attuned to the interests of state, even within fora premised – ostensibly at least – upon internationalist and cosmopolitan ethico-legal foundations. It suggests that a compliant corporatism characterized not only the domestic relationships between the state and major ICFTU affiliates, but also relations between these actors on a global plane: in this case, within intergovernmental organizations such as the United Nations and the ILO.

This corporatist orientation is reflected in editorials and other commentary appearing in the ICFTU's journal, *Free Labour World*. The tenor of these commentaries is very illustrative. What is most evident about the contributions to this journal – focusing here on the volumes issued throughout the 1950s and 1960s – is the seemingly unqualified support for the United Nations and its agencies. These institutions were held in high regard by the ICFTU in this period, with the latter going to great lengths to persuade readers of *Free Labour World* that its proclaimed goals of greater liberty and freedom were inextricably entwined with the growing economic development and progress sought by United Nations agencies.

And yet these pronouncements concealed significant tensions within the movement. Though a commitment to universal emancipation was persistently affirmed, this was at odds with organized labour's preoccupation with national interests. There seems to have been a conflict here between very real, but waning, cosmopolitan motivations, and a communitarianism that found expression in a commitment to state-focused developmentalist and welfarist programmes. In other words, though an impulse towards more intense globalization could be discerned throughout this period, this was an orientation that did not challenge the organic connection to the state. Indeed, organized labour's internationalism throughout this period served to complement states' interests.

Like the ICFTU, the pro-Soviet World Federation of Trade Unions had observer status in various intergovernmental organizations. By 1972 it had gained such accreditation in the most important United Nations specialized agencies. These were mentioned earlier, and included the

United Nations Economic and Social Council, the United Nations Educational, Scientific and Cultural Organization, the World Health Organization, and the Food and Agriculture Organization. The WFTU also maintained a presence within regional organizations such as the United Nations Commission for Europe, and the United Nations Economic Commission for Asia and the Far East. Of most importance, for the purposes of this study, was its involvement in the ILO.

Because of the scarcity of material relating to its involvement in the ILO we are left to speculate as to the precise nature of the WFTU's engagement. Yet in one sense this task is relatively straightforward because of the clear symbiosis that existed between the WFTU's principal affiliate – the Soviet Union's All Union Central Council of Trade Unions – and the Communist Party of the Soviet Union. Indeed, in contrast to the preceding section, we are on firmer ground here because the WFTU was more beholden to the Soviet Union than the ICFTU was to the American labour–government alliance. In other words, the WFTU's position relating to the ILO was *ipso facto* the position taken by the Soviet Union.

Prior to 1954 the Soviet Union had been very antagonistic towards the ILO and had refused to take up membership within it. This mirrored the Soviet Union's policy on all United Nations specialized agencies, as well as on virtually all post-war intergovernmental organizations. The proliferation of these institutions was considered to be 'one of those pseudo-liberal moves calculated by the international bourgeoisie to halt the wave of workers' revolution throughout the capitalist world'.[95] But such outright hostility gradually waned, and in accordance with the post-Stalinist foreign policy shift – later to be dubbed 'peaceful coexistence' – the Soviets joined the ILO in 1954.

Notwithstanding objections from its rivals, the Soviet Union in subsequent years became an active participant within the ILO. Indeed, its record in terms of ratification of conventions was quite impressive throughout this period. Of special interest to the Soviet government–labour–'employer' alliance were conventions relating to freedom of association, forced labour, and discrimination in employment and occupation. One somewhat sceptical observer put this interest down to the Soviet Union government's eagerness to

> lend support to any convention which in any way would strengthen the hands of the working classes in 'capitalist' countries and would therefore constitute an embarrassment for the governments of Western member states.[96]

In terms of gaining political influence through the ILO, the Soviet delegations achieved little. That said, this was also a time when the Soviet Union was becoming a more vocal participant within many United Nations organs and specialized agencies. According to its critics, this participation only served to 'politicize' such fora. In general, the WFTU was motivated to participate in the ILO for a range of reasons. Mainly, it sought to use it as a platform to promote its commitment to peaceful coexistence; to confront there the liberal reformist ideology permeating the ILO; to promote the successes of socialism; and finally, to court states of the decolonized world.

It is important to reiterate that the WFTU represented at the time a vehicle for the articulation of Soviet foreign policy. This was especially true within the ILO. Given this situation, it is not surprising then that much of the WFTU's work in the ILO was directed towards gaining an advantage in the ongoing rivalry with the ICFTU.[97] Overall, the literature available seems to indicate that the WFTU's contribution was overshadowed by its patron state, the Soviet Union. All this is not to say that the WFTU was totally mute within such intergovernmental organizations. Like the ICFTU, it fulfilled an advisory role on the ILO's Industrial Committees, its Governing Body, and International Labour Conference. It also enjoyed consultative status within these ILO organs. The point to emphasize is that its contribution to the formulation of resolutions and ILO conventions were made with an eye fixed on the foreign policy interests of the Kremlin. More broadly, the WFTU experience reaffirms the point that while the transnational network of labour organizations continued to expand, the ideas underpinning such change remained in harmony with the interests of the state. Thus we see a process of stunted globalization, lacking as it did movement autonomy or disengagement from the world of interstate politics.

Leaders of the industry-specific International Trade Secretariats also looked to engage the United Nations and the global political realm in general. In the most important intergovernmental organizations the trade secretariats gained entry mainly – though not exclusively – through the agency of the nation-oriented labour organizations. For example, the Trade Union Advisory Committee – an organization comprising national affiliates of the OECD countries – acted as an intermediary for trade secretariats in their relations with the OECD. And in their transactions with the European Economic Community, it was the European Trade Unions Secretariat that facilitated interaction. Similarly, the ICFTU acted as an intermediary for the trade secretariats in their dealings with the United Nations. This arrangement reflected a tacit and agreed upon division of labour between the secretariats and the ICFTU. The understanding was that the United Nations was largely the preserve of the nation-oriented ICFTU, while the trade secretariats were expected to focus on their respective industries.

Though the extent of involvement in the United Nations varied among trade secretariats, they all expressed strong support for its various agencies. Indeed, a recurring lament in many of the statements issued by the trade secretariat leaders was that the much valued ILO was under threat and needed to be protected from attacks by employer groups in particular.[98] In general, this meant that the trade secretariats had a relatively low profile at the level of intergovernmental organizations. Even though the ILO's Industrial Committees provided the secretariats with a valuable platform within the context of the United Nations, the pre-eminent forum within the ILO remained the Labour Conference, one dominated by the nationally oriented labour confederations.

1945–72: The political dimension – conclusion

Even though the transnational network of labour organizations were now establishing a presence within the United Nations system, this did not mean that the fundamental orientation of the network – and by this I mean the orientation of the peak confederations, their major affiliates, and the latter's own constituent parts – changed in any significant way. It is true that, taken as a whole, the network did shift its gaze 'upwards' in response to the changes in the prevailing structures of production and organization. In reality, the global network of labour organizations continued to defer to the priorities of the interstate community of the day. For this network the United Nations/ILO path led straight back to a preoccupation with the domestic concerns of state.

Though the ILO in particular served as an important platform for international labour, its usefulness always fluctuated according to the interstate tensions shaping relationships between the most powerful states. The interests inherent in these tensions were not only of a geostrategic nature, but also economic. As developmentalism gained currency throughout the 1960s the 'United Nations labor agencies became "service institutions" to the "neocorporatist power structures of the national states" '.[99] It is this notion of incorporation of organized labour into the overall project of national security and development that is relevant here.

The centre of gravity for the loose network of transnational labour organizations remained within the national political realm. If this network was becoming more globalized, such a transformation was only occurring superficially – that is, as an organizational projection rather than as a fundamental change to the movement's political and ideological orientation. It remained a loose ensemble of organizations 'led' by figure-head peak confederations. It was at its weakest at this peak level, with its most politically effective and coherent organs operating on the national and regional planes.

Part I: 1945–72 – conclusion

The aim throughout this review was to discern the orientation of the transnational network of labour organizations from the immediate postwar years and up to 1972. We commenced with a survey of organizational changes that occurred within the network. This showed a proliferation of cross-border labour organizations, manifesting itself in the emergence of rival peak confederations – the International Confederation of Free Trade Unions, and the World Federation of Trade Unions – as well as a re-emergence of a Christian World Confederation of Labour, the International Trade Secretariats, and a host of regional trade union bodies. This growth saw transnational labour increase its geographical reach beyond Europe, the Americas, and the Antipodes. In an organizational sense, it undoubtedly boasted a global presence.

In terms of internal integrative change we saw how more advanced communications media came to be utilized throughout the network. While face-to-face interaction remained a feature of the relationships between the leaderships of the various peak bodies, these technologies made little difference to relations between constituents and the top strata of peak body representatives. Though confederate structures expanded – under the auspices of the peak bodies – virtually all 'authority' resided in the network's nationally anchored constituent parts. The peak confederations dealt almost exclusively in highly symbolic forms of exhortation, while their affiliated parts engaged in a politics that was more attuned to the affairs of state. Indeed – and in spite of some participation in oppositional, counter-state, politics during the late 1960s – the interests and ideas that informed the transnational network of labour organizations derived from the imperatives of Cold War enmity, decolonization, growth-based Keynesianism, modernization, and developmentalism.

Our attention also turned to mapping organized labour's external engagements within the national/global dimensions of the state realm. After reviewing these interactions it became apparent that labour's centre of gravity was situated almost exclusively within the national setting of this 'political' realm. Its connection to state manifested itself through corporatist arrangements, and through commitments to the ideological and strategic priorities of governments of the day. Such commitments were also evident on a global plane, in labour's representations to intergovernmental organizations.

This continuing preoccupation with the state seems unusual, given that the prevailing structural imperatives were resulting in the expansion of markets and a liberal developmentalist sensibility in general. Ultimately, what we see is a network that had established a superficial globalized form while remaining deeply divided and embedded within the state-mediated political realm. To this extent, there was little to suggest that organized labour was globalizing to any significant degree throughout this period.

Part II
1972–89

Prevailing structural imperatives

The so-called 'boom years' of the 1950s and 1960s were followed by a period of tremendous global instability. The 1972–89 period was punctuated by a series of worldwide economic slumps, with the most significant of these occurring between 1973–75, 1980–82, and in 1987. Identifying the principal causes of these slumps is not at issue here; rather, it is enough to note only that a combination of complex events and processes reshaped the landscape inhabited by labour.[100] Economic instability placed immense pressure on important regulatory structures that had been put in place following the Second World War. The collapse of the Bretton Woods system of international currency regulation was perhaps the most important symptom of this prolonged crisis. Subsequently, the world economy was restructured in a way that not only resulted in greater fluidity of capital and the constant relocation of industry, but also a dramatic rise in new companies, mergers, and takeovers.[101] Also of tremendous significance was the collapse of the Soviet Union. While the collapse of this empire cannot be attributed solely to economic factors, the pressures inherent in an increasingly integrated world economy contributed to the rise of the separatist nationalism that played such an important role in its demise. How then can this maelstrom of events be understood in relation to organized labour? These events can again be considered abstractly as structural imperatives bearing down upon labour. If viewed in this way we can better understand the context in which organized labour managed to integrate across borders and enhance its autonomy in relation to the state.

The structure of production

The global structure of production changed markedly throughout the 1970s and 1980s. As previously noted, the expansion and accumulation of capital on a global scale increased dramatically in this period, and was made possible by the revolutionary advances in science and technology. The advances in information, communication, and transport systems freed production from established temporal and spatial constraints. It was within this context that the multinational corporation – acting within a global capitalist economy – became the principal agent of change.

Literature on the subject of this transformation is often framed around notions of the *new international division of labour* or, alternatively, the *global division of labour*.[102] Such theorizing also speaks of the transition in the structure of production hitherto characterized as 'Fordist' or 'Taylorist', to 'post-Fordist' and 'neo-Taylorist'. We also see terms such as 'toyotism', 'flexible specialization', and 'flexible mass production' used to give character to the structure of production with which labour had to contend. In one way or another, such concepts resonate with what Regini refers to as the 'end of the phase of *concertation*'; that is, a shift away from patterns of production that were overseen by the state, and towards those premised upon diversified structures managed from the level of the corporation.[103]

This process affected relationships of employment and consumption in different ways, varying according to region and sectors within the global economy. Broadly speaking, however, this process had two dimensions that were of significance to labour. In societies hitherto reliant upon heavy industry – the societies of the developed world – socio-economic relationships underwent dramatic change as the less labour-intensive service sectors expanded. We refer here to social and personal services, as well as to 'producer' services.[104] Beyond the service sector, a greater emphasis was placed on computer-mediated fabrication at the expense of industrially organized production that was dependent on manual labour. A displacement of skilled labour led to extremely high levels of unemployment among traditional blue-collar workers. Precarious employment became more common as traditional industries closed, only to be replaced by the more decentralized, flexible, and transitory service industries.

In most developing countries there was fundamental change in the socio-economic relationships traditionally determined by agriculture-based forms of production. Here traditional production methods were replaced by growing industrial and manufacturing sectors.[105]

For organized labour, the consequences of the internationalization of production throughout the 1970s and 1980s were profound. Less developed countries were locked into what was becoming a highly integrated global production process. Internal migration in most developing and Third World countries saw rural communities diminish in size as agricultural workers gravitated towards urban areas in search of employment. Fuelling much of this migration was the spread of multinationals' production plants and the establishment of what came to be known as 'free-trade' or 'export-processing zones'. Typically, these production regimes came with few taxation, environmental, labour standards, or social service obligations for the corporate protagonist.

Not only did production plants of this sort fail to accommodate all those searching for employment, but they also shed existing jobs faster than the market economy could replace them. The victims of this process could only gravitate towards a nether world of urban subsistence living within the rapidly expanding informal economies of these countries. Another consequence of this process was the dramatic increase in regional migration as transitory labour joined the growing ranks of refugees seeking asylum in more prosperous countries. Of course, it should be noted that the effects of this process of integration within a global economy were uneven, and on a range of indicators many impoverished countries made significant gains: indeed, the notion of *Third World* itself became a highly problematic generalization.

Central to the integrated systems of transnational production driving change were advances in communication technologies. For organized labour this change was significant because it facilitated a transition from Fordist systems of production to socio-economic relations associated with the 'post-industrial' 'informational society'. One symptom of this transition was the sudden and frenetic increase in the trade of currencies. By the early 1980s this activity had also generated a tremendous growth in the use of derivatives, a type of transaction that was mainly premised upon speculation on future movements in currency prices, and then eventually on commodity values. These developments represented a disjuncture between trade in materials produced from capital investment, and unregulated speculative transactions within a market of intangibles.

In addition to continuing advancements in transport systems, there emerged new telecommunications and broadcasting media, as well as processing technologies with ever-expanding storage capacity. These included the Direct Broadcasting Satellite, computers, fax, compact discs, cable television, video-cassette recorders, telex, fibre optics, and an emerging internet. Such innovation was significant for organized labour because it magnified the effects new production regimes had on socio-economic relations. Markets were integrated, while production methods evolved in a way that could utilize a global pool of labour. Some of the most important conduits for these phenomena were the growth in tourism, and a globalizing entertainment industry. Ultimately, we saw in this period changes that resulted in hitherto unknown levels of interaction: this was evident in terms of intensity, velocity, and stratification of relations.[106] And just as such change impacted upon the structure of production, it also – to a very great extent – determined the nature of the prevailing structure of organization. We now turn our attention to the most important of the organizational imperatives with which labour had to contend during the 1970s and 1980s.

The structure of organization

The developments outlined earlier combined to fundamentally reshape the organizational structures through which power and authority were exercised and which had a direct bearing on labour politics worldwide. By the end of this 20-year period nationally anchored institutions found their capacity to determine outcomes much diminished. Theories that countenanced the diminution of state sovereignty gained prominence as states seemed paralyzed in the face of economic, political, ecological, and security crises. Whether the state lost its sovereign authority during this period was – and still is – a contested issue. What is clear is that there had emerged a layer of transnational institutions that – taken as a whole – began to govern, regulate, and manage alongside the state.

These processes had, by the late 1980s, undermined the legitimacy and efficacy of the welfare state, as well as the centrally planned economies of the Eastern bloc. The steady internationalization of production and communication technologies meant, in effect, the continuing internationalization of the functions of state. The most important of these functions were in the realms of security and economic regulation. In terms of security we witnessed unprecedented levels of integration within two alliance systems. The culmination of American intervention in Indo-China, the subsequent Soviet Invasion of Afghanistan, and the numerous proxy wars waged in southern Africa and Central America increased pressure on states to align themselves with a superpower. Cold War 2, as it became known, gave even greater prominence to NATO and the Warsaw pact alliance systems. Until the collapse of the Soviet Union in 1989, this manifested itself in even greater incorporation of states into vast systems of command, control, and communications, each maintained by rival superpowers. This is of relevance because it highlights the worldwide scope of the conflict, as well as the breadth of its organization form. More specifically, it places into context forthcoming discussions of the involvement of transnational labour confederations in the foreign policy initiatives of the great powers of the day.

For labour leaders the organizational structures of greatest concern were those relating to international economic affairs. Between 1972 and 1989 we saw the emergence of interlocking regimes aimed at facilitating greater trade liberalization and economic deregulation. While integration occurred on both regional and global planes, the most significant changes in the structure of organization manifested themselves at the global level. Here authority and power were increasingly concentrated in institutional forms such as the General Agreement on Tariffs and Trade, World Bank, International Monetary Fund, Group of Seven, Organization for Economic Co-operation and Development, and the Trilateral Commission. By the late 1980s these had become the pre-eminent transnational governing utilities, and though they differed in form, all of them served to remove barriers to trade and to construct a global neoliberal economic order.

During this period labour leaders also had to be cognizant of a wider range of intergovernmental and international *non*-governmental organizations. It was noted earlier that international organizations in general began to proliferate in the immediate post-war years. This trend continued – even though their numbers had by 1985 reached a plateau – with the non-governmental organizations in particular proliferating throughout the 1970s and 1980s.[107] But this proliferation to a great extent masks the degree to which authority was being invested in the few instruments of global economic liberalization mentioned earlier.

Thus, the tendency towards global macro-economic management through international organizations was well entrenched by the late 1980s. It was significant for labour that in spite of the gains made by United Nations specialized agencies such as the Food and Agriculture Organization, and the UN Educational, Scientific and Cultural Organization, the United Nations itself was being bypassed by the plethora of international organizations that emerged. These organizations ranged widely across sectors, offering alternative avenues for states pursuing their national interests.

This broad overview of the prevailing structure of organization has suggested that the post-war managerial internationalism assumed even greater importance in the years between 1972 and 1989. This manifested itself in more important roles for former Bretton Woods institutions. These not only established closer working relationships, but also shared the same aims. Increasingly, they worked in concert to incorporate the majority of states into a single rule-based trading system, and to also ensure that the emerging trading regime accorded with the requirements of the ascendant neoliberal economic ideologies.

The structure of ideology

The years between 1972 and 1989 saw the decline of emancipatory ideologies. Of particular relevance for labour was the continued decline of traditional class-based doctrines. By the mid-1970s anarchistic, Marxist, and socialistic worldviews were much diminished. Other emancipatory ideologies – namely, Western feminism and environmentalism – did, however, gain modest footholds, leaving their mark in the mainstream political consciousness. At the more reformist end of the emancipatory spectrum, traditional liberal internationalism continued to make an impression. After reaching its heyday during the struggles for independence and post-colonial nation-building of the 1950s and 1960s, this form of emancipatory ideology had itself reached a plateau. Even though the late 1980s saw a proliferation of new states, this was due more to the disintegration of the Soviet Union, and a pro-democracy nationalism, than the appeal of liberalism *per se*. Developmentalist ideologies – particularly up to the early 1980s – also continued to manifest themselves in Keynesian welfarism. The latter had reached its zenith in Europe in the mid-1970s and early 1980s.

By far the most important change within the structure of ideology was the emergence of a particular strain of instrumentalism. We refer here to the emergence in the early 1980s of neoliberalism. Premised on limitless economic expansion, mandatory free trade, deregulation, the emasculation of organized labour, and unmediated flow of capital, this form of instrumentalism had by the end of the 1980s established itself as the *lingua franca* within political, economic, and bureaucratic circles. Enmeshed with all these ideological tendencies were the perennial conservative manifestations of statism and nationalism. This combination continued to provide the basis for Cold War antagonisms that remained as intense as they had been in previous decades.

1972–89: prevailing structural imperatives – conclusion

It was apparent throughout this period that powerful structural imperatives served simultaneously to integrate and fragment a myriad of traditional social and economic relationships. These forces also resulted in a reconfiguration of traditional forms of national and global governance.

Central to this dynamic were highly advanced systems of production and communication, as well as emerging ideologies extolling the virtues of unconstrained capital.

In what follows we begin to explore the implications of these structural imperatives for the transnational network of labour organizations. We begin by focusing on one of the principal indicators of globalization – the extent to which organized labour was able to integrate across national borders. Consistent with observations of earlier periods, it will become apparent that whereas labour's continuing organizational presence across continents constituted a globalization of sorts, this did not necessarily entail greater intra-network integration; and nor did it signal a turning away from the particularity of the state. In other words, even though the network's institutions continued to expand across the globe, there was little evidence of a more profound form of globalization.

3
1972–89 – Internal Change: Expansion and Uneasy Integration

The organizational dimension – introduction

Our study of labour's globalizing tendencies recommences with a review of the network's organizational dimension of change during the 1972–89 period. Beginning with a survey of the horizontal organization of the network during the 1972–89 period, we look to identify changes that occurred among the peak confederations. This will be followed by an analysis of the vertical forms of organization that were evident during this time. What will emerge is a profile of a network that has gradually become more integrated within this organizational dimension. By the late 1980s there was a resolution in the struggle between those transnational confederations vying for the position of the network's principal organ. Ultimately, the International Confederation of Free Trade Unions was to emerge as the pre-eminent confederation. Of its rivals, the World Federation of Trade Unions began to slide into obscurity, while the World Confederation of Labour continued to play a relatively marginal role within the world of cross-border labour politics. On the global level this represented a further organizational integration in the network's form. In addition to greater integration on the level of the nationally oriented confederations, we also see the growing relevance of the various industry-specific confederations, as well as the emergence of very important regional trade union bodies. The following survey of the horizontal forms of organization is the first stage of a more detailed account of the changes outlined earlier.

The organizational dimension – the horizontal

In 1972 the transnational network of labour organizations comprised the International Confederation of Free Trade Unions, the World

Federation of Trade Unions, and the World Confederation of Labour. These confederations were themselves comprised of national trade union affiliates. In addition, there existed a number of industry-specific trade secretariats. This basic configuration was to stay in place for most of the next 20 years. This was in contrast to the immediate post-war period when the organizational form of the network at this peak level seemed to be in a constant state of flux.

By the end of this period the ICFTU had established itself as the most representative of all the transnational confederations. As time progressed, it enhanced its reputation by adopting a more supportive and sophisticated approach to trade union actors beyond its traditional European constituency.[108] Its membership increased from 48.6 million in 1972, to 84.8 million in 1983, and to more than of 100 million in 1989 (this translated into 115, 134, and 143 affiliated organizations for each period).[109] By 1972 the ICFTU had established a presence throughout Asia, Africa, and Latin America, as well as permanent offices in Geneva, Washington, and New York. Similarly, its income grew from (bfr)91 million[110] in 1972, to 160 million in 1980, and then to 326 million by 1989. Finally, the ICFTU's expenditure on 'Solidarity Activities' increased from (bfr)43.7 million in 1972, to 69 million in 1980, and then to 89.5 million in 1989.[111] While all this is indicative of the organizational growth of the ICFTU, it masks the true complexion of an actor that was beset by problems of fragmentation, and state-bound political interests.

This period was also noteworthy because it witnessed the slow decline of the ICFTU's major rival, the World Federation of Trade Unions. The WFTU began to lose important affiliates during the late 1970s: by the late 1980s more and more of its constituent parts were defecting to the ICFTU.[112] This was to deny the WFTU legitimacy and relevance, as over half of its remaining membership was supplied by the Soviet Union's sole domestic labour federation. Though its official membership figures throughout the 1970s and the 1980s showed quite a dramatic increase, these figures were widely disregarded.[113] The WFTU continued to fund and direct its industry-specific bodies – the Trade Union Internationals. Like their Western counterparts, the International Trade Secretariats, these bodies focused on industries associated with transport, mining, food, textiles, chemical, education, and construction.[114] But unlike the trade secretariats, these transnational sectoral confederations were not only beholden to a major nation-based confederation – in this case the WFTU – but by extension also to the governing parties in whose countries they operated. In reality – and according to one Trade

Union International president – such confederations were concerned with the need to 'mobilize all national resources for ... economic development'.[115]

Meanwhile, the leadership of the third peak confederation then in existence – the World Confederation of Labour – was attempting to consolidate its presence beyond its traditional European heartland. To a great extent, the Confederation was positioning itself as the most oppositional of the remaining peak bodies. Having shed its brand of Christian-socialism in the mid-1960s, the World Confederation of Labour now embraced what Windmuller and Pursey describe as 'a secular militant programme based on a mixture of humanist, socialist, and syndicalist ideas'.[116] In doing so it aimed to differentiate itself from the reformism of the ICFTU and the doctrinaire Marxism of the WFTU. Yet the gains it did make in this period could not mask its reliance upon the membership of just a few European affiliates. Most notable among these affiliates were the Confederation of Christian Trade Unions of Belgium, and Solidarność of Poland. The relative weakness of the World Confederation of Labour was in no small part due to the lack of patronage from governments, and its reluctance to accommodate the needs of capital or the state. In relation to the WFTU, and the ICFTU in particular, this confederation remained a marginal actor.

To complete this view of the organizational form of peak confederations we must consider the configuration of the industry-specific International Trade Secretariats. The most notable trends impacting on trade secretariats throughout this period was the continuing organizational consolidation and the process of geographical expansion. This mirrored developments within the network of nation-based bodies, wherein organizational consolidation and stability was maintained while the membership and geographic reach expanded. By 1979 the trade secretariats had a combined membership of 56.4 million.[117]

The trade secretariats were, of course, more likely to be configured in ways that mirrored the conditions determined by the global structures of production. Those concerned with industries at the heart of the new global division of labour enjoyed the most growth. Thus, trade secretariats covering industries relating to textiles, chemicals, mining, transport, communications, and manufacturing increased their memberships. The largest of these was the International Metalworkers' Federation. Its membership stood at 13.7 million in 1979, and rose to approximately 16 million in 1989.[118] Notwithstanding the rise in membership, most trade secretariats experienced financial difficulties. Constituent trade unions even from the more prosperous countries found the affiliation fees prohibitive. Those trade secretariats that were concerned with industries predominantly located within developing and Third World countries could not fund activities because of the modest affiliation fees imposed on their member unions. The International Trade Secretariats also bear mentioning because many had in place what came to be known as World Company Councils. These councils were established in order to bring together employees of the same corporation or corporations, but by the mid-1980s most were moribund. Their demise was due mainly to the antipathy of the multinational corporations that they were designed to monitor.[119]

This assessment of the organizational configuration of the peak transnational confederations shows that while the network's outward form remained stable on this global plane, the ICFTU was gradually assuming a pre-eminent position over other nation-oriented peak confederations. In large part, the ICFTU was able to assert itself in this way because it was the most amenable – indeed, the most committed – of all the confederations to the proliferating system of trade and development inclined intergovernmental organizations mentioned earlier. This reformist character also made it a relatively docile actor in the eyes of state elites preoccupied with Cold War antagonisms, and though it was associated with Western interests it still attracted many disaffected affiliates of rival confederations because of its pluralistic form.

The point to be made here is that within this organizational dimension the transnational network of labour organizations extended, *via* one agent or another, across all regions and industrial sectors. To all intents and purposes, this network was by now truly global in scope. And yet notwithstanding this expansion in reach, these peak confederations remained obscure and impotent players in the world of labour politics. Moreover, this form of expansion had little to do with a globalization of the sort outlined at the beginning of this book. Put differently, this expansion was not necessarily indicative of greater network integration, or of the network's autonomy in relation to the state. A better understanding of the undercurrents shaping relationships can be gained by turning to the organizational form of the movement on a vertical plane.

The organizational dimension – the vertical

The most significant change occurring on this vertical plane was the emergence, and growing importance of, the regional organizations. In many ways these labour organizations came to play a more important role than the peak confederations to which they were affiliated. Indeed, while the configuration of the peak confederations remained relatively stable throughout the 1970s and 1980s, there was considerable change occurring among intermediary bodies linking national affiliates to the wider network.

We recall that the major transnational confederations had by 1972 established a loose network of subsidiary, regional, organizations. The ICFTU had representation in Asia, Latin America, Africa, and Europe through its own nation-oriented offshoots. The smaller World Confederation of Labour had also established its own offices in these regions and was represented by important regional organizations.[120] The WFTU had no such organizational structure in place and chose instead to connect with regions beyond Europe through direct affiliation with trade union bodies of different countries. Added to the intermediary organizations already in existence was the Trade Union Advisory Committee, a stand-alone labour body established to represent trade union interests within the OECD.

Between 1972 and 1989 there was a proliferation of new regional and sectoral trade union bodies. These included the Council of Nordic Trade Unions (1972), the European Trade Union Confederation (1973), the Organization of African Trade Union Unity (1973), the All Africa Teachers' Organization (1974), the Commonwealth Trade Union Council (1979), the Federation Africaine des Syndicats des Mineurs et des Energeticiens (1979), the Pacific Trade Union Community (1980), the Southern African Trade Union Co-ordination Council (1984), the International Miners' Organization (1985), the Asia-Pacific Trade Union Co-ordination Committee (1987), and the South Asian Regional Trade Union Council (1988). These joined the ranks of existing regional labour bodies. Apart from those that represented the interests of the peak confederations (those mentioned above), there also existed a number of regional groupings that had been established prior to 1972.[121] The most important of these were the International Confederation of Arab Trade Unions. We might add to this list the many large national organizations that also engaged in cross-border activities. The more prominent of these were the national organizations of America, Britain, Germany, The Netherlands, South Africa, France, Sweden, and Japan.

1972–89: The organizational dimension – conclusion

In one sense all the foregoing can be read as being indicative of a continuing expansion of the global network of labour organizations, and of its taking root in areas beyond its traditional heartland in Europe and North America. Certainly, within this internal organizational dimension there seemed to be evidence of an ever-expanding labour network: this, in turn, hinted at a more profound process of globalization for labour. However, this organizational expansion tells us little about the true extent of organized labour's integration, and its necessary and continued preoccupation with forms of political organization premised upon the authority of the state. Moreover, as we proceed we find that the changes occurring in this organizational dimension – on both horizontal and vertical planes – can be linked to the fact that the state continued to play a pivotal role, be it in relation to changing structures of production, governance, and ideology. We explore these issues by moving beyond the organizational sphere, to the dimension concerned with network integration.

1972–89: the integrative dimension – introduction

What intra-network factors were at play in the organizational reconfiguration outlined earlier? For a better understanding of these processes we now look at the ways in which relationships within the network were mediated and constituted throughout this period. This once again entails a review of the communication media upon which interaction was premised, and consideration of the interests and ideologies that gave shape to this internal integrative dimension. It soon becomes apparent that in spite of the inexorable organizational expansion, intra-network integration proved elusive. This was so because the interests and ideologies informing the various actors created deep divisions. These were motivating factors that made continuing alignment to the state the overriding concern.

The integrative dimension – relationships

Earlier, in the brief analysis of the structure of production for this period, we noted the dramatic technological advancements in areas of transmission, information storage and stratification. This increase in the velocity and intensity of worldwide communication was facilitated by new media, including fax, compact discs, video, personal computers, satellite technology, and fibre-optics, as well as by technological advancement in the fields of transport. A focus on the communication media employed by labour in this context provides another vantage point from which to study change throughout the transnational network of labour organizations. It is here that we might expect to see various media facilitating greater cross-border interaction between labour organizations: and yet we find instead that this media did little to change a *milieu* characterized by fractiousness and statism. It is thus surprising that under such conditions organized labour's globalization was retarded to the degree it was.

Certainly the network's communication regime underwent significant, if gradual, change in this 1972–89 period. As in any political community we see a reliance on both old and new technologies, as well as on media that might facilitate either face-to-face, extended, or detached interactions. The most important medium that facilitated face-to-face interaction within the network of trade union confederations was the conference. The intra-network conference circuit became a site of vibrant exchange and engagement as transport – particularly civil air travel – became cheaper and more accessible. Thus the technologies that had begun to connect people in the realms of business, tourism, and education, also played an important role in expanding linkages within the disparate trade union communities.

In the context of intra-network interaction, the medium of the conference assumed a variety of forms throughout this period. Conferences held under the auspices of the peak confederations – the International Confederation of Free Trade Unions, and the World Federation of Trade Unions – brought together their respective affiliates. There were also conferences whose participants consisted of established, but disaffected, national trade union bodies; as well as those whose participants represented trade union organizations of the newly independent and non-aligned countries. Finally, there were conferences held for the express purpose of courting rival confederations' affiliates in the hope that they would switch their allegiance.[122] Overall, this proliferation of conference sites and events reflected the growing diversity of labour actors and their contending interests. It was indicative of a network whose centre of gravity lay far from the peak confederations that purported to represent the interests of the whole.

What motivated national trade union bodies to participate in conferences that were not sanctioned by their own peak confederation? Most national bodies acknowledged the existence of a global dimension to the problems besetting trade unions. Furthermore, they acknowledged the need to cooperate across borders in order to ameliorate the worst aspects of these problems. However, many also considered the peak confederations to be seriously handicapped – or, at worst, compromised – by their association with the superpowers and Cold War politics in general.

Against this background, leaders of many national organizations began to meet with a view to overhauling the network of transnational confederations. In addition to increasing face-to-face interaction by those seeking to change the existing network's overall political orientation, there were conferences catering for those wanting to give voice specifically to the labour movements of the non-aligned world. This started a trend that saw trade union organizations of the developing and Third World congregating at regional-level conferences. The participants here saw the likes of the ICFTU as representatives of the wealthy labour movements of the 'North', and resented what they perceived as the patronization of their First World counterparts. Thus, far from indicating greater harmony, cohesion or levels of integration within the ensemble of worldwide trade union confederations, this proliferation of cross-border gatherings – this form of global interaction – was evidence of very significant cleavages. Put simply, these somewhat fleeting interactions were not indicative of greater movement integration.

Indeed, for the ICFTU Executive Board the agenda item 'International Trade Union Gatherings' became somewhat of a preoccupation.[123] Throughout the 1970s and 1980s, the number of international conferences without the ICFTU's endorsement or support increased dramatically, and proved to be a cause of great consternation. The ICFTU Executive Board was concerned that its own affiliates would attend these conferences and be lured away by confederations committed to oppositional programmes. It was thought that this in turn might undermine the ICFTU's position as the pre-eminent transnational confederation. This concern prompted a series of communiqués to affiliates pointing out the dangers of flirting with the programmes of rival confederations.[124] For their part the WFTU and the World Confederation of Labour actively promoted such gatherings. The former did so because it lacked an organizational presence at the regional level, and thus relied upon bilateral and multilateral engagements with autonomous players within the network to maintain credibility. The World Confederation of Labour also needed to establish a presence beyond its traditional Christian supporter base in Europe if it was to establish itself as a new, secular, and radicalized advocate for trade unions worldwide. And so it too regularly sponsored and participated in conferences that brought together what the ICFTU regarded as the radical elements within the world of trade union politics. For its part, the ICFTU believed that the WFTU and the World Confederation of Labour mischievously promoted their conferences in ways that implied the events had ICFTU endorsement.[125]

On one reading such changes to the face-to-face medium connecting the constellation of trade union confederations may seem unremarkable. But when considered in the context of the ways in which actors can become more integrated or autonomous – indeed, more globalized – such changes provide food for thought. We witness the reaching-out by many of the constituent parts of the network in ways that might suggest that it was changing in some fundamental sense. Instead, we find that this increased level of connectedness had little to do with a greater sense of network integration, or with the constituent parts transcending parochial concerns.

The focus now turns to the relatively extended relationships enabled by media based on print. Traditionally, such media consisted of pamphlets, newsletters, bulletins, circulars, reports, newspapers, and periodicals. With the possible exception of the pamphlet, these printed forms of communication continued to be used throughout the 1970s and 1980s to integrate the network's constituent parts. The most important of all such printed media was the in-house periodical, a medium employed by each of the confederations surveyed thus far.

Since the 1950s these periodicals had been, by and large, handsomely produced publications that were usually distributed on a monthly basis. Typically, the content included editorial commentary on the major issues of the day, messages from senior officials, dispatches from regional affiliates, previews of upcoming congresses, news of progress in campaigns within or beyond intergovernmental fora, as well as what seemed like the obligatory broadsides aimed at rival confederations. Importantly, these publications also carried within them the texts of official resolutions, statements, and declarations issued by executive bodies. With a few exceptions, the overall production quality of these periodicals up to the early 1980s was very impressive. Distribution was global and without charge to affiliates.

By the mid-1980s, however, the form, content, and production quality of the various periodicals distributed by the peak confederations had markedly diminished. This trend was apparent across the spectrum of confederations. The deterioration in the form was most apparent in the ICFTU's *Free Labour World*.[126] At the same time the WFTU's periodical – *World Trade Union Movement* – was also showing signs of decline. Unlike *Free Labour World*, it survived the 1980s without drastic changes to its format, though its declining fortunes were evident in other ways. Perhaps the most striking of these was the 1987 decision on the part of the editors of this journal of anti-imperialism and radical socialism to carry advertisements.[127] Similar trends were apparent among the publications of other peak confederations; namely, the International Trade Secretariats and the World Confederation of Labour. Though the quality of production varied greatly between trade secretariat publications, these too deteriorated throughout the 1980s.[128]

Perhaps the foregoing has overstated the significance of the form of printed media employed throughout this period. But it is worth dwelling on this aspect because the health or otherwise of these journals may be indicative of deeper trends across the network as a whole. Of course, the content of the media is of paramount importance, as these publications were the confederations' principal means of expressing their interests and ideologies. These interests and ideologies will be covered in some detail in subsequent discussion and need not concern us here. For the moment we can rely on Peter Waterman's observations for a general understanding. According to Waterman, the publications of the peak confederations tended to 'reflect or reproduce interstate or inter-bloc relations'. They encouraged 'factionalism within the third world countries by seeking loyal members, and such member organizations exercise[d] a virtual veto on criticism of "their own" nation-state'. This factionalism, Waterman claims, meant that these 'publications [were] able to respond to new waves of worker protest (Poland, South Africa, Brazil, Philippines) only in a selective and partisan manner'.[129]

What, then, do these observations tell us about the importance of the print media in use during the 1970s and 1980s? One point to be made is that this traditional means of maintaining relationships and, ostensibly, for integrating the network, seemed to be in serious decline at the very moment when the movement, taken as a whole, was expanding its global reach. If the nature and quality of communication media is any indication, we can deduce that in addition to greater estrangement between peak bodies, there was also increasing distance between the confederations and their constituent parts.

Alongside the conferences and print media there was also a reliance on electronic modes of interaction and communication. These facilitated what might be regarded as detached forms of interaction, and can be grouped into media that were employed to reach the constituents directly, and those used to coordinate, administer, and integrate the confederate structures that bound the network as a whole. Included in the former category were radio, television, and the audio-visual, while in the latter we find the telephone, telegram, telex, and fax.

By the 1970s few within the transnational network of labour organizations were relying on radio. The ICFTU's interest in the medium had waned by this stage, with its anti-communist programme – *The Voice of Free Trade Unions* – having lost the relevance that it once had.[130] The WFTU had since 1981 broadcast *World Federation of Trade Unions Calling* using the facilities of Radio Prague. This provided information on the activities of the WFTU Secretariat, news about the issues concerning affiliates, interviews, and reports. Initially, this service was presented in eight languages and consisted of regular ten-minute programmes. By 1985 this format had changed to fortnightly half-hour broadcasts of programmes in 25 languages. By 1989 it catered for just eight languages and was broadcast on a range of days chosen in accordance to language group. Ultimately, the WFTU's use of radio decreased to the point where it barely figured at all.[131]

The role of television was also negligible. Again we see the use of the medium within various national contexts: but here too the experiments were sporadic and short-lived. In 1974 the Belgium Joint Union Front produced a television series consisting of ten programmes that were to be screened three times per week during workers' rest breaks.[132] These were well received but could not continue due to employer resistance. The American Federation of Labor-Congress of Industrial Organizations also utilized the medium of television. In 1982, the Federation worked with its offshoot, the Labor Institute of Public Affairs, to produce and distribute programmes using public access cable television and other network outlets.[133] To these we can add the use of various forms of electronically based audio-visual media such as video and film. However, these were used only by pro-labour organizations that were not formally associated with the network of trade union confederations.[134] Thus, notwithstanding these localized initiatives, the mediums based on radio, television, and audio-visual forms played an insignificant role in the integration and globalization of what remained a very loose network of transnational labour confederations.

The most prevalent electronic media employed up to 1989 were the telephone, telegram, telex, and fax. It is difficult to assess the role of the ubiquitous telephone, suffice to say that as the costs associated with transcontinental connections fell, usage must have increased accordingly. The telegram, telex, and fax were also being utilized, though their usage did not fundamentally transform relationships within the network of labour organizations. Indicators of the significance of these media can be found in seemingly innocuous places. For example, the ICFTU only began to request its affiliates pass on their telex numbers in 1984. Similarly, the first systematic use of telex for campaign purposes came in 1985. It was then that the ICFTU launched its *Telex News*, an electronic communiqué aimed at influencing popular opinion *via* the mass media. In sum, this approach to the use of well established forms of electronic media betrayed a degree of tentativeness within the network, and one that was symptomatic of an estrangement between the network's constituent parts and of a lack of integration in general.

In a sense, we should not read too much into this survey of the different media in use throughout the 1970s and 1980s. It must be acknowledged that at various times each media had different audiences and served different functions. Conferences were a relatively unconstrained two-way form that served to bring together – face-to-face – delegations of leaders from disparate political communities. Periodicals and print were carefully controlled and tailored forms, employing language familiar only to the literate and politically attuned. They imparted information one-way – and at a remove – and were principally concerned with influencing labour leaderships. Ostensibly aimed at the broader membership, these periodicals in practice served to reassure, exhort, and galvanize support among the officials of each affiliated organization. The electronic media highlighted here seemed to be either ineffective and ephemeral (in the case of radio and television) or employed predominantly as an administrative tool (in the case of telex). In addition, these media were utilized concurrently, so clear transitions from one to another are not easily discerned.

Yet, these media are worthy of our attention because their use facilitated different forms of interaction, be they face-to-face, extended, or detached. Focusing on them provides insight into the process of movement re-configuration and, in particular, into change in levels of integration. For instance, focusing on the medium of the conference reveals that face-to-face interactions were increasing at a time when the network as a whole was very divided. At the same time, less emphasis was placed on the extended print media. This was illustrated by the deteriorating quality of the principal form, the periodical. And finally, the use of electronic media up to 1989 seemed to hardly matter in terms of movement cohesion and integration, though it was becoming more important as the 1980s came to an end.

Overall, this focus on the media at work within the internal integrative dimension of transnational labour politics indicates that throughout this period there emerged a constellation of confederations that was becoming a more vibrant site of interaction with an ever-increasing number of participants. To this extent we can identify the expansion of the network in ways that had the potential to loosen the bonds to the state. This was evident in the growing connectedness – especially *via* the conference – of parties whose engagement up to this point was limited. However, this process did not bring with it greater network integration. While change was occurring in the ways in which relationships were mediated, the 'centre-pieces' of this already loose system of confederacies – those peak confederations identified earlier – remained largely estranged not only from one another, but from their own affiliates.

Once again – and as was evident in the preceding analysis on the organizational dimension – one cannot be convinced of any substantive or profound re-alignment in the network's orientation by focusing only on one dimension of change. While it is apparent that the new media enabled greater intra-network engagement, this is not in itself proof of increasing integration across national borders – or of a turning away from the state. If anything, such change is an indication of intra-network discord. For a better understanding of this internal integrative dimension, we need to revisit the interests and ideologies that permeated the network throughout the 1970s and 1980s. Here it becomes apparent that while some of the foregoing changes in internal organization and media suggested a deeper form of globalization pertained, they were in reality symptomatic of a movement that remained fixated on the authority of state.

The integrative dimension – interests, ideologies

The interests and issues of concern to the transnational network of labour organizations were inextricably tied to changes wrought by the aforementioned structural imperatives. How did these imperatives affect cross-border trade union politics? The dynamics inherent generated a range of both divisive and integrative factors. In what follows we look first at the interests that either divided or integrated this sprawling ensemble of cross-border trade union organizations. Attention then shifts to the interplay of ideologies evident within the network at this time. Ultimately, we see that the interests and ideas that permeated the network throughout this period – be they divisive or integrative – all in one way or another served to keep trade union confederations within the orbit of the state, thus mitigating a globalization of any substance.

Organizational decentralization was a serious concern for labour leaders of the peak confederations. This decentralization – often referred to as 'regionalism' – was manifest in the growth of a new layer of trade union representation that in effect served to widen the gap between the peak confederations and their affiliates. For transnational organized labour the most important development in this regard was the formation in 1973 of a new regional body, the European Trade Union Confederation. A result of a merger of the European Confederation of Trade Unions and the European Free Trade Area Trade Union Committee, this organization was comprised of the affiliates of existing peak confederations. From its inception and throughout the 1980s it served as a lobbying body within European Community institutions. The European Trade Union Confederation can also be considered a response to the prevailing structures of organization in the region. This had resulted in European states joining together to harmonize regulatory regimes in relation to the movement of goods, services, capital, and labour, as well as in relation to common agricultural and transport policies.

The establishment of this European trade union organization caused consternation within the International Confederation of Free Trade Unions in particular. As one author observed:

> the desire of most of the European affiliates to form a separate organization was seen as an affront to trade union internationalism and a threat to the continuity of the ICFTU as a world body.[135]

The World Confederation of Labour was also dealt a blow by this regional turn when the members of its own European offshoot chose to affiliate with the European Trade Union Confederation. For these established peak confederations – as well as for the International Trade Secretariats – the emergence of a new and autonomous regional body had the potential to trigger widespread fragmentation. In addition to the threat of fragmentation, many labour leaders of the West feared that such a body might accept as affiliates trade union organizations of the communist states. Tensions between many important labour organizations increased markedly when the European Trade Union Confederation proceeded to consider such requests for membership.[136]

Over time, cordial relationships were established between this new regional body and the transnational confederations, with most national organizations choosing to affiliate to both. But the underlying problem persisted: because the peak confederations did not cater for their affiliates' most pressing needs, the latter sought to build relationships of a more relevant and intimate sort at a lower level than the 'global'. These were, importantly, relationships and alliances that were designed to accommodate changes occurring in the organizational form of the state. To this extent the proliferation of cross-border interactions on the part of trade union organizations mirrored the states' own shift towards regionalism, especially as it pertained to trade and security matters. And so what in one sense can be regarded as increased cross-border interaction on the part of organized labour – on the regional level – can also be read as a retreat from the global. This is especially so if one takes as an indicator the various actors' (waning) confidence in their network's peak confederations.

The case of the European Trade Union Confederation is illustrative of just some of the tensions evident throughout the transnational network of labour organizations. The tenuousness of the confederate relationships – between transnational bodies and their often ambivalent affiliates – was apparent in other ways during this period. And in these cases we also see tensions that were inseparable from developments in the field of interstate politics.

Another contentious issue was *détente* between the superpowers. This brought to the fore tensions and contending interests evident among not only European trade union bodies, but also among those throughout the network as a whole. In the early 1970s national affiliates to the ICFTU began to form their own relationships and policies in relation to communist countries and their trade union movements. These initiatives took different forms. In seeking closer contacts with their counterparts in Eastern Europe, the labour movements of West Germany and Austria aligned their policies with those of their respective social-democratic parties. At the same time national labour organizations of the United Kingdom and Belgium pursued bilateral contacts with the WFTU, as well as with the World Confederation of Labour. Similarly, national organizations of The Netherlands and Belgium also moved to establish closer ties with the left-leaning World Confederation of Labour. These interactions with 'rival' organizations alarmed the leadership of ICFTU, as it remained committed to a policy aimed at isolating trade unions of the Eastern bloc.

Intra-network tension over priorities and interests were also plainly evident in relations between the ICFTU, its regional offshoots, and many autonomous national or regional bodies beyond Europe. For example, the lure of Pan-Africanism meant that network integrity and cohesion in the African setting was extremely difficult to attain.[137] Hostile to neo-colonialism, national(ist) trade union leaders in this region often accused the ICFTU of paternalism. In Asia, the network of transnational labour organizations had to contend with the full spectrum of contending interests and priorities. Coordination and integration was mitigated under these conditions. These conditions saw national trade union movements subjected to extreme repression in countries such as China, Indonesia, Thailand, and Burma. Civil wars in the Philippines and in Sri Lanka complicated matters further. Economic underdevelopment, extreme poverty, gender inequality, religious and cultural impediments – such as the caste system in India – all meant that common cause throughout the network was elusive to say the least.

Economic development was a high priority for newly independent nations. Within this context the leaderships of national trade union organizations were frequently enlisted to serve the national project. This aspect of the study will be further explored when the research turns to the movement's external political dimension. For the time being it is worth noting that under such circumstances service to the state was paramount for many leaders of national trade union organizations, and the drive towards economic development made governments very intolerant of protests on behalf of workers' rights. This was especially so in the case of many public sector trade unions whose members were already engaged in servicing governments. Coercion aside, there were those who willingly submitted to such imperatives. The leaderships of the trade union movements in Japan and South Korea can be placed in this category.

In Central and South America throughout the 1970s and 1980s a number of formidable hurdles stood in the way of movement integrity. The region comprised only a few industrialized countries – for example, Brazil, Chile, and Argentina – with most engaged in the export of raw products and agricultural produce. All peak confederations were experiencing difficulties in maintaining relations with – and between – national affiliates in these regions as the latter endured tremendous hardship. Poverty and underdevelopment had increased dramatically in this period as governments embraced neoliberal, free-market orientated economic programmes. This exacerbated existing socio-economic problems of inequity in land ownership, and in the rights of ethnic and indigenous minorities. Throughout this period repressive regimes subjected trade unionists to extreme violence, with the governments of Colombia, Guatemala, El Salvador, and Chile among the worst offenders. In addition, civil wars in Nicaragua and El Salvador meant that those countries' labour movements were all but disabled for much of the 1970s and 1980s.

Figuring in this landscape was ORIT,[138] the ICFTU's regional organization. This was an unusual organization in that it pre-dated the ICFTU itself, having had a previous incarnation as the Confederación Interamericana de Trabajadores (1948–1951). This prior history is relevant because even though it now represented the ICFTU in the region, ORIT still retained a considerable degree of independence. When the American Federation of Labor-Congress of Industrial Organizations withdrew its affiliation from the ICFTU, its participation in ORIT continued.[139] The Americans asserted their influence in the region through the latter, and changed the complexion of the ICFTU's regional body in a way that made it far more amenable to the conservative political forces in the region. At a time when right-wing coups and dictatorships were commonplace, the approach taken by the American federation and ORIT enraged many affiliates of the ICFTU in that region and beyond.[140] Undeterred, the Federation also threatened to withdraw its funding from ORIT unless its chosen leadership team was installed.

The ICFTU Executive Board was, for a time, divided over how to counter this form of interference. This was a delicate issue not least because the Federation's financial contribution to ORIT was crucial.[141] These differences over political and ideological allegiances reverberated throughout the network. Some important European affiliates to the ICFTU threatened to cease financial contributions because of what they considered to be the latter's ambivalence over such conservative tendencies, especially as they related to Central and South America.[142]

We have dwelt, once again, on the ICFTU – and in this case, its regional representative – because its experiences at this time reveal the nature of the discord and competing interests within the world of cross-border labour politics. But it is important to also emphasize the fluid nature of these tensions during this period. Indeed, throughout the 1980s ORIT was to some extent rehabilitated as it began to place greater emphasis on opposing human rights abuses and economic austerity policies. This episode is important because we see here the effects of a large number of contending interests, with questions of autonomy, political allegiances to state, and paternalism coming to the fore. The point to be stressed is that labour politics – and the interests and priorities upon which such politics was founded – remained virtually inseparable from the politics of state.

In a sense, all this represents a 'bottom-up' survey of the pressures, interests and priorities that served to divide the constituent parts of the network. Broadly, these contending interests stemmed from tensions over economic integration, *détente*, colonialism, neo-imperialism, development, repression, and human rights violations, usually within the context of civil strife. Across the European, African, Middle Eastern, Asian, and American settings these constraints served to keep national trade union actors orientated towards the state. Such turmoil placed immense obstacles in the way of the peak bodies, thwarting efforts to attain integration, even within their own confederacies. Reconciling these contending interests was an immense task. Establishing a presence in all regions was difficult in itself; maintaining and asserting that presence was harder still.

Yet in spite of these differences the peak confederations also shared many 'integrative' interests. Even though political sensitivities and alignments largely determined the tone of declarations on contentious issues[143] – declarations that cast the peak bodies as bitter rivals – there was also consensus on fundamental matters. There continued to be agreement on such matters such as opposition to apartheid, the nuclear arms race, the abuse of power by multinational corporations, Third World debt, discrimination based on race and gender, the growing violence inflicted on trade unionists, as well as on support for the United Nations.

At a still more abstract level we can characterize the various confederations in ways that reveal even deeper ideological similarities. Ultimately, these similarities can be distilled to the point where a consensus emerges over one ideological tendency: virtually all peak and regional trade union bodies expressed a deep commitment to the ideological tendency that privileged development, modernization, and progress. What is more, this commitment – one that by no means excluded other ideological influences – orientated the network as a whole in a way that made a turning away from the state all but impossible throughout the period under review.

This claim needs elaboration. Throughout the 1970s and 1980s the ICFTU maintained its determined commitment to development, as well as to an equitable redistribution of wealth across nations. The ICFTU repeatedly stressed the importance of generating economic growth for the sake of such development. Its commitment to economic growth and progress went hand-in-glove with support for free trade within a worldwide capitalist market. There were any number of pronouncements, declarations, and resolutions issued over this 20-year period that demonstrate the ICFTU's commitment to attaining development in this manner. The following are typical of the statements made to encourage development and economic growth under a more just global economic order.

> [the ICFTU] recognises the importance in the GATT negotiations of further liberalization of all aspects of trade between the industrial countries in order to ward off the danger of the creation of rival and inward looking economic blocks.[144]
>
> The open world trading system is threatened ... A programme for balanced development must include a strong international framework for the coordination of trade and adjustment policy. The forthcoming GATT Ministerial Council should build on the recent Tokyo round and counter protectionism.[145]

In sum, the ICFTU espoused the view that 'only economic growth can provide the means for more jobs and incomes, whether in the North or

South'.[146] It was by virtue of its support for this economic model that the ICFTU became known – among its critics – as the standard-bearer for reformism and accommodation.

Whereas the ICFTU's rival, the WFTU, proclaimed itself to be anti-capitalist, this did not preclude it from also committing to a modernizing and developmentalist mission. The importance of 'economic and social development' became a constant refrain in the published material of the WFTU throughout this period. The following statements are indicative:

> What is needed ... is the mobilization of all the productive forces around specific and commonly agreed upon short and long-term plans for economic development.[147]
>
> There is no 'development crisis' in the world as such but only in the capitalist world ... The socialist countries have shown that through planning, with the participation of workers and trade unions, high rates of growth of the national economy, balanced industrialization and social progress can be ensured.[148]

Like the ICFTU, the WFTU considered economic and technological advancement to be crucial for delivering to its constituents a form of emancipation from material want. And like the ICFTU, the WFTU – in contrast to the preceding 1945–72 period – also began to stress the need for free trade, albeit in somewhat cryptic terms. Calls were made for 'an end to discrimination in trade and politically-orientated trade and economic boycotts organized by imperialism', and 'mutually advantageous commerce'.[149]

One can also attribute a commitment to developmentalism and progress to trade union organizations in the post-colonial settings. Here pride in recently won independence was very strong. Complementing this was a commitment – especially prevalent among the leadership class within labour organizations – to a form of nation-building that was synonymous with technological, economic, and social development.[150] In this context, to enhance national independence was to embrace a modernizing project. Like their transnational counterparts – the ICFTU and the WFTU – leaders of these national organizations set about the sometimes impossible task of reconciling a commitment to development with the pursuit of global justice and equity.

To claim that throughout the 1970s and 1980s organized labour – across the spectrum – was committed to the development imperative is not in itself so significant. What makes this claim relevant is that in each of the contexts mentioned above development was dependent upon the smooth functioning and integrity of the state and, more specifically, upon the cooperation of governments. The authority of the state was integral to achieving the desired levels of advancement. This applied equally to trade union cultures of the West, the East, or the developing world.

If we were to distil the above we would conclude that while the peak confederations had distinct political and philosophical dispositions, they also shared quite fundamental aims. The most important of these was the commitment to development. Their shared commitment to these ideals – however understood – implied an investment in the authority of government, an investment that continued to mitigate processes that would figure in a deeper form of globalization for labour.

1972–89: the integrative dimension – conclusion

This is an appropriate point at which to review all the foregoing discussion of the internal dimension of change within the network of transnational labour organizations. We commenced by noting that the network's organizational configuration had long ago assumed global proportions, but that this was not necessarily indicative of an integrated, outward-looking, or globalized political community. In the survey of the prevailing forms of integration within the network we first highlighted the roles of the various media through which relationships were constituted. Here conclusions were somewhat tentative. The increase in face-to-face interactions – seen here mainly in the form of the conference – was interpreted more as a symptom of internal discord than of the emergence of an integrated and globalized network. In relation to print and electronic media, the conclusions were also very speculative. The proposition was put that the apparent decline in the importance of in-house publications indicated an ever-widening gap between the peak confederations and their audience of national labour affiliates. And while it was evident that various electronic forms of communication had been in use for some decades, such media were not altering relationships in any profound way, at least not in the period under review.

The role played by interests and ideologies concluded the review of the 1972–89 period. Interests were identified as being either divisive or unifying, and the commitment to developmentalism was seen to be the most important commonly held aspiration throughout the network of transnational confederations. There were no grounds to believe that any of these interests provided the basis for a turning away from the authority of the state. Even the commitment to the universalistic notion of developmentalism in no way put organized labour at odds with the state. On the contrary, the developmentalist imperative increased trade unions' dependence on the state, and mitigated any profound form of movement globalization.

4
1972–89 – External Change: From Incorporation to Partial Disengagement

The political dimension – the national

To 1989, developments on the national plane of this external dimension of change hinted at a partial disengagement between organized labour and the state. And yet, at best, these changes represented only portents of more fundamental changes to come. To elaborate we first look at the fate of the corporatist, and then the functional, relationships between organized labour and the state in the 1972–89 period. These were the relationships that had, for decades, kept trade unions within the orbit of the state. In the earlier survey of organized labour's engagement with this external dimension (1945–72) it was ascertained that the national–political was by far the most important realm of interaction. This predictable finding emerged after a review of corporatist regimes – in both voluntaristic and statist forms – and also of the various ways in which the leaders of trade union organizations committed themselves to defending the interests of the state. Implicit throughout this was the assumption that the labour actors at furthest remove from the national–political realm – that is, the peak transnational confederations – acted as disengaged agents, rather than pivotal actors within the transnational network. In other words, the fixation on the national ensured that this transnational confederacy remained very weak indeed, in spite of its ever-increasing global reach.

What changed in the two decades following 1972? Some of the most important changes related to the voluntarist and statist corporatist arrangements outlined earlier. We noted then the increased level of incorporation from the early 1970s and how this had involved respective actors – businesses, governments, and trade unions – 'exchanging legitimacy' within highly politicized forms of negotiation, as well as highly centralized regimes of collective bargaining.[151]

The prevailing structures of production and organization were to trigger significant changes to these corporatist regimes. The recession of 1973–75 was followed by economic slumps in 1981–83 and in 1987. The subsequent upsurge in neoliberal and conservative ideologies combined to sweep aside many social-democratic governments. In many contexts we saw the decline of such phenomena as the Keynesian welfare state, Fordist production methods, and of social-democratic parties in general. In the workplace, systems of production were – by the mid-1980s – characterized as 'flexible' and 'post-Fordist'.

Beyond the workplace these changes manifested themselves in the dismantling of many centralized-bargaining systems, reduced state intervention, a greater emphasis on adversarial dispute resolution, and the shifting of power from unions to employers. In these turbulent conditions, according to Regini, trade unions were considered by elites to be a

> constraint on the choice among different policy options facing employers and governments as they responded to the double challenge of rising inflation coupled with growing recession ... [These] actors came to regard the participation of trade unions in the management of economic policies as a second-best solution.[152]

The following examples reveal how this trend impacted on the nexus between national trade union organizations and governments in various Western countries. They show that in some cases the labour–government nexus – as it was sustained by voluntarist corporatist relationships – had weakened considerably by the late 1980s. While important actors within the transnational network of labour organizations continued to work closely with governments, others drifted – or were pushed – away from the centers of political authority.

Earlier, we touched upon the Mexican setting, suggesting that trade unions in that country had for many decades been enlisted to serve as stabilizing influences by ruling parties. When the incumbent labour-inclined party – the Partido Revolucionario Institucional – embraced neoliberal ideology in the early 1980s, it set about reversing traditional policies of state expansion, protectionism, and rigid labour markets. The subsequent increase in trade liberalization and privatization contributed to high levels of urban unemployment and instability. Embracing what some have labelled 'savage flexibility',[153] the Partido put in place an industrial relations regime that had a dramatic impact on the once symbiotic relationship between trade unions and government. One aspect of this new regime was the undermining of the status of trade unions.

This happened when reforms were made to the traditional system of highly inclusive collective contracts that had hitherto offered protection to workers across industries. These contracts were reconstituted in a way that accommodated the needs of predatory capital, and that ensured that trade unions were marginalized. In many cases the existing trade unions were replaced by sham 'company unions'. The greatest impact was felt among the trade unions representing employees of the privatized state utilities, and those in the burgeoning system of *maquiladora* assembly-line plants within free-trade zones in the country's northern regions.[154]

Of particular relevance here was the effect this change had on Mexico's principal trade union confederation at the time, the Confederación de Trabajordores de México. In order to retain relevance as a corporatist partner, the Confederación eased its opposition to privatization, wage-restraint, and other reforms aimed at increasing flexibility.[155] This restraint on the part of the Confederación only served to diminish its importance to government, and severely undermined its own legitimacy in the eyes of its affiliates. Thus, by the end of the 1980s, the once-strong corporatist relationship between the Confederación and the ruling Partido Revolucionario Institucional had weakened significantly.

At the same time, a divergence of a similar sort was occurring in Venezuela. The protagonists here were the strong social-democrat party, Acción Democrática, and its trade union partner, the Confederación de Trabajordores de Venezuela. A symbiosis had existed between the two since the 1960s. Whereas the Acción Democrática provided the trade unions with social and political benefits, and labour leaders with political influence, the trade union organization provided the party with logistical and administrative assistance during elections, support for reform programmes, and a union leadership eager to be integrated into mainstream party life.[156] In common with the Mexican experience were the extremely high levels of national indebtedness and the consequent pressure to adopt neoliberal economic reforms. In the case of Venezuela, the implementation of these reforms was delayed somewhat because the nation's oil revenue provided a significant buffer. When this declined, and the level of debt reached crisis proportions, the Acción Democrática embraced policies that were to threaten the long-standing corporatist relationship with the Confederación de Trabajordores de Venezuela. These policies included the removal of subsidies on important staple food items, and the enforcement of a series of wage freezes. Under these circumstances, according to Coker, 'pact-making deteriorated, and labor increasingly acted outside of its corporatist constraints'. As in the

Mexican example, this also served to deny the trade union organization the influence it once enjoyed, resulting in the 'deterioration of corporatist bonds in Venezuela ... [and the Confederación's] steady loss of legitimacy among workers'.[157]

In Europe, the voluntarist corporatist arrangements between governments and trade union organizations were also subject to great stress during this period. The British experience is illustrative. Here, the Trades Union Congress was connected to government through its association with the Labour Party, and through a long-established and elaborate network of tripartite relationships with the civil service. This hitherto uncodified relationship was formalized in a 1974 agreement dubbed the 'Social Contract'. For the remainder of the 1970s, this agreement delivered to the union movement increases in pensions, food subsidies, a rent freeze, price controls, and a strengthening of union rights. It also delivered to the Trades Union Congress unprecedented levels of political influence. Ultimately, the deteriorating economic conditions, and the consequent wage-restraint obligations embodied within the Social Contract, undermined domestic trade union support for the Congress. This, in turn, led to the abandonment of the agreement in 1979. Subsequently, the incoming Conservative government set about dismantling any residual ties between organized labour and government, marking the end of a period in which trade unions had invested heavily in this version of 'state fixation'.[158]

In Italy, a similar pact – the *solidarietà nazionale* – also failed to withstand the pressures associated with the wider structural changes to production and organization. The largest national trade union organization, the Confederazione Generale Italiana del Lavoro, entered into this agreement in 1977. Through the agency of this contract, the Confederazione gained unprecedented influence over industrial and labour market policies. In return, it committed itself to wage restraint. However, like its British equivalent, the *solidarietà nazionale* pact was abandoned by the national trade union body because of a reluctance on the part of affiliated trade unions to endorse the compromises inherent. There followed a period of reform entailing more decentralized collective bargaining throughout Italy, and the marginalization of major trade union organizations. There also followed years of industrial unrest, as all parties attempted to withstand the effects of greater neoliberal reform.[159]

In Sweden – the quintessential corporatist state – strains were also evident in relations between government and the country's major trade union organization. The much-vaunted Swedish model suffered a serious blow in 1976 when the social-democrat party, Svenska Arbeter Partei, lost power after 44 years in office. The country's main trade union organization, the blue-collar Landsorganisationen i Sverige, had to that point been party to a strong corporatist relationship based on the 1938 'Basic Agreement'. Pivotal to this agreement was a commitment to a system of centralized collective bargaining. The gradual breakdown of this system and its replacement with local bargaining followed in the wake of Svenska Arbeter Partei's loss of power. This breakdown was the result not only of this party's demise, but also of the clamouring on the part of business for greater flexibility in the labour market and in wage determination across all sectors. Further weakening this voluntarist corporatist arrangement was the Landsorganisationen's waning influence relative to the emerging white-collar trade union organizations.[160] The latter's rise to prominence was itself a symptom of important change in the structure of production; change marked by the reduction in the numbers of manufacturing jobs in Sweden at the time.

Voluntarist corporatist relations in the then German Federal Republic had also been characterized by relatively durable, longstanding ties between government and organized labour. While the peak national body, the German Federation of Trade Unions (or Deutscher Gewerkschaftsbund), was tied symbiotically to the German Social Democratic Party, it had managed to remain relatively neutral in relation to other political parties. It was to a great extent connected to government through formalized representation in all major ministries. Its influence was most evident during the formative stages of the drafting of legislation, where its views were channelled through the Ministry of Labour. Notwithstanding the hostile economic environment of the 1980s, corporatism in the Republic continued to endure in ways that differed from the previous examples.[161] Yet the 1980s also saw cracks appearing in this regime. In a climate of rising political conservatism, the Social Democratic Party lost office in 1982. This ushered into power those less sanguine about trade union participation in policy-making processes or about Keynesianism in general. The mid-1980s saw high levels of industrial conflict. In an attempt to repackage itself, the German Social Democratic Party distanced itself, from the country's principal trade union organization.[162]

The same trend towards disengagement and decentralization occurred in other Western countries. The early 1980s saw the United States' highly flexible regime of collective bargaining loosened even further. In the absence of formal links to government, the American Federation of Labor-Congress of Industrial Organizations had for many years relied upon the same lobbying methods used by all interest groups.

This meant employing professional lobbyists who would seek to influence legislators and those administering the complex Senate and House committee system. To this extent, organized labour was generally considered a legitimate player – albeit one of countless others – that could petition government in this way. But the Reagan-era policies 'led to a reaction against [labour's] status in a way that would have been [previously] unthinkable',[163] and in a way that curtailed its access to the corridors of the bureaucracy. As well as rejecting the requests of labour's lobbyists, the Republicans excluded organized labour by deregulating key industries, and by decentralizing bargaining processes. Though some might argue that this shift pre-dated Reagan by a number of years, the most crucial changes occurred in 1982 and 1986 – especially in the auto industry – and signalled a sea-change in this area of industrial relations.[164] As in the case of its European counterparts, all this served to marginalize the Federation from the state's decision-making processes. In Canada and Australia, the process of decentralization was also under way. Privatization of the transport and communications utilities in Canada in the 1980s weakened both the main trade union organizations.[165] Their decline continued as various provincial governments embraced industrial relations systems in which bargaining was usually conducted on a single enterprise basis. In Australia, the 1988 incarnation of the tripartite 'Prices and Incomes Accord' introduced a two-tiered bargaining mechanism that opened the way for even greater decentralization in the coming years.[166]

What these various examples shared in common were conditions in which incumbent social-democrat parties had either lost power, or were in such a state of retreat that concessions to organized labour were difficult to honour.[167] In addition, we saw during this period, the rise of non-labour parties that shared a zealous commitment to neoliberal ideology. Finally, common to all settings was what Western refers to as the gradual 'decentralization' of the 'nationally anchored institutions'[168] that had hitherto facilitated trade unions' involvement in matters of policy formation and governance in general.[169] All this points to a separation between the state and organized labour across many national settings. It shows that the state's participation in voluntarist corporatist arrangements had, by the late 1980s, all but disappeared at the national level.

This trend points to a profound shift; to a transformation wherein important elements within the transnational network of labour organizations were compelled to adopt a more autonomous orientation. However, the trend was by no means universal. Lange highlights this point in his study of corporatism among Nordic countries. He finds that – at least in terms of wage fixation – corporatist institutions in some Nordic states proved to be far more resilient than one would expect. Developments in the Japanese setting also defied the trends noted above. Here, we saw organized labour on a trajectory that led to even greater incorporation.[170] Overall, however, this review of voluntarist corporatism in the period leading up to 1989 shows that many nationally anchored trade union organizations experienced a disengagement *of sorts* from the processes and actors linking them to governments.

A more complete examination of labour's relationship within the national–political sphere requires a look at trade unions engaged in statist corporatist regimes. In the earlier review of this form of corporatism – with the focus mainly on Eastern bloc countries – it was established that up to the early 1970s, trade unions served an important functional role on behalf of the party/state. Notwithstanding the cultural and political variations across states, this usually entailed a commitment to achieving production goals, and to serving as intermediaries in relation to enterprise-level management. More broadly, this occurred within systems characterized by central planning, party political control, and state ownership. This was to change throughout the 1970s and 1980s. Gradually, this entanglement with state-controlled systems of management began to loosen. These transformations were closely linked to the changes in structural imperatives mentioned earlier. The deteriorating worldwide economic climate and rapid technological change were very important factors. Developments that were quite unique to communist countries were also significant in triggering a shift away from the traditional dualist model of trade union representation. Though referring here to the Polish context, Kulpinska identifies a number of factors that were evident across many settings at the time. These include

> decentralization, autonomy from the central organs, and administrative management obtained by enterprises, the introduction of market mechanisms, the depoliticization of management, changes in the structure of ownership and in that of economic entities.[171]

Changes also occurred in the disposition and composition of the workforce in these countries. Specifically, there emerged a more educated and technically proficient strata of workers who increasingly voiced their disenchantment with traditional forms of labour representation. More significant still was the gradual relaxation of systems of command management. In their account at the time, Pravda and Ruble observed the following:

> Party and state pronouncements now urge managers to be efficiency-conscious, to extract more and higher-quality production from dwindling resources ... Such demands distinguish more sharply between management and labor interests and increase the likelihood of friction between them.[172]

The corollary of this was that trade unions were forced to assume the unfamiliar role of semi-autonomous bargaining and negotiating agents. As economic growth declined further, and governments anxiously implemented reforms, trade unions assumed even greater importance as intermediaries between the state, the party, management, and workers. Though the nature of change in labour relations varied, each country witnessed the same tendency towards decentralization, flexibility, and greater labour autonomy. In Bulgaria and Poland, for example, the 1980s saw attempts to introduce the *self-management* model of labour relations. Such reforms in Poland were entwined with the changes forced on the government by the Solidarność movement. The latter's demands were expressed through its *Three S* program, representing the call for greater self-management, self-finance, and self-rule.[173] The Czechoslovak government sought greater trade union autonomy by implementing what it referred to as the *brigade form* of labour relations.[174] In the Soviet Union, this process of distancing trade unions from state-managed enterprises was manifest in such concepts as *business democracy, workers' brigades, work collective councils, teams,* and *cost-benefit incentive* schemes.[175] In the German Democratic Republic, the transformation from transmission-belt unionism to limited autonomy was facilitated by such initiatives as the *comanagement* model of labour relations.[176] And finally, the Hungarian experience saw the introduction of *enterprise councils*. Here as elsewhere, trade unions were forced to adapt by getting 'rid of functions alien to their nature'.[177] In broad terms, the liberalization of traditional statist models of labour relations demanded that trade unions reorientate themselves for the sake of the state's pursuit of greater productivity and flexibility.

All this represented a form of gradual, incremental, separation from state control that was not dissimilar to that experienced by trade unions engaged in voluntarist corporatist relationships in the West: though, of course in the case of the communist countries, the degree of autonomy from the state was still negligible in the period up to 1989. Clearly, it would be wrong to claim that there was a schism between organized labour and the state. However, there was an apparent loosening of the formal linkages with government. When considered alongside changes to voluntarist corporatist relationships, there emerges what seems like a more widespread re-orientation. Indeed, it seems that labour relations with governments in many contexts during this period were characterized by a certain degree of disengagement – a process that might, in turn, be a precursor to a more autonomous and, hence, more globalized disposition.

Our examination of such change in the national–political dimension remains incomplete. The above accounts of both voluntarist and statist corporatist relationships are set within the comparatively genteel political environments of the industrialized world. But the world of trade union politics also consisted of engagement premised upon fear, violence, intimidation, and compulsion in many developing and Third World states. Even though a complete survey of this form of repression is clearly beyond the scope of this book, we must acquaint ourselves with relationships that did not fit easily into the categories used so far. This is important because so many of the relationships that came to be premised upon coercion involved government and labour actors that had earlier worked cooperatively during struggles for national self-determination.

Reference was earlier made to such labour–state relationships when the focus was on the role played by trade unions – and their leadership in particular – in achieving independence in many Third World countries. It became apparent that trade union leaders often made the transition into the ranks of the government or the civil service, once independence struggles had been concluded. In subsequent decades – leading up to 1989 – many governments in developing countries adopted strategies aimed at emasculating trade unions. Harris captures well the bleakness of the 1980s for trade unions in these regions:

> Everywhere in the newly industrializing countries they [trade unions] are banned or neutralized, from the tame CGT of Mexico and the yellow unions of Brazil ... to the government-controlled NTUC in Singapore and the explicit legal prohibition on the intervention of 'third parties' (that is, national trade unions) in South Korean industrial disputes.[178]

Governments looking to hasten development sought to render trade unions impotent by using various 'systems of labour control'.[179] Deyo argues that in contrast to the immediate post-independence phase in which governments generally adopted policies of 'populist inclusion' *vis-à-vis* organized labour, the 1970s saw many regimes across Asia and Latin America adopt 'politically exclusionary' approaches premised on violence and repression. Alternatively, many regimes chose to emasculate labour organizations through the use of 'authoritarian corporatist framework[s]'.[180] Under these conditions, according to Petras and Engbarth, the

> ubiquitous state institutions and their highly centralized structures penetrate and control trade unions at the apex – the leaders of federations and confederations frequently appear to be functionaries of government labour ministries.[181]

This swing towards repressive and coercive corporatist arrangements reflected the determination of many single-party states to maintain control, and to provide stable economic environments for foreign investment, economic expansion, and development.[182]

For organized labour, the state loomed large in these contexts. This was so regardless of whether national relationships were characterized by exclusion or by coercive corporatist frameworks. In the case of the excluded trade union organizations, the state ensured separation through intimidation. In those characterized by coercive corporatism, organized labour's incorporation was imposed. The existence of these types of relationships merely underscores the fact that there was no universal model in this period. There were, in fact, clearly discernible trends towards exclusion from decision-making processes, as well as incorporation, albeit through a high degree of compulsion. All this provides a view from the perspective of the transnational labour network's base constituency; that is, the national organizations and their affiliates within specific national contexts. This view of organized labour's relationships with the national–political realm also focuses mainly on changes to industrial relations. But as was apparent in the 1945–72 period, relationships were also marked by a strategic, or foreign-policy, dimension. We must also re-connect with this aspect and consider the extent to which parochialism and functionalism determined the disposition of influential trade union organizations, and the extent to which these labour actors were committed to the defence of the state's strategic interests up to 1989.

The earlier review of strategic and functional relationships in the 1945–72 period ascertained that the American Federation of Labor-Congress of Industrial Organizations and the British Trades Union

Congress had played important roles in the service of their respective state's foreign affairs establishments. Throughout the 1970s and early 1980s, the Trades Union Congress changed its orientation in this respect. Even though the Congress continued to accept direct financial assistance from the incumbent labour government – for various projects in the Third World – it exhibited, according to Press, 'the more moderate aspect of the state/union foreign policy convergence'.[183] To an extent, this withdrawal on the part of British labour was an outcome of tensions in national industrial relations that increasingly saw it excluded from the corridors of power. It was also due to the fact that the Trades Union Congress' traditional commitment to the state was premised more on the need to help maintain Britain's colonial empire than it was on a hostility to the spread of communism.[184] As the British empire receded, so did the Trades Union Congress' enthusiasm for the type of covert operations it had engaged in throughout the 1950s and 1960s. To this extent, the Trades Union Congress began to gravitate away from those concerned with protecting the state's strategic interests, and instead placed greater emphasis on bilateral, solidaristic, cross-border activity.

In contrast, the functional relationship between organized labour and government in the American context followed the same pre-1972 trajectory. The American Federation of Labor-Congress of Industrial Organizations continued to make available its various offshoot organizations for use as tools of foreign policy and for dubious cross-border activities in general.[185] The nature of these activities varied. Beth Sims differentiates between activities involving the education of 'free' trade unions, development of agrarian unionism, funding of social projects, information dissemination and visitor exchanges, political actions, and institution-building. These activities appear to be relatively benign, but when considered within the context of the 'Reagan-Bush "Democracy Offensive" ' they represented valuable tools for those seeking to undermine Left-nationalist or social-democrat labour movements across many developing and Third World settings.[186] Much has been written about this chapter in the Federation's history and we need not engage it in great detail here.[187] Sims' reflections from that period suffice:

> US-funded labor projects create patronage networks which enhance the appeal of allied unions and school up-and-coming union leaders in the principles and tactics of "business" and [American-style] "bread-and-butter" unionism. In addition ... emphasis on directly political activities ... has magnified the political impact of the institutes, as

they directly fund and guide programs aimed at selecting political leaders overseas.[188]

The nexus between the American trade union movement and the state during this period also had a financial dimension, with government largesse flowing to the Federation's offshoots, administering overseas projects. Indeed, the money provided by the Agency of International Development and the National Endowment for Democracy together accounted for 98 per cent of the Federation's activities abroad, with the central executive of the Federation providing the remaining 2 per cent.[189] The scale of this dependence was remarkable and extended beyond the two government institutes mentioned here. Beyond these, there existed a complex network of public and private bodies that acted as conduits for government funding of this sort. In return for this financial assistance the various organs of the Federation ensured that American strategic interests were advanced.

It would seem then that the American example also belies the existence of a universal trend of disassociation of labour organizations from the state. But it should also be acknowledged that during this period – and up to 1989 – there were signs that even this most conspicuous, long-standing relationship of mutual dependence between organized labour and the state was beginning to change. These signs took the form of increasing criticism of the Federation's 'foreign policy' by the rank-and-file groups and officials in the American trade union movement. Throughout the 1980s, trade unionists staged large demonstrations against support for repressive regimes throughout the world, and also engaged in heated debate over these issues at Federation conventions and regional meetings. While this challenge was repulsed by the then leadership, it did indicate that by the late 1980s, ties with government would no longer be uncritically accepted throughout the nationwide network of American trade unions.[190] And while such dissent may not, in itself, have constituted a sea-change in relations between the peak American trade union body and government, it did, according to Sims, 'produce cross-pressures on the [Federation] whose outcomes [were] unpredictable'.[191]

Meanwhile, a functional relationship of a somewhat different kind was emerging in the Asia-Pacific region. In Japan throughout the 1970s and early 1980s, trade unions were aligned with either of two domestic federations. These were the left-leaning General Council of Trade Unions of Japan (or Sohyo), and the conservative, American-supported Japan Confederation of Labour (or Domei). The economic recessions of the 1970s had had an important moderating and pacifying effect on Sohyo. It subsequently followed in Domei's path and established even closer ties with the incumbent Liberal Democratic Party.[192] In 1987 the two labour organizations merged to form Japan's Confederation of Public Sector Trade Unions (or RENGO).

Though corporatism was already a feature of the Japanese setting, this merger heralded the arrival of a still more intimate and functional regime. RENGO was determined to act on behalf of its corporatist partners beyond the Japanese setting. Indeed, we witnessed here a concerted attempt by all protagonists – RENGO, the state, and business – to project their state's influence throughout the Asia-Pacific region. The most important element here was the spread of a Japanese-style 'business unionism'. By virtue of its affinity with the American Federation of Labor-Congress of Industrial Organizations, RENGO was from the mid-1980s able to dominate the International Confederation of Free Trade Union's regional body, APRO.[193] Like its American counterpart, RENGO financed a range of international programs. It did this through its international organ, the Japan International Labor Foundation. Though not so overtly concerned with the geostrategic interests of state, RENGO was preoccupied with expanding Japan's export-oriented corporate economy. It was determined to play a role in the internationalization of Japanese production at a time when that country was an ascendant regional power: so determined, in fact, that it devoted much time and energy to lobbying its government to increase Japan's role in foreign affairs, particularly in the Asian region.[194]

Before concluding this section – and our assessment of the extent to which trade union organizations in this period turned away from the national-political setting – there is a need to take account of functional and strategic relationships within communist countries. Recall that the 1945–72 period saw how the major communist powers – the Soviet Union and China – exploited trade unions and their representatives as front organizations in bitter interstate conflicts. Also apparent, was the extent to which the peak confederation of the Left – the World Federation of Trade Unions – was beholden to the Soviet Union. Then it was established that during the 1970s and 1980s statist–corporatist relationships began to show signs of disentanglement. We now contemplate whether communist trade union organizations continued to serve the interests of state beyond the confines of national industrial relations settings.

Change in this regard is difficult to discern. While there were signs of greater trade union autonomy in matters relating to foreign policy, these were limited. A review of the Russian setting shows the extent to which this was so. What becomes apparent is that the major domestic trade union organization in the Soviet Union was indeed given greater latitude in the 1970s to develop a foreign policy that deviated from that of the state. But like the change noted in most statist corporatist relations, this increased level of autonomy was of a very limited kind.

Like its American counterpart, the domestic organization representing all Soviet workers – the All Union Central Council of Trade Unions – maintained an offshoot body concerned with foreign affairs. The Central Council's International Department was responsible for overseeing every contact made with foreigners, as well as with formulating policy directions for the WFTU itself. Blair Ruble's study of the development of Soviet trade unions in the 1970s offers some insights into the changes that occurred within the International Department; changes that suggest autonomy from the state did increase somewhat throughout the 1970s.[195]

Ruble firstly notes the expansion of the International Department in the 1970s, with a doubling of its staff to over 100. This, he claims, created greater diversity of opinion in a hitherto ossified and insular body. He also notes that whereas prior to this expansion – when 'foreign policy decisions affecting the unions came directly from the Communist Party's Secretariat' – the 1970s saw 'some deviation, be it ever so slight, in union positions on international issues from those of the Party'.[196] This was especially so throughout the 1970s and early 1980s when this principal WFTU affiliate developed broader ties with trade unions in Western Europe. This exposure allowed the International Department and, by extension, the Central Council itself, to develop a more sophisticated worldview than would otherwise have existed.

During this period, the Central Council exploited the withdrawal of American trade union organizations from the ICFTU-led network of Western trade union organizations. The withdrawal by the Americans, lasting until 1982, provided an opportunity for Soviet labour leaders to engage with trade unions of the West and this, in turn, helped trigger the aforementioned change in the Central Council's outlook. Yet, notwithstanding this newfound autonomy, the role of the Central Council continued to be prescribed by the Communist Party. While some change can be discerned, it was indeed marginal, and confirms that the WFTU itself remained very much a transnational confederation beholden to the Soviet Union.

No account of change in labour–state relationships in communist countries during this period would be complete without mention of the

Polish Solidarność movement. The connection between Polish trade unions and the state was not strategic if this is taken to mean an ongoing commitment to the service of states' interests. To this extent the relationship between Polish trade unions and the state does not sit squarely with the examples used earlier. However, this episode is important because it reveals a fault line in the labour–government nexus that went beyond those identified in other statist–corporatist relationships of the day. It is all the more significant because the geo-political importance of Poland to the Soviet Union – the WFTU's superpower patron – would suggest that this setting would be the least accommodating of all for those trade union organizations seeking greater autonomy.

It is not possible to do justice here to the complex nature of the Solidarność trade union, or to the socio-political dynamics of the day. However, we can consider a broad-brush outline. The independent trade union, Solidarność, came into being following the Gdańsk ship-yard strike of August 1980, though its origins can be traced to the emergence of a broad range of social movements in the 1970s. This landmark strike triggered a backlash from the state that included the imposition of martial law and the imprisonment of many Solidarność supporters. The existing national trade union organization in Poland, the Central Council of Trade Unions, was typical of the incorporated democratic-centralist federations throughout Eastern Europe at this time. Like most important affiliates of the WFTU, the Central Council of Trade Unions was closely related to the country's ruling party, the Polish United Workers' Party. In essence, this episode involved a dispute between those wedded to party administered 'democratic-centralism', and those demanding non-hierarchical 'horizontalist' structures of governance.[197] The strategic, instrumental imperatives of the sort found in the previous examples were not so evident here. However, we have in this case an example of trade union disengagement from a state supported, national organization – the Central Council of Trade Unions – as well as a profound rejection of the authority of the state.[198]

Overall, what has this examination of engagements in the national–political dimension revealed? The review of change within voluntarist-corporatist relationships suggested that in many respects organized labour was turning-away – or being turned away – from the state. This view was tempered somewhat after consideration of change in the statist–corporatist regimes within the Eastern bloc countries. Here we saw a barely discernible loosening of labour–state relations that had for decades been structurally determined. The waters were muddied still further in the review of the functional relationships existing between governments and some of the major national trade union organizations. All the examples used here show that while partial disengagement was occurring in important sectors of trade union politics worldwide, there remained strong residual ties between some very powerful national trade union organizations and their respective governments. Yet it is safe to say that even in relationships in which organized labour remained committed to serving the interests of state there appeared faint signs of more profound, future change.

Indeed, in comparison with the preceding historical period – 1945–1972 – there is evidence here of a widespread, yet uneven, drift by organized labour away from the corridors of state power. While acknowledging this shift, we should note that the apparent drift did not constitute an estrangement or disengagement from the state *per se*. Clearly, these indicators alone do not prove that the constituent parts of the transnational network of labour organizations were globalizing in any profound sense. In order to make more definitive statements in this regard, we need to assess the nature of organized labour's engagement with the global-political realm.

The political dimension – the global

A return to this level of analysis necessarily brings back into view the peak confederations. Throughout the 1970s and 1980s, these remained the weakest of all the constituent parts of the transnational network of trade union organizations. Nonetheless, their orientation during this period provides us with an interesting juxtaposition. For at the very historical moment when many affiliated, national, organizations were loosening formal connections to state, the peak confederations were further insinuating themselves into the inter-governmental organizations representing the collectivity of states.

Throughout the 1970s and 1980s, there was a dramatic intensification of interaction between the peak labour bodies and inter-governmental organizations. Indeed, all confederations clamoured to engage with this level of state-mediated governance. This development shows that the process of disengagement identified at the national–political plane did not in itself represent a turning away from the state on the part of the transnational network of confederations. What might be read in one context – the national-political – as a move away from relationships premised upon corporatism and functionalism, appears to be countered here by a concerted move towards integration with the instruments of state on a global plane. To gauge the extent to which this was so, we once more turn our attention to some of the major players within the transnational network of labour confederations.

The International Confederation of Free Trade Union's already strong commitment to dialogue with states within intergovernmental organizations intensified still further in the early 1970s. It was then that the upheavals produced by changes in the structures of production, organization and ideology presented the ICFTU with issues that were increasingly global in scope and intensity. These were manifest in, for example, human rights abuses – including violence directed at trade unionists, discrimination against women, apartheid, and child labour – as well as the nuclear arms race, global economic instability, mass unemployment, and the inexorable spread of the multinational corporation. An important factor in the ICFTU's increased engagement was the developing countries' push within the UN General Assembly to have accepted the Charter of the Economic Rights and Duties of States. This was the mechanism through which demands for a New International Economic Order were channelled. The ICFTU was an enthusiastic supporter of this proposal, and tailored its campaigns on free trade, development, and debt reduction in ways that complemented this goal.

In addition, there was a growing appreciation among senior ICFTU personnel of the increasingly complex nature of the worldwide system of intergovernmental organizations. Many leading figures in the ICFTU believed that if it did not adapt to this new landscape it would lose the little influence it then enjoyed.[199] The subsequent increase in participation took many forms. The ICFTU re-doubled its efforts to assert its presence in the UN Economic and Social Council and its offshoots, the UN Conference on Trade and Development, the UN Industrial Development Organization, the Food and Agriculture Organization, and the UN Educational Scientific and Cultural Organization. It also extended its commitment to the International Labour Organization (ILO). In most of these bodies – with the exception of the ILO – the ICFTU had to be content with 'category A' consultative status, and continued to lobby for the right to participate more fully and present its views in a more formal manner. Beyond this, the ICFTU sought to participate in United Nations events that lay outside the normal framework of meetings and conferences.[200] Even though specialized agencies such as the General Agreement on Tariffs and Trade and the International Monetary Fund continued to deny the ICFTU official status, the latter persisted in its attempts to gain recognition and influence proceedings.[201]

Significantly, the ICFTU's decision to more fully engage with the panoply of inter-governmental organizations also meant that the ILO was no longer its sole focus of attention. While the ILO remained a crucial – indeed, indispensable – component throughout the 1970s and 1980s, it also became one of many avenues open to organized labour. This shift on the part of the ICFTU reflected a greater willingness to engage in questions that had not traditionally featured on the labour rights agenda; those issues relating to global trading regimes, regulation of global finance, and investment. On another level, this intensified integration within the system of intergovernmental organizations necessarily cast the ICFTU in the role of chief advocate for a labour-orientated developmentalism.

Finally, the United Nations took on special significance for the leaders of the ICFTU in this period for reasons to do with intra-network rivalry. Throughout the 1970s and 1980s the ICFTU's principal rival, the World Federation of Trade Unions, intensified its campaign for 'trade union unity'. The mantra of unity resonated through countless statements and resolutions appearing in the WFTU's publications. In stressing the need for cooperation between all confederations, the WFTU sought to join in campaigns with trade union organizations of the West. It also sought to engage with them in conference fora outside of those provided by the 'reformist' inter-governmental organizations. The ICFTU itself was committed to many of these campaigns – the anti-apartheid struggle was a case in point – but considered calls for unity by the WFTU to be part of a ploy aimed at splitting the ranks of ICFTU affiliates.

This placed the ICFTU in an awkward position. Given the nature of the issues at stake, the rejection of such overtures would reflect badly on the ICFTU. The ICFTU leadership hoped to out-manoeuvre its rival by agreeing to cooperate only if their dealings were within United Nations fora, most notably within the ILO. The United Nations system provided the ICFTU with a relatively safe site of engagement with its rival, and one in which it enjoyed favoured status among states and national trade union organizations alike. Thus, by confining all such engagements within the established United Nations system, as well as within other intergovernmental organizations, the ICFTU was able to ensure that its rival was circumscribed by the ideology of reformist–developmentalism upon which the relevant intergovernmental organizations were founded.[202] Whether the ICFTU's increased participation in inter-governmental organizations produced commensurate gains is not of direct relevance to this discussion (it is certainly the case that such involvement did little to defuse intra-network tension).[203] What is important is that in this 20-year period the ICFTU made a determined effort to further embed itself within the United Nations system and other intergovernmental organizations. It did this in order to facilitate the petitioning of governments beyond the ILO, and to seek to create an international regulatory framework that would compel governments to support its policies. There is no doubt that of all the peak confederations, the ICFTU was the most committed participant in the fora of intergovernmental organizations. This is not to under-state the enthusiasm of the other major players within the world of cross-border labour politics. Indeed, the WFTU, the industry-specific International Trade Secretariats, and the World Confederation of Labour, were also investing heavily in such forms of global governance.[204]

After abandoning its initial post-war hostility, the WFTU became an ardent supporter of the United Nations system. Increasingly, throughout the 1970s and into the 1980s, it participated in the proceedings of the ILO, the Food and Agriculture Organization, the UN Educational Scientific and Cultural Organization, and other such bodies overseen by the UN Economic and Social Council. It also participated in sessions of the UN Organization for Industrial Development, and the UN Conference on Trade and Development.[205] And like the ICFTU, the WFTU took part in events held outside the United Nation's normal operational framework.[206] It also mounted campaigns supporting the UN International Women's Year (1975) and, in the 1980s, the UN's second Disarmament Decade, as well as for events related to its third UN Development Decade. The WFTU was also fully supportive of the UN Commission on Transnational Corporations in its attempts to draft a code of conduct for regulation in this area.[207] Thus, the WFTU had by the late 1980s become as dedicated to the United Nations as had the ICFTU. Indeed, like the ICFTU, it was quick to defend bodies such as the ILO and the UN Educational Scientific and Cultural Organization in the face of attacks made on them by the American representatives.[208]

In contrast to the ICFTU, however, the WFTU was not enamoured of the inter-governmental organizations situated beyond the United Nations system. WFTU leaders railed against intergovernmental organizations such as the International Monetary Fund, the World Bank, the General Agreement on Tariffs and Trade, the OECD, and the Trilateral Commission.[209] Unlike the ICFTU, the WFTU did not seek acceptance within these organizations, choosing instead to establish links with the informal sector comprising both nation-based and autonomous, like-minded, movements from across the globe. This process, we recall, manifested itself in the numerous conferences held outside the auspices of established intergovernmental organizations – conferences that caused much angst within ICFTU leadership circles.

What might this contrast between these two major players signify? If the WFTU's rejection of these market-oriented intergovernmental organizations was indicative of a network-wide sentiment there might be grounds for believing a more profound autonomous, oppositional dynamic was at work. This might, in turn, suggest a tendency towards ever greater disassociation from the state in the future. But this was not the case. The peak confederations during this period – the ICFTU and the WFTU – were more committed than ever to the United Nations system of inter-governmental organizations. While the WFTU was highly critical of the inter-governmental organizations upon which global capitalism relied, it nevertheless considered the United Nations to be of tremendous importance. To this extent these peak confederations were by now more deeply entrenched within the global political realm than ever before.

The industry-specific International Trade Secretariats were similarly investing heavily in inter-governmental organizations. As in the preceding decades, the trade secretariats continued to gain *entrée* in to the intergovernmental organizations through the agency of the peak nation-oriented confederations. Hitherto, these secretariats' direct and unmediated interactions with inter-governmental organizations were largely confined to the industry committees of the ILO. Throughout the 1970s and 1980s a wider range of inter-governmental organizations came to preoccupy the trade secretariats, with those such as the UN Food and Agriculture Organization, the UN Centre on Transnational Corporations, the OECD, and the European Economic Community coming to play an increasingly important role. Here too the trade secretariats usually relied on the various nation-oriented confederations to act as their proxies.[210] This is not to suggest that the interests of the trade secretariats were at all times, and in all fora, expressed through the ICFTU and other nation-oriented organizations. Indeed, secretariats continued to have unmediated relations with the aforementioned ILO industry committees and other United Nations agencies.[211] The point to emphasize is that increasingly over this period, the trade secretariats interacted with a wider range of intergovernmental organizations, though more often through the agency of the nationally oriented confederations. To this extent we see a universal trend among the world's peak confederations to engage more enthusiastically than ever before with this global-political realm.

1972–89: The political dimension – conclusion

In sum, organized labour's engagement on both national and global planes was aimed at enlisting states' help in the amelioration of problems associated with change in the structures of production, organization, and ideology. For the ICFTU and the labour organizations of the West more broadly, the involvement of the state was also crucial because governments were expected to put in place the legislative and regulative frameworks that would encourage free, but fair, trade.[212] For the WFTU – and especially for its affiliates in Eastern Europe – the state was considered the embodiment of the socialist ideal, and its interests were conflated with those of the working class. It was, at once, the engine of development and the distributor of the fruits of labour. For the leaders of trade union organizations of the developing world the state represented a symbol of emancipation from historical servitude. Under such circumstances trade unionists invested a great deal of faith in governments' ability to not only maintain the integrity of the sovereign state, but to also deliver the material benefits associated with modernity. With all this in mind, one cannot assume that the aforementioned examples of disengagement signalled the emergence of a more globally integrated and autonomous labour network.

Part II: 1972–89 – conclusion

These observations of the external resonate with those made in earlier sections concerning internal movement integrity. Indeed, the tensions identified there are very evident in organized labour's external relations throughout this period. The effects of these tensions were played out in the realm of the peak confederations, and were reflected in the nature and effectiveness of the advocacy at that level. They determined the nature of the engagement with the state in relations external to the network.

Throughout the 1972–89 period, the transnational network of labour organizations had grown in ways that further enhanced its 'fit' with the state. When the opportunity to go beyond the state-mediated political realm arose, endogenous and exogenous barriers combined to impede such efforts. We recall earlier discussions on organized labour's growing commitment to instrumentalist and developmentalist ideologies. All this resulted in a worldwide movement that only had at its disposal structures and political practices that usually led to a growing reliance on the state. This was so in spite of the loosening of corporatist and functionalist constraints. Though this continued to be a time of organizational expansion – and, to some extent, integration – for labour worldwide, the political practices and relationships underpinning the movement remained state-orientated.

Part III
1989–2005

Prevailing structural imperatives

If the 1972–89 period can be characterized as a time of great instability, the subsequent years were nothing short of tumultuous. We witnessed the dismantling of the Soviet empire and the subsequent creation of new and autonomous republics in that region. We also witnessed conflagrations in the Persian Gulf and the Balkans, ethnic blood-letting throughout Africa, shocking acts of terrorism and equally shocking reprisals. Human suffering was compounded by the effects of pandemic disease, cataclysmic earthquakes and tsunamis, as well as global warming and ozone layer depletion. All this combined with hyper-liberalism and endemic levels of corporate theft, resulting in the 'failed state' phenomena and a consequent increase in famine and displaced peoples. Many considered such developments to be symptomatic of a sea-change in world affairs, entailing a growing sense of borderlessness, immediacy, and non-territorial linkages that appeared to be undermining traditional centers of authority and social formations. But how can all this be understood in terms of change to the structural imperatives referred to throughout this book?

The structure of production

The landscape now inhabited by labour is one in which transnational business networks span the globe, and in which joint ventures and strategic alliances between multinational corporations are commonplace.[213] While the propensity for capital and industry to take flight may at times be exaggerated, manufacturing plants continue to gravitate to semi-peripheral settings. Regardless of national base, global profitability is the central imperative for multinational corporations in what is now a highly competitive and export-obsessed world. Notwithstanding the advent of non-hierarchical systems of control, the multinational corporation has become the principal determinant of the structure of production. By the end of the 1980s, the expansion of production beyond the developed world, the integration of systems of management, and the concentration of economic power had become pre-dominant, entwined processes. Labour leaders have had to be cognizant also of the dramatic change in the nature of the commodities and services exchanged within this system of production. Incessant commodification has meant that growing trade in intellectual property – along with advances in biotechnology – entails multinationals invoking intellectual property rights over a vast array of biological resources. Similarly, negotiations are underway within the World Trade Organization to assess the viability of trade in hitherto publicly provided natural resources and services. The corollary of this may be the mandatory privatization of public utilities concerned with water supply, postal services, and other necessities.

Of real concern to trade unionists has been the contraction of labour intensive industries. Financial-service sectors have displaced heavy industry in much of the developed world. Currency speculation is frenzied, with such activity symptomatic of a highly dynamic, unregulated, and unstable global economy. While high-technology industries exist on all continents, textile and agriculture production continues to underpin the economies of the periphery.

How has this prevailing structure of production impacted on labour, and on socio-economic relations in general? In the developed world, precarious employment, dislocation, and high levels of stress have become endemic. High levels of under employment and unemployment also prevail, as heavy industry recedes and boom-bust cycles become more concentrated in the finance and communications sectors. At the same time, there are tremendous disparities in wealth.[214] In Third World and developing countries, subsistence living is often the norm. This is so not only in rural areas, but in those urban settings that have attracted transient populations seeking employment. Elements of this landscape resemble conditions in earlier periods. However, what sets today's structure of production apart is the scale and intensity of the inherent processes. Specifically, the expansion of production, the integration of markets and management systems, and the concentration of power, have all reached unprecedented levels of intensity and, together, now present labour leaders with extraordinary challenges.

Such changes in the structure of production are, of course, linked to advances in communication technology. Similar patterns – of expansion, integration, and concentration – can also be discerned in the changing communication regimes. At present the available communication technology consists, at one level, of a late-modern, global, information network comprising radio, television, telecommunications, and digital networks. At another level, it consists of classical media such as postal services and the press. Both coexist in ways that have resulted in the integration of all regions across the developed and developing worlds.

The late-modern network is one in which the earth orbiting satellite is a permanent feature, and in which text, sound, and images are translated into a common format – digital or binary – that is available, in theory at least, to anyone instantaneously. Everyday manifestations of this late-modern network include the ubiquitous personal computer, digital money, cryptography, the internet, e-mail, intranets, cellular phones, info-processing algorithms, as well as display and storage technologies with remarkable capacities. Of particular concern for labour has been the continued growth of a 'cyber-financial structure' that, in the words of one, 'came to dominate virtually all other forms of social organization'.[215] All these advances have fostered expanded, increasingly integrated – and yet highly unstable – networks of interaction. In sum, the late twentieth century advances in communications technology have permitted a seemingly contradictory process entailing a concentration of power within a worldwide network of corporate entities, as well as the unmediated and instantaneous engagement through and around structures of authority. It is to these organizational and administrative structures to which we now turn.

The structure of organization

Throughout this period the organizational structure has been constituted by, and yet also a major influence on, the structures of production discussed above. The contemporary structure of organization is one that continues to be premised upon the authority of the state. And yet, this period is also one characterized by the increasing tendency on the part of governments to defer to a range of powerful commercial entities as well as to transnational and regional inter-governmental bodies.

From 1989 – and since the dissolution of the bipolar system of military alliances – the number of independent states has burgeoned, increasing from the 1989 figure of 156 to 191 in 2002. The Cold War has been replaced as the principal organizational narrative by neoliberalism. The rivalry that once found expression through Cold War antagonism and brinkmanship increasingly manifests itself in the competition for markets. This has meant the growth of what Karns sees as 'glomerations of governance' concerned with mediating relations between actors in all spheres and at all levels.[216] It has also meant the formation of the World Trade Organization and the ever-increasing concentration of authority in it and its sister-bodies, the International Monetary Fund and the World Bank. Another tier of governing networks – those comprising, for example, the Group of Seven and the Trilateral Commission – has been joined by those such as the Group of Twenty. The latter, formed in 1999, comprises leaders of both developed and Third World countries and also supports many aspects of the existing neoliberal financial order. Confronting labour is what amounts to a network of interlocking regimes of governance committed to administering a global neoliberal market-based system. Latterly, this form of enmeshment has entailed regional free-trade regimes – a subject to which we shall return – expanding rapidly to include new member-states, and to also incorporate smaller, existing, inter-governmental organizations.[217] Such regimes have, to a great extent, marginalized many of the more established post-war inter-governmental organizations; most notably, those within the United Nations system that are concerned with normative issues relating to social, cultural, and economic well-being.

Apart from the ever-expanding networks of inter-governmental bodies, there is now a formidable community of international non-governmental organizations that continue to insinuate themselves into decision-making processes within the United Nations and beyond.[218] Even though the United States reigns as *the* global empire – the dominant force in terms of military, political, economic and cultural influence – the structure of global governance is nevertheless complex and multi-layered. Increasingly, this structure integrates the system of states within an over-arching regime of neoliberal, market-oriented interactions, while at the same time serving more traditional purposes relating to state security.

The structure of ideology

Throughout this study a framework has been utilized to identify change in ideological trends. It has grouped many ideological tendencies under the category headings of conservative, instrumental, developmental, and emancipatory worldviews. By the new millennium the landscape inhabited by labour was one characterized by the prominence of instrumental worldviews. This ensemble of ideologies privileges calculating and technocratic programs designed to maximize political and economic gain. Incorporated in this are the ideas associated with neoliberalism, an ideological tendency that has attained the status of commonsense.

And yet this instrumentalist neoliberal characterization does not fully capture the prevailing mood.

Combining with instrumentalism are enduring conservative creeds such as statism and nationalist parochialism. Also evident within this conservatism is the increasingly significant levels of religiosity. Of course, there is tension between these instrumental and conservative ideological tendencies. This should not surprise given the dynamic nature of neoliberalism, and the system-maintaining inclinations inherent in conservatism. That conservatism persists should also not surprise, given that prevailing structures of authority play a facilitating role in programs of neoliberal reform.

Of significance still are elements of developmentalism. Whereas associated notions of liberal internationalism, Keynesianism, and corporatism have indeed waned in recent times, the modernizing imperative within developmentalism continues to buttress more radical and dynamic elements within instrumentalism. In contrast, emancipatory ideologies – those comprising radical and reformist collectivism, environmentalism, and feminism – assert moderate influence, at least within policy-making and corporate circles. Ultimately, the ascent of capitalist neoliberalism from the early 1980s has meant that both developmentalist and emancipatory ideologies have, in varying degrees, been marginalized. This has led to a structure of ideology dominated by a commonsense that at once celebrates dynamic instrumentalism and conservatism.

1989–2005: prevailing structural imperatives – conclusion

All this represents a sketch of the structural imperatives with which organized labour has had to contend throughout this period. We have seen, for example, a structure of production premised upon post-Fordist flexibility and an expansion and integration of corporate power. This has been facilitated by tremendous advances in communications technology. Such expansion has also been replicated within the prevailing structure of organization as new layers of governance have emerged on regional and global planes. Importantly, the organizational structure throughout this period has also been marked by fragmentation as new states proliferate. Finally, we have seen how all this is informed by a capitalist instrumentalism that is buttressed by a statist conservatism. It is within this context that we situate the contemporary transnational network of labour organizations.

Before moving on to once more examine organized labour's internal and external dimensions of change, it is important to point out that this part of the book will differ from those that preceded it. Even though it also sets out to map organized labour's orientation within a given period – in this case, between 1989–2005 – it does so in a way that incorporates insights gleaned throughout the entire study. It attempts to establish a correspondence between the various dimensions of change as they have spanned the post-war history of the transnational network of labour organizations. Expressed differently, this section attempts to reconcile the present with the past – the *what is*, with the *what was*. It is framed thus in order to highlight the deeper trends, or trajectories, that may be evident in the ways in which organized labour has integrated across national borders, and the ways in which it has engaged with the state.

Without pre-empting that conclusion, this section will confirm a trend that has emerged throughout this study. It will show that while the process of globalization has in many ways been a constant feature of the transnational labour network's evolution, this has been a globalization of a peculiar sort. In terms of integration, the transnational network of labour organizations has indeed evolved in ways that enable it to assert a more unified presence across state boundaries. To this extent, it appears to fulfill one of our main prerequisites for the existence of a deeper form of globalization. However, this has not been a globalization of *separateness* from traditional forms of governance and authority; on the contrary, the process has entailed an ongoing re-configuration that has, in one way or another, maintained the state at the epicentre of the network.

5
1989–2005 – Internal Change: Consolidation and Integration

The organizational dimension

A profile of today's transnational community of labour organizations reveals a network 'headed' by the International Confederation of Free Trade Unions. Greater organizational consolidation continues, with plans to form a single, unified peak body incorporating all leading confederations revealed ahead of the ICFTU's Eighteenth World Congress in Japan, December, 2004.[219] A reduced number of industry-specific trade secretariats continue to work closely with the ICFTU. On a vertical plane, there exist a myriad of regional organizations that together represent a secondary level of representation. Highly extended and detached forms of internal relationships prevail. These manifest themselves in high levels of delegated representation – be it in distant intra-union fora, or in those associated with inter-governmental organizations – and also in the use of web-based advocacy. This profile also reveals a community of labour organizations committed to statist developmentalism; but at the same time, one that is strident in its advocacy in defence of human rights. Let us now dismantle this profile, and contrast each dimension of change – the organizational, integrative, and political – with those of previous eras. In so doing, we will gain a better understanding of the ways in which organized labour has integrated across national borders, as well as the ways in which it has projected itself outwards and away from the realm of state-mediated politics. Ultimately, we will find that a more integrated network has in some ways engaged in a deeper form of globalization; but it has done so in ways that do not necessarily entail a turning away from the state.

Organizationally, the transnational network of trade union confederations continues to integrate and expand. In this respect it has today a well-established global presence. On the horizontal plane – that is, in relation to the peak bodies – the network now revolves around one major confederation, the ICFTU. It has emerged as the unrivalled peak confederation following the post-Cold War demise of the Soviet-backed World Federation of Trade Unions.[220] The ending of the Cold War and the collapse of state socialism – first in Central and Eastern Europe, and then in the Soviet Union – triggered a sudden re-configuration of labour relations in those settings, changes that have resulted in a wave of new affiliates for the ICFTU. This has enhanced the ICFTU's pre-eminence.[221] In addition, the ICFTU's regional offshoots are now acknowledged as important players within the transnational network of labour organizations. The third nation-oriented peak confederation – the World Confederation of Labour – remains an active, though marginal player.[222] While the ICFTU is the organizational hub of the network, the industry-specific trade secretariats also remain important actors. Like their nation-oriented counterparts, they have consolidated in number. Amalgamations were common throughout the 1990s, with the total number of trade secretariats decreasing from the 1996 figure of 14 to 10 by 2002.[223] With plans of further integration mooted, there is certain to be still fewer peak bodies of all kinds in the coming years.

Organizational integration of a different sort also occurred in 2001. The ICFTU, the trade secretariats, and the Trade Union Advisory Committee to the OECD collaborated to form a joint news and campaign website. This now appears under the banner 'Global Unions'.[224] The extent and significance of this kind of integration will be addressed when the discussion turns to the internal, integrative dimension of change. For now it is important to note that the organizational integration – witnessed on this horizontal plane – now also entails an additional, somewhat abstract, form.

On a vertical plane, the network of labour organizations has expanded. Added to the twenty or so regional organizations not structurally tied to peak confederations are the European-based Union of Workers of Arab Maghreb, as well as over 30 Inter-regional Trade Union Councils.[225] Beyond the European setting there have appeared new regional organizations such as the ICFTU-aligned South Pacific and Oceanic Council of Trade Unions, and the Asia Pacific Labour Network. The network expanded further when the trade secretariats formed offshoots in regions such as the Asia-Pacific, Russia, Africa, and the Americas.[226] This now represents another layer of representation in the regions, and one that complements those regional organizations already in existence.

All this has not only signalled a break from the network's traditional Euro-centrism, but has also extended the web of cross-border trade union organizations to all corners of the globe. While this overview provides only a glimpse of a very complex ensemble of organizations, it does show that the organizational configuration of today's network of transnational labour bodies has at once integrated – with the ICFTU establishing an unrivalled leadership position, ahead of further consolidation in the years to come – and also expanded, as bodies dedicated to specific regions proliferate. Indeed, representation in the regions has become a priority for all the major players within the network.

Another interesting medium for labour advocacy that emerged at this time was the European Works Council. This regime emerged from the social protocol of the 1993 Maastricht Treaty, and was in large part a product of many years of lobbying by the European Trade Union Confederation. In essence, works councils were designed to ensure on-site representation for workers of the same multinational corporation operating across the European Union. By 1998, approximately 500 of these works councils – covering at least 15 million employees – had been established throughout some 1500 multinational corporations.[227] The European Works Councils are interesting because they have an organizational dimension that connects workers with corporate actors on an ongoing face-to-face basis. And yet the council regime does not reserve a place for trade unions *per se*. Commenting on the directive underpinning the regime, one prominent labour leader stated that '[in] its final and present form it does not mention trade unions at all, so that unions ... have to fight to nail down the right of the union officials to be part of the EWC'.[228] Thus, while these councils bear mentioning they are not strictly speaking a part of the transnational network of labour organizations. Indeed, the regime is itself underpinned by the authority of the state, and is a regional mechanism imposed on the various protagonists by the relevant governments.

We can make sense of all these developments by referring to earlier trends within this organizational dimension. As we have seen, a process of organizational integration and expansion began long ago. More significantly, this form of integration and expansion seemed to reflect – or perhaps was determined by – similar trends occurring in the prevailing structure of organization. In other words, the imperatives of interstate relations have always proved decisive in determining the organizational configuration of the worldwide trade union network. In the years following the Second World War – and as regional and international intergovernmental organizations proliferated – trade union actors embraced organizational forms that enabled intimate engagement with governments. In the post-1945 period, labour's organizational fixation with Europe also began to wane as new independent states began to emerge, and as governing regimes premised upon the authority of the state began to expand to encompass all regions. At that time, significant and influential elements within the transnational network of labour organizations were enlisted to serve the interests of state. Indeed, in the context of the Cold War the (instrumentalist) statist orientation of labour leaders had as much to do with appeasing state elites, as it did with furthering the interests of trade unions worldwide. There was apparent at this time an organizational re-configuration on the part of labour that reflected the dynamics of Cold War 'bloc' politics. It followed that the ending of the Cold War determined another organizational re-configuration within the network, one that resulted in the ICFTU assuming a pivotal role, and the World Federation of Trade Unions all but lapsing into obscurity.

It is not surprising that the organizational changes within the network should mirror those of the overall structure of organization. As changes in this structure entailed the abandonment of interventionist, welfarist, and corporatist policies by governments, organized labour consequently re-configured in ways that enabled it to petition regional and international inter-governmental organizations. Thus, regimes such as the World Trade Organization, the European Union, the Association of South-East Asian Nations, the North American Free Trade Agreement, as well as the International Labour Organization, all came to represent important points of entry for organized labour.

Change in other structural imperatives – most notably in the structures of ideology and production – have also shaped labour's organizational form. We have already noted the ways in which organized labour's re-configuration mirrored those of the states. But such re-configuration also reflected the demise of anti-statist ideologies, and the corresponding commitment to developmentalism. In addition, the structure of production has had a considerable impact, especially on the constellation of industry-specific trade secretariats. The growing integration of management and systems of production worldwide has meant that secretariats must now be cognizant of the need for an organizational presence in regions beyond Europe. For these reasons, we should once more emphasize the interplay between the various structural imperatives mentioned throughout.

1989–2005: the organizational dimension – conclusion

A summary of this historical transition necessarily re-focuses attention on our principal concern; that is, on the ways in which the transnational network of trade union organizations has evolved in terms of integration across national borders, and in terms of autonomy in relation to the state. In an organizational sense, this network has indeed expanded across national borders, and is poised to undergo further consolidation at the level of the peak bodies. But a principal determinant in shaping the network in this way has been change in the wider structural organizational imperatives as they relate to interstate relations. Labour leaders thus continue to embrace organizational structures that best complement national identities, allegiances, state-mediated governing bodies and, at times, the interests of individual states.

1989–2005: the integrative dimension – introduction

What internal integrative factors have been at play in labour's organizational expansion and consolidation? To what extent is such expansion and consolidation indicative of greater movement integration? For clues we once more turn to the internal integrative dimension in order to shed light on the ways in which relationships within the network have been mediated and constituted. This entails a review of the communication regimes that facilitated interaction, and then an analysis of the interests and ideologies that gave shape to this internal integrative dimension.

The integrative dimension – relationships

Relationships within the transnational network of labour organizations are today mediated by a combination of computer-based information technologies, as well as by more traditional communication forms such as print, conferencing, and the already established electronic forms. A closer examination of these communication regimes – and how they contrast with those of previous decades – shows that while new communication media have facilitated more instantaneous forms of interaction on both horizontal and vertical planes, they have not in themselves radically altered forms of representation or levels of integration within the network.

The 'information revolution' has heralded the arrival of technologies that have permitted an extraordinary range of interactions within the network of trade union organizations. The use of the worldwide-web and e-mail – the former enhanced by recent advances in language translation software – has made possible movement-wide electronic bulletin boards, e-mail-based discussion groups, global on-line video-conferences, and access to global interactive databases.[229] These forms of media and interaction are apparent in a multitude of trade union settings, though it is perhaps easier to conceive of them as belonging to three overlapping areas of use: the informational, organizational, and solidaristic.[230] Among the most important informational tools utilized by organized labour are the interactive databases containing information on multinational corporations, management strategies, and economic analysis in general. Such resources have become indispensable in contemporary labour's national and international collective bargaining negotiations.

An innovator in this area was a trade secretariat known as the International Federation of Chemical, Energy and General Workers.[231] This trade secretariat began producing an in-house electronic newsletter in 1987, and by the early 1990s had launched its computer-mediated campaign for 'electronic solidarity'.[232] This involved gaining, and then providing, access to 1,500 databases, establishing company-specific computer bulletin boards, and encouraging affiliates to join the GEONET e-mail network.[233] This informational application of new technologies now also involves the easy dissemination of less complex material – bulletins, campaign updates and the like – to countless people beyond the immediate setting of the trade secretariat. Another good example of an information-based service is *ICFTU Online*, an e-mail circular maintained by that confederation's media department. It provides updates on ICFTU's advocacy within inter-governmental organizations such as the ILO and the World Trade Organization, as well as on its campaigns against human rights violations in specific countries.

Change in the way information is accessed and disseminated has been an important factor in the organizational re-configuration of the entire network. Not only have the largest labour organizations been able to more efficiently maintain and administer their own affiliated networks, but such technology has also enabled the most unlikely players to form alliances. This is because a reliance on low-risk virtual communion has helped to overcome financial, cultural, logistical, and ideological differences existing within the network. This is evidenced in the formation of Global Unions, the alliance alluded to in earlier discussions about changes in the network's organizational form. This is a newly formed virtual-alliance established by the ICFTU, the trade secretariats, and the Trade Union Advisory Committee of the OECD. According to the website's banner

> Global Unions is a website which is jointly owned and managed by a number of international trade union organizations ... The website gives its members the ability to draw the attention of their partners, their members, and the press to the news they produce and the campaigns they run.[234]

The impact of new communication technologies is also apparent at levels that are far removed from this global plane. For individual trade unions, these technologies have provided the means by which recruitment strategies and service to members are improved, and internal democratic processes refined and expanded.[235] Closely associated with these informational and organizational aspects of new communications technology is the potential for innovative solidaristic activities. New technologies have enabled peak confederations to construct what Lee refers to as an 'early warning network on trade union rights'.[236] In the case of the ICFTU, such messages are disseminated through *ICFTU Online* updates, while other labour organizations have employed the technology during the cut-and-thrust of battle.[237]

And yet while many trade unions and their organizations have embraced information technology, others have been slow to do so.[238] Indeed, in spite of the adoption of these technologies, traditional media continue to fulfil important functions. The conference, for example, remains a pivotal form of interaction, combining as it does the intensity of face-to-face interaction with a reliance on extended agents (that is, the delegate). This form has endured for two main reasons. First, it has become more important since states began to invest more in regional governing regimes. This regionalism necessarily spawns intergovernmental organizations that labour seeks to engage. Second, the conference form remains crucial to labour actors aiming to exploit the growing sentiment against neoliberalism, while simultaneously promoting growth and market-oriented developmentalism. We will discuss this aspect further when our attention turns to questions of ideology. It is enough to say now that this 'contrary developmentalism' was to become the movement's common-sense view, gradually smoothing over many of the previous tensions that had, through the 1970s and 1980s, made the conference such a fraught site.

The old medium of print endures, though it now plays a less important administrative, integrative, and informational role. For instance, by the mid-1980s, the printed material of the peak confederations – in particular, the periodicals distributed to affiliates – carried far fewer detailed accounts of resolutions, statements, and executive board reports. Instead, the periodicals of the main confederations grew thinner, and tended towards bolder, more combative editorial styles. Perhaps, this was a reflection of the parlous financial state of the main confederations. More likely, it reflected the residues of intense intra-network competition, wherein proselytizing and exhortation had become more important than detail. These periodicals had earlier served an important function for the various constituent parts of the transnational trade union network as they sought to differentiate themselves, and also to attract new affiliates.

In the contemporary setting, we see a continuing and more generalized move away from this printed material. Today, information that was once made available in periodical form is distributed through computer-mediated communications systems. To a great extent, these systems have also supplanted traditional electronic forms. Media such as the telegram, telex, and fax were much used in earlier times, but are now being replaced by on-line technologies. The older forms were utilized primarily for internal communications, and less for movement-wide awareness and solidaristic purposes. Newer technologies such as e-mail have been adopted for both functions.

Overall, there is now an interesting juxtaposition between those media that promote face-to-face and also disengaged forms of communication. The relatively intimate medium of the conference has been supplemented by a remarkable increase in instantaneous on-line interaction. This has meant that vital information is now disseminated across the network of transnational labour organizations in a way that ultimately increases cooperation. This is to be expected given the communication technologies now prevalent.

But although it is easy to claim that an integration of sorts has occurred, it is more difficult to explain the nature of the integration. Under this communication regime, the peak confederations have been able to attain a level of integration that is, in many respects, based on symbolic rather than personalized forms of interaction. The best example of this is the web-based Global Unions alliance mentioned above. And the unity that this implies – apparent in most confederation websites – cannot fully erase the often conflicting interests that have since the mid-1940s distinguished the constituent parts of the transnational network of labour organizations. Even though jointly managed websites and instantaneous computer-mediated interactions can help the top-level leadership portray themselves as champions of the working masses, it is questionable whether these regimes change relationships fundamentally on both horizontal and vertical planes. Hodkinson expresses his doubts about this symbolic integration thus:

> when net-internationalism does take place, it tends to take the form of an 'e-greeting' card – the uni-directional sending of solidarity messages to striking or struggling workers to let them know that other people support their struggle, know about it and are behind its continuation.[239]

This review of communication media, and the relationships they have shaped, goes some way to revealing the nature of integrative change. But a survey of the prevailing communication regime offers only a partial explanation of such change. An account of the interests and ideologies that permeate the movement is required, before more definitive claims can be made. This will provide a clearer picture of the movement's internal integrative condition.

The integrative dimension – interests, ideologies

The focus now is on the issues and interests that impact on the integrity of the transnational network of labour organizations. Accounting for these interests enables us to then reflect upon the network's ideological complexion and, ultimately, to gain a clearer understanding of the ways in which organized labour has assumed a more integrated, and/or autonomous disposition. After contrasting all this with earlier periods, it becomes apparent that many of the issues and interests that once divided the network have either lost potency, or have disappeared altogether. Notwithstanding enduring tensions over many diverging interests, there is now a higher level of convergence, as well as of cross-border, intra-network, cooperation. Moreover, a higher degree of ideological integration has strengthened the ties between national trade union actors and their peak and regional organizations. In addition, consensus on key interests, greater movement integration, and a more global orientation, are all closely related to ideological tendencies – principally, those tending towards developmentalism – that continue to underscore the reliance upon, and commitment to, the authority of the state.

Clearly, when regarding such a complex ensemble of political organizations, any talk of network-wide consensus is fraught. As Form puts it, tensions are always endemic, and can be attributed to an infinite number of causes.

[the] segmentation of labor is based on autonomy, hierarchy, locality, technology, factionalism, ideology, and external politics. Barriers to political consensus within and among unions also arise from the social heterogeneity of their members based on skill, wealth, gender, education, ethnicity, race, and religion.[240]

When applied to relationships between trade union organizations engaged in cross-border activities, tensions also persist because of conflicting interests at the intersections of North – South, as well as East – West power relations.

On the national level, these conflicts make it difficult for prominent trade union organizations to reconcile the promotion of growth-dependent economic development with the need to maintain autonomy. Tensions also frequently reflect the enduring commitment to the local; usually manifest in a close affinity with the interests of state. And even though we see – on the level of the peak transnational and regional organizations – far greater convergence of views, we should not read the emergence of a more centralized, hierarchical structure into this: the network remains a loose confederacy of confederacies. Indeed, as the following examples show, divisiveness is still endemic.

Preceding the 1994 signing of the North American Free Trade Agreement, there was tension between the labour organizations of the countries involved.[241] The American Federation of Labor-Congress of Industrial Organizations opposed the agreement because it did not contain effective labour protection measures. The Confederación de Trabajordores de Mexico, on the other hand, opposed moves to incorporate labour protection clauses and was, like its government, an enthusiastic supporter of the free-trade agreement. This principal Mexican labour organization hoped the agreement would attract foreign capital and also stem the tide of emigration to the north.[242] For its part, the Canadian Congress of Labour was animated by a nationalism that opposed the agreement on the grounds that it would lead to greater penetration of Canada's economy by American corporations.[243]

Tensions of a similar kind also surfaced in response to the proposed Multilateral Agreement on Investment. An OECD initiative that came to prominence in the mid-1990s, this proposal had as one of its central aims the liberalization of investment regimes in ways that would also privilege the interests of multinational corporations. As Goodman and Ranald have it, the Multilateral Agreement on Investment was 'a treaty designed to protect investors against governments'.[244] In this instance, important players within the transnational network of labour organizations – most notably the national organizations of Canada, New Zealand, Australia, and the United States – were at odds with their peak confederation, the ICFTU. At a time when national affiliates were helping to mount a worldwide campaign against the Multilateral Agreement on Investment, the ICFTU and the Trade Union Advisory Committee to the OECD were assisting those drafting it.[245]

North–South divisions also created tensions within the transnational network of labour organizations. These surfaced during the ongoing campaign to have a labour-friendly social clause incorporated into regimes of economic governance.[246] According to O'Brien, this campaign has attempted to 'link the ILO's supervisory machinery with the [World Trade Organization's] enforcement mechanism'.[247] Whereas the benefits of such clauses are self-evident for many labour actors, others are concerned that the new standards might be used as protectionist devices that will favor the wealthier economies of the North. ICFTU affiliates from the Asia-Pacific region have been the most sceptical about having workers' rights linked to trade. In some cases these affiliates have sided with their governments to thwart progress of the social clause initiative. This scepticism was most apparent in the stand taken by some Indian labour leaders in the mid-1990s. Working in tandem with their government, they blocked progress in the social clause campaign within the ILO's International Labour Conference and, ultimately, within World Trade Organization negotiations. Similarly, leading figures within the Malaysian Trade Union Congress were highly sceptical about this regulatory regime. In the face of this resistance, the ICFTU tempered its approach in ways that mollified affiliates in the developing and Third World countries.[248]

Relationships along this North–South axis were also strained after the demise of the World Federation of Trade Unions. Many of its former national affiliates found it difficult to accept the fact that the reformist, development-oriented ICFTU was now the only remaining transnational confederation of any standing. This posed difficulties for trade union organizations that were informed by oppositional, emancipatory programs. One such organization was the Congress of South African Trade Unions. As pressure to affiliate with the ICFTU intensified, this – and like-minded – national federations hesitated to endorse a peak body known to harbour within its ranks a number of quisling national affiliates.[249] It was in the years preceding the South African organization's affiliation to the ICFTU that debate grew more heated between those pursuing economic growth and development, and those seeking structural change.[250] Such disagreements reflected differences between those purporting to represent the trade unions of the South, and those representing labour in the North. Though a highly circumscribed form of economic liberalization now has the in-principle support from the majority of trade union organizations – especially those within the orbit of the ICFTU – many continue to question this trend.

Disagreements also stemmed from former Cold War divisions. The most intense manifestation of these differences were evident in Central and Eastern Europe during the immediate post-Cold War years. Trade union politics throughout Central and Eastern Europe underwent significant change in the wake of the Cold War. With the exception of the All-Poland Trade Union Alliance, the WFTU's national affiliates – along with their post-Cold War successor organizations – abandoned that peak body. In the transition all these affiliates underwent fundamental political re-orientation. This occurred even when many chose to retain their pre-Cold War organizational form. One outward manifestation of such change was the re-naming of national trade union organizations in ways that featured the words 'free' and 'independent'.[251] In countries such as Hungary and Czechoslovakia, a number of new trade union organizations were formed, thus signalling a complete break from the past. Virtually all of these 'official' (old) and 'independent' (new) trade union organizations sought affiliation with the ICFTU.[252]

Many tensions were associated with this realignment, posing what Ashwin calls a 'somewhat bizarre victor's dilemma' for the ICFTU.[253] This peak confederation was slow to adapt to the end of the Cold War and remained, well into the 1990s, very wary of trade union movements of the East. Tensions were exacerbated by the activities of the American Federation of Labor-Congress of Industrial Organizations. Determined to pursue its anti-communist crusade, the American trade union body embraced those Central and Eastern European organizations that were most willing to abandon past political allegiances. This support more often took the form of considerable financial assistance.[254] Many of the ICFTU's Western European affiliates feared that the Americans' approach would pave the way for neoliberal economic reforms in the region, and then a consequent increase in 'social dumping' throughout the continent.[255] In addition, European affiliates of the ICFTU resented the way in which their long-standing relationships with counterparts in Central and Eastern Europe were now being disregarded and undermined. This tension between pragmatism and crusading anti-communism also had ramifications for relationships between the International Trade Secretariats and the ICFTU. Many trade secretariats also objected to the extent to which the legacy of anti-communism was permitted to interfere with their own relationships with trade union movements of Central and Eastern Europe.[256]

All this represents a survey of the more contentious issues that trade union organizations worldwide have confronted throughout the 1990s. Yet, in spite of all these tensions, it is apparent that by the new century there had emerged a far more integrated network of transnational labour organizations. This network has grown more coherent and unified as still more interests converge. While much of this convergence is attributable to the events of 1989, it is also a part of a much wider process.

One cannot overstate the importance to network integrity of the passing of the Cold War. For much of the twentieth century, the imperatives of the Cold War demanded that pivotal actors within the ranks of trade union organizations assume a functional, if not mercenary, role for the sake of superpowers' strategic interests. This, in turn, poisoned many intra-network relationships and for many decades hindered network integration. Cold War antagonisms also exacerbated divisions indirectly. For instance, the trend towards regionalism – most evident in the 1972–89 period – and the related emergence of the non-aligned movement, were in varying degrees reactions to the polarities of Cold War politics. These developments had a marked effect on the political disposition of trade union organizations, particularly those in developing and Third World countries. And, suffice to say, these tensions also determined these organizations' relationships with the ICFTU and the WFTU, the world's peak confederations of the time.

The relationship between these peak bodies had itself been marked by a hostility that prevented meaningful interaction within intergovernmental fora. Support for dictatorial and quisling governments – direct or through regional proxies – further damaged relations between these pivotal actors within the network in the regions and in Europe. As a result, their European affiliates were hindered in their attempts to establish bilateral relationships with trade union counterparts in rival superpower camps.

These direct and indirect Cold War-related tensions have since dissipated. Now that the aforementioned problems associated with the transition from command-economy to free-independent unionism have receded, the interests underlying network integrity have come to the fore. In the economic realm, we see the agendas of peak and regional organizations featuring programs, initiatives, and exhortations aimed at ameliorating the deleterious effects of neoliberalism, while at the same time looking for ways to boost world economic growth and development. Evidence of a consensus around these themes and, hence, greater integration, can be found in the statements, programs, and campaigns of the network's leading actors. This trend is evident across the network, and is often manifest in collaborative efforts between confederations. The following examples are illustrative.

The Sixteenth and Seventeenth World Congresses of the ICFTU were watershed events, during which a renewed concern for social issues became apparent. The Sixteenth World Congress, held in Brussels in 1996, saw the ICFTU's General Secretary, Bill Jordan, table a report that focused on 'A world of widening divisions', 'Building solidarity, attacking poverty, and creating jobs', and 'Strengthening the voice of working men and women through international trade union solidarity'.[257] This report, and the subsequent congress proceedings, concentrated on specific areas of concern; the most notable being the defence of trade union rights, the promotion of employment and labour standards, the need to confront multinational corporations, diminishing trade union membership, and the fight for equal rights. Also featured were statements and resolutions aimed at establishing collaborative relationships with other peak trade union bodies. One of the areas of common concern here was the aforementioned trade-related social clause.[258]

The Seventeenth World Congress held in Durban in 2000, was also notable for the extent to which affiliates emphasized issues relating to global social justice. The degree of commitment to this agenda was evident in a raft of ICFTU statements and resolutions on such issues as the social clause, relations with non-government organizations, equality for women, Third World debt, and poverty.[259] Both of these congress gatherings built on initiatives already in place since the early 1990s. The most important of these was the 1994 campaign – launched in conjunction with the International Trade Secretariats – to combat exploitation of children, and violations of trade union rights by repressive regimes.[260]

This agenda was replicated in the programmes of other transnational, regional, and national labour organizations. In the case of the World Confederation of Labour, the similarities were especially apparent in its initiatives on child labour, advancement for women workers, the social clause, sustainable development, and multinational corporations.[261] Collaboration with the ICFTU has become increasingly important to the World Confederation of Labour. Joint statements are commonplace, while initial signs of 'structural cooperation' are set to translate into a still more profound integration by 2006 or 2007.[262]

As interests across the network of labour organizations converge, we also see the European Trade Union Confederation's relationship with these peak bodies grow closer. This organization also focuses on such issues as discrimination in the workplace, and the use of the social clause as a vehicle for securing improved standards of human rights. As a consequence, the European Trade Union Confederation has joined the search for ways of achieving 'decentralized cooperation' with other peak bodies.²⁶³ At the same time, the interests of the Trade Union Advisory Committee to the OECD have also become more closely aligned with the main peak and regional trade union bodies. While the Committee's brief is limited to providing a select group of trade unions *entrée* to the OECD, it nevertheless has more in common than ever with its counterparts. Since the mid-1990s, the Committee has stressed the importance of core labour standards, and has become an enthusiastic advocate of a social clause component of World Trade Organization regulation.²⁶⁴ And like its counterparts, it too has been outspoken in its condemnation of labour rights violations.

As noted in previous discussion of the network's organizational form, the Trade Union Advisory Committee's affinity with other peak bodies – specifically, with the ICFTU and the trade secretariats – is such that it has joined in a loose alliance known as the Global Unions. This represents another medium through which common concerns are aired. One of the most important common aims is the promotion of growth and development through a boost in trade and economic activity in general. Indeed, virtually all the principal actors within the transnational network of labour organizations 'demand [a] boost to [the] world economy', look to 'prevent economic slowdown', and promote 'trade for development'. Typical are statements claiming that 'now is the time to reflate the global economy', and that 'the promotion of trade goes hand-in-hand with enabling workers to exercise their basic rights'.²⁶⁵

Of course, this is not an exhaustive account of the interests motivating the contemporary network of transnational labour organizations. What all this does show, however, is that there has been a discernible shift in priorities across the entire ensemble of labour organizations. It shows a trend away from the instrumental, parochial, and functional; and to a set of interests that reflect concern for human rights, equity, and justice. We have seen through the 1990s, a renewed and concerted focus on the amelioration of the most pernicious aspects of the prevailing neoliberal order. These bread-and-butter issues relate to child labour, discrimination, safety and environment, the power of multinational corporations, and labour rights. Linked to all this is the re-doubling of efforts to have social clauses – in their various guises – inserted into trade agreements, and into various compacts with governments.²⁶⁶

This assessment of the network's interests enables more abstract observations about its ideological orientation. Prior to 1989, change in the labour movement's ideological orientation had seen class-based emancipatory worldviews – in their various Marxist, socialist, and anarcho-syndicalist manifestations – gradually recede. Receding also were those emancipatory worldviews associated with anti-imperialism, anti-colonialism, bourgeois cosmopolitanism, and republicanism. By the 1980s, the most prevalent ideological tendency combined developmentalism – that is, an orientation that privileges modernizing, growth-orientated programmes – with instrumental and conservative statism. The latter were fuelled by the Cold War, and by post-colonial nation-building.

In subsequent years, the worldviews that have most characterized organized labour are those that combine the developmentalism mentioned earlier, with what seems to be an echo of past emancipatory inclinations. In a sense, we see here the commitment to economic growth inherent within the developmentalist inclination tempered by an urgent and pragmatic opposition to extreme neoliberalism. This finds expression in calls for 'sustainable economic growth', a 'human face [for] globalization', and an end to 'ideologically-driven privatization programmes'.[267] Though this ideological tendency is still inclined towards the ameliorative and reformist, it nevertheless represents a more contrary and oppositional ideological disposition than has been the case in recent decades.[268]

However, while there has been a discernible shift away from the conservative and instrumentalist ideological tendencies – those that committed organized labour to the strategic interests of state – this has not meant that statism *per se* has waned. It is the nature of this statism that seems to have changed. Hitherto, the state represented, on the one hand, an emancipatory ideal – seen in the context of struggles against colonial rule – and, on the other, an agent through which imperial designs, or socialist utopias, could be realized. Today's statism is one that has organized labour looking to government – individually or collectively – to play the role of a guardian legislator, and to provide refuge for those facing a neoliberalism that poses a serious threat to social welfare and security. This form of a statism also sees organized labour mounting actions in defence of national autonomy and sovereignty. At the transnational level, it is labour's hope that the perennial goal of growth and development will be facilitated by the intergovernmental organizations whose role it is to manage trade; but whose legitimacy, ultimately, derives from the authority of the state. An ideological profile emerges from all this. The ideological disposition of today's transnational network of labour organizations can best be characterized as one that combines an enduring commitment to humane developmentalism with a pragmatic and somewhat enlightened form of ameliorative statism.

1989–2005: the organizational and integrative dimensions of change – conclusion

In an organizational sense, this network has over the decades integrated and expanded. However, it continues to embrace an organizational structure that reflects – albeit implicitly – national identities, allegiances and, at times, the interests of states. This is unlikely to change even as the peak confederations continue to merge. In relation to the internal integrative dimension, there have been rather dramatic changes to the ways in which relationships are mediated. The traditional face-to-face relationships have been transformed by a remarkable increase in computer-mediated interaction. Under this communication regime, the peak confederations have been able to increase intra-network cooperation. As a result, there has emerged what can be regarded as a degree of symbolic integration. The *symbolic* is stressed here because there remains very distinct areas of specialty and responsibility that differentiate the various constituent parts of the network. Moreover, while the contemporary relationships necessarily entail more horizontal interactions – that is, between the leaders of the peak confederations – integration on a vertical plane remains very elusive. Indeed, it must be stressed that suggestions of increased ideological and symbolic integration are not in any way meant to imply a centralization of authority within the network. There has been no surrender of autonomy by constituents to the peak confederations. The transnational network of labour organizations remains just that – a loose ensemble of confederations held together to a greater or lesser degree by commonalities of interests and ideologies.

It is in the realm of interests and ideologies that important changes, and continuities, are evident. There has been a shift in priorities away from the instrumental and parochial, to a set of interests focusing more on human rights, as well as on questions of global distributive justice. These are reconciled with the ongoing support for trade and economic expansion. Both tendencies have at their core a dependence upon the authority of the state.

6
1989–2005 – External Change: Eviction and Insinuation

The political dimension – the national

In this section, we build on the foregoing by reflecting upon the network's external relations: ultimately, we find that notwithstanding significant tensions within the political dimension, the labour network continues to adhere to a form of ameliorative statism – an orientation that belies its globalizing pretensions.

We begin by once more reflecting on organized labour's political-realm engagement at the national level. This is an important point of departure because, as we have seen throughout, it is within this national *milieu* that the vast majority of the network's affiliates exist. By this section's end, we find that there is little to suggest that labour – considered broadly – has become estranged from the state, in spite of the existence of some forces for disassociation on this national plane. We explore this phenomenon by firstly outlining the forces undermining the labour–state nexus: these are then contrasted with forces that continue to bind organized labour to the state.

The importance of the Cold War was outlined in previous discussion of the network's internal integration. There, it was noted that the Cold War had greatly hindered network integrity – when understood in terms of interests and ideology – by compelling many labour organizations to serve the strategic interests of state. That this particular aspect of the labour-state nexus has been broken is by now self-evident, and there is no need to dwell on it further. Instead, we ought to consider a wider range of factors that may be creating a rift between organized labour and the state.

Throughout the 1990s, powerful forces continued to undermine trade unions' institutional links to the state. The structures of production, organization, and ideology were such that trade unions had to confront not only the seemingly omnipotent multinational corporations and, more broadly, 'turbo-capitalism', but also what some refer to as the 'competition state'.[269] This refers to a disposition on the part of states that has them championing neoliberal articles of faith – trade liberalization, reduced tariffs and subsidies, financial deregulation, privatization, and casualization. It was a form of governance that in many contexts rounded savagely on labour and its representative bodies.

There was a tendency on the part of many governments throughout the 1990s to reform the legal and institutional frameworks that had protected organized labour, or that had given it *entrée* into decision-making settings. In many cases such changes served to emasculate systems of arbitration and also decentralize processes of collective bargaining. These reforms saw the locale of most collective bargaining negotiation – particularly in the English-speaking countries – shift from the macro to the micro level; that is, from economy and industry-wide bargaining, to negotiation at the enterprise or even individual level.[270]

Earlier we looked at the way corporatist arrangements changed through the 1970s and 1980s. Some of the subtle – and not so subtle – changes to voluntarist, statist, and coercive corporatist arrangements were mapped. The trends identified in that period, though mixed, showed a degree of disassociation: estrangement at one end of the spectrum (throughout Europe and the West); and imposed flexibility and autonomy for labour protagonists at the other (throughout Central and Eastern Europe). In the most recent period, governments' aversion to voluntarist forms of corporatist relationships have only intensified, and the statist corporatism of the former Eastern bloc has all but disappeared in the wake of the Cold War.

Another important feature of industrial relations in the 1990s, was the increasing influence of managerial ideologies. These management fads began to permeate public-sector management and resulted in the marginalization of unions.[271] These management stratagems ranged from the somewhat amorphous notion of Human Resources Management, to notions of Best Practice, Lean Production, Toyotism, and the many variants of the Just-In-Time management systems. They had in common the use of subtle, yet all-pervasive, systems of control and surveillance for the sake of flexibility, competition, cost reduction, and the emasculation of organized labour.[272] While the extent to which these ideologies shaped labour-state relations varied considerably, they nevertheless played an important role in ostracizing trade unions from employer–employee interactions in the public sector and beyond.

They were also instrumental in assuring uncritical acceptance of high levels of casualization in many industrialized countries.

The list of factors resulting in an estrangement between organized labour and the state could be extended to include the continuing decline of social-democrat parties, and of social-democracy itself. But there is no need to expand further on such developments: suffice to say that together they continued throughout the 1990s and then beyond 2000 to severely undermine the capacity of labour leaders to assert themselves within policy-making circles at this national level. Indeed, in many cases leaders were accorded pariah status. This happened when trade unions were perceived by the 'competition state' to be an impediment to progress, as defined by the neoliberal orthodoxy. As an aside, the processes outlined earlier also go some way to explaining the declining status of trade unions in general and, more specifically, of falls in union membership throughout the 1990s.[273]

In the developing countries, national labour movements were also undermined by the effects of market liberalization, structural adjustment programs, and the subsequent decline in public sector employment. Many of these movements had hitherto played prominent roles in struggles for independence and in nation-building. Added to this was the upsurge throughout the late 1980s and 1990s of state-sponsored violence directed at unionists. This, as one ICFTU researcher wrote,

> confirms that international competition is responsible for the majority of union rights violations because many governments have abdicated responsibility from their obligations and allow foreign investors to systematically flout labour laws and regulations so as to stop them from taking their investment elsewhere.[274]

And yet in spite of the findings that point to an emerging schism between organized labour and the state, research also suggests that such change does not constitute a universal trend. Indeed, while the aforementioned tensions are evident, the connections between an ever-expanding and integrated labour network and the state in many areas remain strong. As scholars within the field of comparative industrial relations point out, there remains a great deal of heterogeneity in the institutionalized industrial relations regimes still in place. These writers suggest that cross-cultural responses to exogenous structural change have varied dramatically.[275] This means that even though neoliberalism has undermined established regulatory systems, as well as traditional corporatist arrangements, there have emerged a range of alternative forms of engagement and cooperation between organized labour and the state.

For example, in Central and Eastern Europe there now exist industrial relations systems that feature tripartite forms of governance that include trade unions as active participants. In what Reutter calls 'tripartism without corporatism'[276] we see a proliferation of such regimes between governments and organized labour. These are borne out of a consensus about the need for social stability during times of dramatic economic change. While these arrangements are usually *ad hoc*, and by no means institutionally grounded, they nevertheless point to an enduring connection between the state and trade unions throughout the region. As Reutter argues:

> These relations have to be cooperative ... [and] this means that the parliaments or parties accept the 'semi-public' role and functions of the unions and the agreements of the tripartite bodies.[277]

Moreover, this form of engagement has in many ways been imposed on organized labour by the state, and as such belies notions of a fundamental schism.[278]

Many developing countries also have in place what Bamber refers to as 'statist-micro-corporatist relationships'.[279] These represent variants of the coercive corporatist regimes mentioned earlier, and have emerged mainly in countries such as Japan and other 'tiger economies' of Asia. And finally, we also see the emergence of a similar, highly flexible, 'supply-side' corporatism within the Western European setting. By this it is meant that forms of corporatism may be emerging that are specifically tailored to the needs of the market; forms that 'tend no longer to be the single feature which characterizes entire political systems'.[280]

Signs of enduring connection are also apparent, if we look at the contradictory phenomenon of the 'anti-globalization' movement, of which organized labour is increasingly a part. This movement is contradictory because it can express both cosmopolitan or communitarian intents. It is possible that trade union activism here can be interpreted as a manifestation of what Laxer calls 'left-wing nationalism'.[281] Along with the right-wing variant, this disposition can be interpreted as a rearguard action *in defence of the state* in the face of worldwide economic and cultural integration. While it is difficult to assess the extent to which this left-wing nationalism represents an inward-looking retreat into nationhood, it nevertheless seems to make even more problematic claims of a break in the nexus between organized labour and the state.

Throughout the earlier discussion about relationships on this national-political plane, it was asserted that the orientation of organized labour remained inward-looking, if not statist, in character. Notwithstanding an end to the most extreme forms of instrumental and strategic labour-government alliances – as well as the loosening of more subtle cooperative regimes throughout the 1980s and 1990s – there seems little to suggest that there has been a cleavage between the constituent parts of the transnational network of labour organizations and the state. This is not to say that the continuing marriage between organized labour and the state on the national plane is a happy one. Indeed, underscoring the relationship have been the very fraught symptoms of exogenous structural imperatives; be they in the form of Cold War antagonisms, the influence of the multinational corporations or, more broadly, the deleterious effects of neoliberalism.

To conclude these reflections on organized labour's engagement with this external-political dimension, we return to the global plane. Here, it becomes evident once again that while this transnational labour network continues to assert itself within the global context, this has not necessarily meant that the state is of less importance in labour's overall worldview. Thus, we cannot regard organized labour as having engaged in a profound form of globalization; that is, the nature of intra-network integration, and of its autonomy, belies such a process.

The political dimension – the global

By and large, trade union organizations have been very eager to pursue their interests within the global – state-mediated – political realm. Notwithstanding an initial wariness of the ILO in the early 1920s, and the fleeting opposition to that body by the World Federation of Trade Unions prior to 1954, the peak confederations and their constituent parts have, over the decades, clamoured to insinuate themselves within inter-governmental organizations. Since 1989 – when intra-network rivalry diminished – this form of engagement assumed a greater level of intensity. This was because the network's advocacy in these fora became more coordinated, with the remaining confederations aligning themselves according to common interests and ideology.

Recall that the heightened level of (symbolic) integration within the network was premised on the need to somehow insulate organized labour from the effects of contemporary neoliberalism. Such integration was also based, in large part, on a developmentalist consensus. Subsequently, this consensus enabled the peak confederations to gain easier access to intergovernmental organizations especially to the former Bretton Woods institutions. Because an integral part of this consensus has been the (qualified) support for free trade, a bridge of sorts emerged linking labour leaders and those inter-governmental organizations concerned with achieving limitless economic growth through trade and financial liberalization. Thus, labour's engagement at this level has necessarily entailed a degree of incorporation within a political realm premised upon the authority of the state.

Throughout the 1990s, the peak confederations further intensified their efforts to establish footholds within the growing number of intergovernmental organizations.[282] What sets this episode apart from earlier times has been the breadth and intensity of engagement at not only the global, but also at regional levels of governance. On the global plane, organized labour's determination to insinuate itself was typified by the ICFTU's efforts – made on behalf of all the major confederations – to be heard within the World Trade Organization. We have touched on this relationship a number of times, most recently when highlighting the convergence of interests that had developed around the issue of labour standards. Without dwelling too much on this aspect of the study, it is important to illustrate the degree to which efforts to deepen such relations intensified throughout the 1990s.

The labour-wide campaign to gain a seat at the trade negotiation table began in earnest in 1994, and then intensified in subsequent World Trade Organization Ministerial Meetings in 1996 and 1999. That the results of this engagement ultimately proved disappointing for organized labour is not a central concern here. Nor is the fact that in searching for more effective monitoring mechanisms, the transnational network of labour organizations seemed to be shifting its emphasis away from the International Labour Organization, in favour of the World Trade Organization. What is most important is that in its attempts to 'take up a position as one of the principal parties in the global rule-making process',[283] organized labour continued to gravitate closer to those international regimes that are premised upon the authority of the state. To this extent the nature of labour's 'globalizing' process has been one that entails a statist orientation, whether manifest in relations with the World Trade Organization, or with the Bretton Woods institutions such as the International Monetary Fund and the World Bank.[284] We could easily add to this list of encounters between intergovernmental organizations and peak confederations.[285] Increasingly, the peak confederations – often under the banner of The Global Unions federation – have coordinated their statements and presentations within such fora. As well as reflecting the intra-network consensus mentioned above, the increasing frequency of such engagements with intergovernmental organizations is also indicative of the movement-wide efforts to be accepted within this global political realm.[286]

The same increase in state-centred forms of advocacy is evident on the regional level. As the proliferation of regional intergovernmental organizations has expanded to facilitate and manage liberalizing and developmentalist programs, organized labour's efforts to engage at that level have also intensified. The already well-established institutional connection between the European Trade Union Congress and the European Union, as well as that existing between the Trade Union Advisory Council and the OECD, have already been noted and do not need repeating here. However, it is worth listing some of the relationships that have emerged more recently, given that these represent qualitative and quantitative shifts in relations with the external-political dimension of change throughout the 1990s.

In the Americas, the ICFTU and the national affiliates of its regional body, ORIT, participated in preparatory talks with states planning to establish the Free Trade Area of the Americas (proposed for 2005). They did this with the aim of persuading governments to attach a labour-friendly social clause to the trading regime. This trade union grouping also established the first formal institutional relationship between trade unions and a multilateral development bank. It did this when it joined with the Inter-American Development Bank to form a labour-oriented working group in 2000.[287]

In an engagement of a similar kind, the ICFTU/ORIT combination – in conjunction with the World Confederation of Labour and its own regional representative[288] – helped to draft the Social and Labour Declaration incorporated within the Common Market of the Southern Cone countries (also known as MERCOSUR). They did this through the agency of the MERCOSUR Trade Union Commission, and through its tripartite Consultative Forum on Economic and Social Issues. Likewise, the Caribbean Congress of Labour has been actively engaged with Caribbean Common Market countries, with particular emphasis on proposals for a Caribbean Social Charter.

In the Asia and Pacific regions, trade union bodies have also attempted to assert themselves within regional inter-governmental organizations. The latter include the Asia Pacific Economic Cooperation Forum (APEC), and the Association of South East Asian Nations (ASEAN). One of the most important bodies facilitating interaction with APEC has been the ICFTU Asia Pacific Labour Network, a network that consists not only of ICFTU affiliates in APEC countries, but also of trade unions associated with the industry-specific trade secretariats. Here resistance to the involvement of organized labour has been intense, with APEC granting limited access to labour leaders. In spite of concerted efforts, labour delegations to ASEAN have also met with little success, though the ICFTU and its regional body, APRO, continue to issue communiqués in response to ASEAN policies, and to establish closer contacts with important ASEAN associates such as the Asian Development Bank.

Interaction in Southern Africa is facilitated through the annual meeting of the Labour Commission of SADC, an offshoot of the Southern African Development Community. Similar interaction and dialogue occurs at the Organization for African Unity annual Labour Commission meeting. The transnational network of labour organizations – led, principally, by the ICFTU and its regional body, AFRO – also asserts itself in Africa by sponsoring major conferences on issues of regional import, and by encouraging representatives of major inter-governmental organizations to attend.[289] The African Development Bank is one such body, and at every opportunity, the ICFTU continues to cultivate its relationship with the bank. In general, these conferences provide settings in which national trade union leaders can engage with delegations from employer groups, the International Labour Organization, the International Monetary Fund, the World Bank, as well as with those of their own governments. This overview does not offer an extensive account of all interaction at the burgeoning regional level of governance (for reasons that will become evident, I defer an assessment of labour's participation in bilateral and regional free trade negotiations until the book's conclusion.) The snapshots provided serve merely to underscore the type and breadth of labour engagement in contemporary times. More specifically, they show that on the global and regional planes organized labour continues to seek deeper institutional connections with the state-mediated political realm.

As Robert O'Brien *et al* argue, organized labour remains locked into this political realm because 'labour issues [can only] remain on the WTO agenda to the extent that labour can influence ... states'.[290] Though these comments are in reference to the labour-World Trade Organization relationship, they might just as well have referred to organized labour's relationships with inter-governmental organizations in general. One might add that the labour-government nexus continues to loom large – in spite of organized labour's globalizing pretensions – because influence within the political realm comes only at the behest of states. Such influence is, according to O'Brien and his colleagues, 'extended through the state [and thus] labour groups continue to rely on the good will of particular states to advance their cause'.[291]

1989–2005: the political dimension – conclusion

Leaders of the transnational network of labour organizations have sought out, and attained, a degree of enmeshment with governing institutions on national, regional, and global planes. This intent has been apparent even when there have been structural forces at play that tend towards disengagement. Thus, the labour network continues to mirror, as it were, changes in the global structure of organization. As forms of global governance change, so too does organized labour's configuration in relation to the external political realm. From labour's perspective, this adaptation is necessary if it is to persuade governments to mitigate the effects of neoliberalism, and also if it is to satisfy the developmentalist imperative that is such an ingrained aspect of organized labour's worldview.

These closer relations with the state are more evident in the contemporary period when labour – as a network – has become more globally oriented and, symbolically at least, internally integrated. To this extent we can say that even though it is possible to discern the emergence of a more globalized movement, this is a globalization that does not come at the expense of close – indeed, symbiotic – relations with the state across national, regional, and global levels. In other words, this has not been a globalization of detachment from traditional forms of governance and authority. The transnational network of labour organizations has been – at least in its twentieth century incarnations – reluctant to stray too far from the corridors of state power.

Conclusion: The Past and Future Globalizations of Organized Labour

At the commencement of this book emphasis was placed on the need to give meaning to 'globalization' as it relates to agency and, specifically, on the agency of organized labour. We have set about this task by gauging the extent to which labour has integrated across national borders, as well as the extent to which it has become estranged from the state. We have been able to carefully dissect the political community that organized labour constitutes, and to explore the complex interplay of relationships – internal and external – and characteristics that bind this sprawling transnational network. We have also been able to isolate structural imperatives and note the ways in which they have impacted on labour over time.

In these concluding reflections, I am not concerned with providing an exhaustive summary of all that subsequently emerged – the previous chapter served that purpose. When distilled this research has revealed the following. Organizationally, the transnational labour network has since 1945 – indeed, since the 1860s – spread to all points of the globe. Its peak bodies have consolidated in number, and have also been joined by a myriad of regional bodies that now give substance to the network on a vertical plane. While this network is more integrated than ever it continues to represent a very loose ensemble of actors. In external relations, organized labour remains oriented towards the state – considered individually or as intergovernmental organizations – in spite of some indicators suggesting a disengagement of sorts may be occurring. When considered against the criteria used throughout to assess network globalization – that is, the extent of cross-border integration, and autonomy in relation to the state – we find that just as the transnational network of labour organizations has attained a form of symbolic integration, it seems to have also attained a form of symbolic autonomy.

The former is marked by a greater reliance on contemporary media technologies and the diffuse nature of intra-network representation; and the latter by a network striving to maintain relations with the state while simultaneously asserting itself as a more outspoken advocate for trade unionists worldwide. But what of the future? What might these trends mean for those seeking to promote labour internationalism and provide a bulwark against threats inherent in the contemporary phase of capitalist development? In spite of the persistent attacks and endemic threats we have entered a period that in some respects presents organized labour with opportunities not hitherto open to it. To elaborate, it is first necessary to bring to the fore aspects of labour's growing affinity with what might be termed oppositional civil realm actors; and secondly, its historical reaction to the structure of organization. Both of these were noted in the preceding chapters – the former tangentially – but assume greater significance when cast in a slightly different light.

Effective advocacy across the transnational network of labour organizations is now more likely due to a shift in organized labour's disposition *vis-à-vis* oppositional civil realm actors. These comprise actors informed by an emancipatory ethic, and who are engaged in progressive struggles in relation to distributive and social justice, environmentalism, peace, national autonomy, or gender rights. Traditionally, the relationship between organized labour and oppositional movements had been characterized by tense and uneasy interactions. By the mid-1930s organized labour had turned its back on a number of class-based internationals, and at every level shown itself to be wary of antisystemic movements in general. Notwithstanding fleeting cooperative interaction during the late 1960s, organized labour remained wedded to a statist, developmentalist orientation. From the perspective of both the 'old' and the New Left, labour was considered little more than a hopelessly reformist and compromised actor.

Leaders of peak confederations had long considered the encroachment of non-governmental organizations into labour's spheres of influence as at best a nuisance. The statements of a prominent labour leader are indicative.

> We insist that the UN recognize that representative, democratic organizations like the ICFTU and the ITSs are not the same as the thousands of non-governmental organizations and 'one person think-tanks' swarming like honey bees around UN summits.[292]

Labour's estrangement from oppositional civil realm actors began to give way throughout the 1970s and 1980s. Opposition to the Vietnam war, increasing unease in trade union ranks over American intervention in Latin America, increasing levels of violence directed at trade unionists, the struggle against apartheid, the spread of export processing zones and, more generally, the harm inflicted by the omnipotent multinational corporation, were just some of the factors that led to a thawing in relations between labour movements and oppositional movements. By the late 1990s, the statements and declarations issued by labour leaders began to hint at a shift. Statements issued at successive ICFTU World Congresses and in that confederation's publication, Free Labour World, serve as good examples. We read here that the 'ICFTU aims to be at the centre of a worldwide social movement',[293] and that it is looking to 'deepen and extend its relationships with NGOs'.[294] We also read statements emphasizing that

> coalition building with relevant non-governmental organizations is crucial to ... success ... and that congress insists that contacts be expanded to encourage ... collaboration between the respective national-level structures of the NGOs concerned and ICFTU or ITS affiliates.[295]

One notable example of closer cooperation in the transnational level can be seen in the efforts to end the exploitation of child labour. This has necessarily brought the ICFTU into close contact with a range of civil realm actors – within and beyond the confines of intergovernmental organizations – many of whom could be considered to be oppositional in character.[296] The ICFTU's launch in 1994 of a global campaign to eradicate child labour was followed by a Charter against Child Labour, and then participation in the Global March Against Child Labour in 1998.

The World Confederation of Labour also sought to 'reinforce its efforts to build or participate in a series of networks dealing with social rights'.[297] By 2000, its reports and publications were peppered with references to nongovernmental organizations and 'peoples organizations'.[298] This confederation acted on its rhetoric by strengthening its ties to many non-governmental organizations, particularly those active in South East Asia, Latin America, and Africa. These included Human Rights Watch, Social Alert, the World Organization Against Torture, and the Clean Clothes Campaign. The tendency towards more frequent engagement with civil oppositional actors was also evident among the trade secretariats. The more active secretariats are now engaged in broad-based campaigns against existing international institutions, as well as in building relationships with civil realm actors campaigning against child labour, slavery, and for women's rights.[299] This shift is also important because it has entailed closer relations between labour and oppositional knowledge based centers of critique. Their ranks include the Transnationals Information Exchange, the International Center for Trade Union Rights, the International Labor Rights Education and Research Fund, Labour Notes, The Resource Centre of the Americas, Asia Monitor Resource Center, the Centro de Información Laboral y Asesoría Sindical, Third World Network, and Focus on the Global South. A tentative engagement with civil oppositional actors has also been manifest in – and facilitated by – the medias employed. We refer here to the online interactive medias now commonly used by all labour and civil oppositional actors. Indeed, the realm of 'cyber space' has come to represent neutral ground for engagement. It represents a relatively risk-free realm where labour and civil oppositional actors can benefit from the loose, *ad hoc*, and symbolic nature of interaction.[300]

On the national plane the growth in what has come to be known variously as 'social movement unionism' or 'new social unionism' is an outcome of traditional trade union organizations' exposure to oppositional movements of the civil sphere.[301] This form of trade unionism arose in countries such as South Africa, South Korea, and Brazil. It has entailed an involvement with actors and issues that are not within the immediate purview of trade union politics, and greater levels of social connectedness in general. Importantly, it is also characterized by a more autonomous orientation in relation to the state. Emblematic of this type of unionism was the emergence of the Congress of South African Trade Unions, an umbrella body that emerged to combat the apartheid regime in throughout the 1970s and 1980s. This organization was formed out of a merger of the Federation of South African Trade Unions and the grass root unions affiliated to the United Democratic Front. The emergence of the Congress of South African Trade Unions brought together two political trends then evident throughout the South African trade union landscape. These contrasting tendencies represented, on the one hand, the industrialized shop floor unions and, on the other, the more community based general unions. Subsequently, a distinguishing feature of the Congress' development was the extent to which it formed 'union-community alliances'.[302] In practice, this meant establishing links with local youth, women's, and civic organizations with a view to addressing community issues such as the crisis in education, rent boycotts, the availability of transport, and poor living conditions. It also meant connecting to a network of over 600 grassroots social movement organizations that together 'developed organizations of direct democracy such as street and area committees, people's courts and defence committees'.³⁰³

Beyond the Americas, similar engagements have also become commonplace. In South Korea, the Federation of Korean Trade Unions has worked closely with a range of social movement organizations to campaign against proposed International Monetary Fund reforms. The associated rallies, strikes, and campaign actions throughout the late 1990s, involved not only oppositional movements, but also more conservative civil realm actors. These included the churches and farmer organizations. Of increasing importance in this loose alliance has been the Korean Women Workers' Associations United, an umbrella group of more than 25 women's advocacy groups.³⁰⁴ At the same time, similar coalitions and alignments have become a feature of Australian labour politics. In 1998 a landmark waterfront dispute saw the relevant trade union, the Maritime Union of Australia, enlist the support of not only the wider labour movement – local and international – but also of numerous community organizations and religious groups.³⁰⁵ Also of interest in the Australian setting has been the existence of a humanitarian aid agency sponsored by the Australian Council of Trade Unions. Known as Union Aid Abroad-APHEDA, this agency represents a medium through which the Australian trade union movement interacts with numerous human rights advocacy groups in far removed places such as East Timor and the Occupied Territories. We note also that similar adjunct foreign aid bodies are maintained by organized labour throughout the Scandinavian countries, as well as in The Netherlands. These are only a handful of instances of what appears to be a network wide shift with network wide ramifications. They serve to highlight that social movement unionism grows out of the most vibrant grassroots elements of worldwide network of labour organizations and kindred civil society movements.

Another reason for believing that the coming years may present labour with unique opportunities stems from the emergence of new terrains of engagement; terrains that may prove amenable for the assertion of organized labour's presence across borders. Moreover – if current trajectories hold true – labour will continue to embed itself deeper into such terrain alongside the aforementioned oppositional actors. Once again we can elaborate with reference to historical tendencies. As we have seen, in spite of labour's eviction from the corridors of power on the national plane, labour leaders remain highly attuned to the state, and to petitioning governments wherever they are able. Organized labour continues to shadow the collectivity of states as inter-state relations assume different organizational forms: to this extent, wherever the state leads, labour continues to follow. Thus, the consolidation of the modern nation-state had earlier resulted in labour's close affinity with social democrat parties and a commitment to parliamentarianism. The proliferation of international public utilities and then multi-layered forms of global governance opened a new arena for labour advocacy, and led to the insinuation by labour's peak transnational bodies within such systems. The Cold War led to the fragmentation of the worldwide labour and a drift towards instrumental statism on the part of the principal actors within the network. Keynesianism entailed the inclusion of labour within national and, to some extent global, forms of governance, and manifested itself in corporatist relationships between labour and the state. Likewise, nation-building and the associated programmes of modernization and development in the post-colonial era also entailed organized labour's incorporation. And in more recent times, the growth of regional intergovernmental organizations and trade agreements has led to a corresponding move on the part of organized labour to establish shadow trade union regimes at that regional level. It is the last of these developments that bears closer examination.

The scale of the shift towards bilateral and regional free trade agreements is spectacular, and is marked by an expansion beyond regional affiliations to include regimes linking faraway states on the basis of their shared commitment to trade liberalization. By mid-2003 the number of such agreements either in operation or under negotiation stood at 265, with approximately half of these coming into being in the preceding 8 years.[306] Coupled with this has been the aforementioned proliferation in regional intergovernmental organizations designed to facilitate trade liberalization. All this is important because it opens up before labour a new terrain of engagement and advocacy. Indeed, developments on this plane may be one factor in a resurgence in cross-border labour activity, or even a catalyst for a *renaissance* in labour internationalism.

Greater and more effective mobilization around the phenomena of the bilateral and regional free trade regime ought not only be possible, but also ought be considered essential. It is of course possible with the assistance of the ever growing number of regional trade union organizations mentioned in earlier chapters. Given that intra-network harmony is at unprecedented levels, this strata of labour organizations is well placed to represent the interests of both peak confederations and the nationally bound domestic federations. These may provide an organizational platform for nationally bound federations that are now compelled – by virtue of the dangers inherent in free trade agreements – to engage in cross-border campaigns with kindred labour bodies in negotiating states. In this sense, free trade negotiations serve to catapult important domestic (formally inward looking?) labour actors beyond their traditional spheres of influence.

We add to this dynamic the plethora of oppositional civil actors that are increasingly joining forces with labour to either oppose outright free trade agreements, pressure governments to incorporate labour standards, or ameliorate the effects of – or alter provisions in – existing agreements. In the wake of the North American Free Trade Agreement such coalitions were formed with the aim of protecting workers in the burgeoning number of export processing zones. Two examples of such alliances were the San Antonio-based Coalition for Justice in the Maquiladoras, and the San Diego-based Committee to Support Maquiladoras. These were sustained by the combined efforts of trade union organizations and members of civil bodies concerned with the defence of citizen and immigrant rights. Primarily involving the American Federation of Labor-Congress of Industrial Organizations (AFL-CIO), these relationships have, according to Carr, 'galvanized ... US union actors with little prior experience with trans-border work in the Americas'.[307] Another body that brings together organized labour and civil realm actors in this way is the Mexican Action Network on Free Trade. This network was formed in 1991, and has sought to ameliorate the worst effects of the North American Free Trade Agreement. Comprising mainly Mexican and Canadian organizations, it is exceptional because it connects over 100 labour, environmental, women's, peasant, and urban community groups.[308]

More recently, we have seen a number of campaigns straddling the domestic, regional, and transnational planes. These have seen labour organizations and oppositional civil realm actors cooperate at various levels of intimacy. The kind of relationships spawned by the NAFTA experience are being replicated as progressive movements formulate their responses to such regimes as the Free Trade Area of the Americas, the Central America Free Trade Agreement, the Australia–United States Free Trade Agreement, as well as to the symptoms of such liberalization. Among the relevant players in these cases are the Canadian Auto Workers, the AFL-CIO, the Minnesota Fair Trade Association, the Miami based Citizens Trade Campaign, the Campaign for Labour Rights, the United States Anti-Sweatshop Movement, and Fair Wear International.

A marriage of forces at this bilateral/regional intersection – between national and regional labour actors, and progressive social movements – holds out interesting opportunities for labour. Cross-border collaborations may come to be infused with greater energy not least because the protagonists are rooted in the particular and yet informed by broader concerns. Because the issues at stake are proximate and of an immediacy, these alliance partners will remain within reach of the centers of national power and authority. But at the same time they may well be able to determine – through the agency of regional and bilateral free trade negotiations – legislative outcomes in faraway states. Moreover, this intersection may in the future become the epicentre of the transnational network of labour organizations: where the transnational confederations come to interact more closely with their national, federated, constituents. It is conceivable that the transnational confederations will themselves devote fewer resources to advocacy within the established multilateral embodiments of the community of states, and more to sustaining their nationally bound affiliates during protracted regional or bilateral free trade negotiations. Indeed, if a more profound vertical integration of this kind were to occur it would be premised upon better organizational, communicative, and intellectual support for national constituents than presently exists.

Thus, the free trade agreements may come to represent an important site at which the struggle for greater control of the state takes place. And, following Gramsci, we might say that a form of 'industrial legalism' writ large (insinuation into free trade agreements) may yet prove to be a useful strategy, so long as regional corporatism does not become an end in itself. The likelihood of this occurring will be minimized for as long as organized labour continues to gravitate towards the more fluid and spontaneous social movements; movements that for so long have eschewed close relations with labour and that remain, by definition, wary of close association with governments.

This sanguine view of organized labour's prospects is posited with reservations. One should not overestimate the degree of unity between affiliates of transnational and regional confederations and, in turn, between the domestic trade union affiliates of national federations. Trade liberalization continues to be a more pressing concern for some trade unions than for others. For example, leaders of trade unions within manufacturing and textile sectors are doubtless more attuned to issues of trade liberalization than are those overseeing transport industries. From another perspective, cross-border collaboration between progressive movements of the north and south remains problematic while protectionist manoeuvring on the part of northern unions persist. And finally, there is nothing to suggest that the trend on the part of states towards bilateral and regional trade agreements is inexorable and irreversible. It may well transpire that states once again veer towards governance regimes overseen by traditional multilateral organizations such as the United Nations, and return with vigour to the now fraught site of the World Trade Organization.

But given the trajectories noted throughout this book – within the various dimensions of change, and across the various layers of engagement noted – it is clear that organized labour's particular form of globalization will continue apace. Its organizational form is now well established on a global plane, and its integration – when considered in terms of internal communicative regimes, issues of common concern, and ideological consistency – is now at unprecedented levels. And yet as we have seen, this remains a globalization of a peculiar kind. This is so because it is driven in large part by statism, albeit a statism premised on a commitment to a progressive and civically informed communitarianism.

Notes

Introduction

1. Alain Touraine, 'Unionism as a social movement', in *Unions in Transition: Entering the Second Century*, edited by Seymour Martin Lipset (San Francisco, 1986), pp. 153, 173.
2. Ellen Meiksins Wood, Peter Meiksins, and Michael Yates, eds, *Rising from the Ashes?: Labor in the Age of "Global" Capitalism* (New York, 1998).
3. The following titles are representative of an ever-expanding literature on the subject. Barry Carr, 'Labour internationalism and the North American Free Trade Agreement', in *Protest and Globalisation*, edited by James Goodman (Sydney, 2002), Jeffrey Harrod and Robert O'Brien, eds *Global Unions? Theory and Strategies of Organized Labour in the Global Political Economy*, RIPE Series in Global Political Economy (London, 2002), Ronaldo Munck, *Globalisation and Labour: The New 'Great Transformation'* (London, 2002), Beverly J. Silver, *Forces of Labor: Workers' Movements and Globalization Since 1870* (Cambridge, 2003), Peter Waterman, 'The new social unionism: A new union model for a new world order', in *Labour Worldwide in the Era of Globalization: Alternative Union Models in the New World Order*, edited by Ronaldo Munck and Peter Waterman (London, 1999).
4. Robert O'Brien *et al.*, *Contesting Global Governance: Multilateral Economic Institutions and Global Social Movements* (Cambridge, 2000), Jane Wills, 'Great expectations: Three years in the life of one EWC', *European Journal of Industrial Relations* 6 (2000), Jane Wills, 'Taking on the Cosmocorps: Experiments in transnational labor organization', *Economic Geography* 74 (1998).
5. Andrew Herod, 'Labor unions and the making of economic geographies', in *Organizing the Landscape: Geographical Perspectives on Labor Unionism*, edited by Andrew Herod (Minneapolis, 1998), Andrew Herod, *Organizing the Landscape: Geographical Perspectives on Labor Unionism* (Minneapolis, 1998).
6. The following scholars approach the notion of globalization using structural imperatives as their point of departure. Joseph A. Camilleri and Jim Falk, *The End of Sovereignty?* (Aldershot, 1992), Philip G. Cerny, 'Globalization and the changing logic of collective action', *International Organization* 49 (1995), Ian R. Douglas, 'Globalization and the retreat of the state', in *Globalization and the Politics of Resistance*, edited by Barry K. Gills (London, 2000), Barry R.J. Jones, 'Globalization in perspective', in *Globalization and its Critics: Perspectives from Political Economy*, edited by Randall D. Germain (New York, 2000), Jan Aart Scholte, 'Globalization: Prospects for a paradigm shift', in *Politics and Globalization: Knowledge, Ethics and Agency*, edited by Martin Shaw (London, 1999).
7. Representatives of this perspective include the following. Stephen Castles, 'Globalization from below', *Arena Magazine* 2000, Ian Clark, *Globalization and International Relations Theory* (Oxford, 1999), Richard Falk, 'Resisting "Globalization-from-Above" through "Globalization-from-Below" ', in *Globalization and the*

Politics of Resistance, edited by Barry K. Gills (London, 2000), Allen Hunter, 'Globalization from below? Promises and perils of the new internationalism', *Social Policy* 25 (1995).
8. R.B.J. Walker, 'Social movements/world politics', *Millennium: Journal of International Studies* 23 (1994): 699.
9. I am indebted to Professor Paul James of the Globalism Institute, RMIT University, Melbourne, for introducing me to his 'theory of abstract community'. He has used this method in research on nationhood, though it is applicable to analysis of all social formations. His method works 'across various levels of analytical abstraction' to make sense of empirical generalizations, modes of practice, modes of integration, and categorical change, as these relate to the dynamics of communal existence. See Paul James, *Nation Formation: Towards a Theory of Abstract Community* (London, 1996).
10. Jan Aart Scholte, 'Global capitalism and the state', *International Affairs* 73 (1997).
11. This interpretation borrows from the Gramscian perspective on ideology. See Antonio Gramsci, *Selections from the Prison Notebooks of Antonio Gramsci*, edited by Quintin Hoare and Geoffrey Nowell (translators) Smith, tenth printing 1989 edn. (New York, 1971), p. 323, or Terry Eagleton, *Ideology: An Introduction* (London, 1991), pp. 113–16.
12. John Boli, 'Conclusion: world authority structures and legitimations', in *Constructing World Culture: International Non-Governmental Organizations Since 1875*, edited by John Boli and George M. Thomas (Stanford, 1999), p. 286.
13. Lewis L. Lorwin, *The International Labor Movement: History, Policies, Outlook* (New York, 1953), p. 31.
14. Ibid., pp. 37–9.
15. Ibid.
16. J.P. Windmuller, *The International Trade Union Movement* (London, 1980), pp. 26–7.
17. Also commonly known as the Red International of Labour Unions. The less cumbersome appellation – the *Profintern* – is preferred here.
18. Lorwin, *The International Labor Movement*, pp. 148–9.
19. Wayne Thorpe, 'Syndicalist internationalism before World War II', in *Revolutionary Syndicalism: An International Perspective*, edited by Marcel Van der Linden and Wayne Thorpe (Aldershot, 1990).
20. Known at the time as the International Secretariat of Trade Union Centres.
21. Windmuller, *The International Trade Union Movement*, p. 35.
22. Lorwin, *The International Labor Movement*, p. 148.
23. Michael Forman, *Nationalism and the International Labor Movement* (University Park, 1998), p. 9.
24. André C. Drainville, 'Left internationalism and the politics of resistance in the New World Order', in *A New World Order: Global Transformations in the Late Twentieth Century*, edited by David A. Smith and József Böröcz (London, 1995), p. 221.
25. For an excellent analysis of the relationship between British labour and imperialist governments of the day see John Saville, 'Britain: internationalism and the Labour Movement between the wars', in *Internationalism in the Labour Movement: 1830–1940*, edited by Frits Van Holthoon and Marcel Van der Linden (Leiden, 1988).

Part I 1945–72

26. Unemployment in North America, Western Europe, Japan, Australia, and New Zealand doubled – from five to ten million – in the years 1967–71.
27. As one commentator noted, 'In 1965, 87 corporations (of which 60 were domiciled in the United States) had sales greater than the gross national product of 57 sovereign states'. Joseph Nye, 'The strength of international regionalism', in *Transnational Industrial Relations: Proceedings of a Symposium held at Geneva by the International Institute for Labour Studies*, edited by Hans Günter (London, 1972), p. 51.
28. Mathew Horsman and Andrew Marshall, *After the Nation-State: Citizens, Tribalism and the New World Disorder* (London, 1995), p. 29.
29. See Nye's examination of the gradual process of regional integration, and the extent to which this reflected a nationalistic counter to the spread of multinational corporations. Nye, 'The strength of international regionalism'.
30. Craig N. Murphy, *International Organization and Industrial Change: Global Governance Since 1850* (Cambridge, 1994), p. 7.
31. The meaning of the term 'corporatism' is contested. Here we adopt Crouch's economical definition: that is, 'the hierarchical, non-conflictual integration of the state and organized groups representative of both capital and labour' See Colin Crouch, 'The changing role of the state in industrial relations in Western Europe', in *The Resurgence of Class Conflict in Western Europe Since 1968*, edited by Colin Crouch and Alessandro Pizzorno (London, 1978), p. 197.

1   1945–72 – Internal Change: Antagonism and Shallow Integration

32. These included the American Congress of Industrial Organizations, the French Confédération Générale du Travail, and the Soviet all Union Central Council of Trade Unions.
33. Brussels was chosen as the headquarters, the leader of the International Transport Workers Federation, J.H. Oldenbroek, was named the General Secretary, and a Belgian, Paul Finet, assumed the role of President. See Gary K. Busch, *The Political Role of International Trade Unions* (London, 1983), pp. 67–71.
34. These also came to be known as Trade Unions Internationals. They were in every sense dependent on the WFTU and were not prominent actors. Heinz Bendt, *One World, One Voice, Solidarity: The International Trade Secretariats* (Bonn, 1996), p. 19.
35. The terms of the relationship between the trade secretariats and the ICFTU are set out in the 1951 'Milan Agreement', a document that was subsequently updated and revised in 1966, 1967, and 1969. See Ibid., pp. 8, 18–19.
36. It would be wrong to regard the International Trade Secretariats as homogeneous. The network of trade secretariats has always comprised those of very different political and social dispositions. For example, the International Metalworkers' Federation has traditionally comprised affiliates active at the coal-face of national and international labour politics. It played a pivotal role in averting secretariat incorporation into the fledgling World Federation of

Trade Unions. Others have assumed far more subdued and unobtrusive dispositions, with notable examples – such as the then International Secretariat of Entertainment Trade Unions – coming from non-manufacturing sectors.
37. The IFCTU represented only 20 members in 1952. These comprised 12 from Europe, 6 from Latin America, 1 from Asia and Canada respectively. By 1968, the IFCTU/WCL had 74 affiliates in 68 countries. Of these 19 were based in Europe, 29 in Latin America, 20 in Africa, 5 in Asia and 1 in North America.
38. It is worth mentioning the main sources of income for the ICFTU during this period. The movement was sustained through affiliation fees and voluntary contributions to its International Solidarity Fund. Throughout the 1970s the proportion of contributions to the Fund declined, as a corresponding increase from affiliates redressed the balance. By the early 1970s the burden of financing the ICFTU fell mainly on the European, Antipodean, and North American affiliates. Burton Bendiner, *International Labour Affairs: The World Trade Unions and the Multinational Companies* (Oxford, 1987), pp. 37–8.
40. Kim Moody, *Workers in a Lean World: Unions in the International Economy* (London, 1997), p. 229.
40. The Confederación's close association with the Soviet dependent WFTU won it few friends throughout the 1950s, and in time its legitimacy eroded to the point where the organization folded in 1964. Its successor – also WFTU aligned – was the Permanent Congress of the Unity of Latin American Workers. Ironically, the latter established an even closer relationship with the WFTU, acting as its *de facto* regional organization in that sphere. See Busch, *The Political Role of International Trade Unions*, pp. 142–6.
41. The reports of the ICFTU's Executive Board at the time reveal a leadership searching for the most effective means of integrating their confederate network. The following reports contain opinions for and against the print and electronic technologies then available. ICFTU, 'Executive Board (report/document 7EB/7)', (Brussels, 1952), ICFTU, 'Executive Board (report/document 9EB/8)', (Brussels, 1952).
42. A good example of this can be found in the following article hailing the WFTU's gains in Africa. WFTU-Editorial, 'A great moment in the history of the WFTU and of the AATUF', *World Trade Union Movement* 4 (1969).
43. The first of these comments was made by Mikhail Tarasov, leader of the principal Russian trade union confederation; and the second reflected the view of even the more radical of the American trade union leaders. Both are quoted in Anthony Carew, 'Towards a free trade union centre: The International Confederation of Free Trade Unions (1949–1972)', in *The International Confederation of Free Trade Unions*, edited by Anthony Carew, et al. (Bern, 2000), pp. 173, 175.
44. ICFTU-Editorial, 'Moscow's agents in the tribunes of the free world', *Free Labour World* 59 (1959): 3–6, ICFTU-Editorial, 'The WFTU in the service of the Kremlin's foreign policy', *Free Labour World* 64 (1955): 7–8, ICFTU-Editorial, 'Where "unions" stay silent', *Free Labour World* 193–4 (1966): 33.
45. See the editorial entitled 'Repression and revolt' taken from issue 247 ICFTU, *ICFTU Viewpoints: A Selection of editorials from Free Labour World* (Brussels, 1970), p. 34.
46. Karel Hoffmann, 'The role of trade unions in the socialist countries', *World Trade Union Movement* 12 (1980): 5.
47. Ibid.

48. Pierre Gensous, 'Concluding speech (of the 22nd Session of the WFTU General Council)', *World Trade Union Movement* 11 (1972): 4–5.
49. WFTU, *In the Thick of the Struggle: 10 Questions and Answers on the Activities and Policies of the WFTU* (Prague, 1965), p. 55.
50. For a fascinating insight into the difficulties the ICFTU encountered in its early forays into the 'regions' see the following report by its Asian Regional Secretary, D. Mungat. ICFTU, 'Report of the Asian Regional Secretary to the ICFTU Executive Board (report/document 7EB/7d)', (Brussels, 1952).
51. While we continue to rely on 'primary' sources – most notably, the various reports and publications of the confederations in question – it must be said that these often tend towards the platitudinous and polemical. Nevertheless, the following reference gives some indication of the complexity of the relations being cultivated in the region at this time. Hector Santibanez and Standing Congress for Latin American Trade Union Unity Executive Secretary, 'The road to unity – The achievement of common aims', *World Trade Union Movement* 1 (1970): 9–11.
52. Understandably, Algerian trade unionists had an aversion to the WFTU because of the latter's connection with the French affiliate, the Confédération Générale du Travail.
53. Agostino Novella, 'WFTU: 5th World Trade Union Congress' (paper presented at the 5th World Trade Union Congress, Moscow, 4–16 December 1961), p. 3. A report to the ICFTU Executive Board on the proceedings of the 1966 WFTU Congress also notes the tensions that exist between these affiliates and the peak body. See ICFTU, 'Executive Board (report/document 39EB/23)', (Brussels, 1966).
54. Peter Waterman, A spectre is haunting labour internationalism, the spectre of communism [Web] (Hartford Web Publishing, 2000 [cited 15/8/2001 2001]); available from http://hartford-hwp.com/archives/26/035.html.
55. MacShane's research reveals the extent to which internecine conflict between movements of the left in this period played a crucial part in determining the WFTU's post-war configuration. Dennis MacShane, *International Labour and the Origins of the Cold War* (Oxford, 1992), pp. 167–87.
56. Respectively: ICFTU, 'For economic equality: notes on the ICFTU World Economic Conference' (paper presented at the ICFTU World Economic Conference, Geneva, 24–26 June 1971), ICFTU, 'Resolutions adopted by the ICFTU Sixth World Congress' (paper presented at the Sixth World Congress of the ICFTU, Brussels, 1–3 December 1960), ICFTU-Editorial, 'The decolonization of trade', *Free Labour World* 173 (1964), ICFTU-Editorial, 'Labour's plan for trade and aid', *Free Labour World* 166 (1964).
57. Pierre Gensous, 'The role, tasks and responsibilities of the unions (extracts from a report presented by Assistant General Secretary of the WFTU at the Seventh World Trade Union Congress)', *World Trade Union Movement* 11 (1969): 14.
58. The following issues of the WFTU's *World Trade Union Movement* publication contain striking images of this sort: June–July, August, September, October, November 1969, and January 1970.
59. Mark E. Rupert, *Producing Hegemony: The Politics of Mass Production and American Global Power* (Cambridge, 1995), p. 82.

60. Patrick Pasture, 'Feminine intrusions in a culture of masculinity', in *The Lost Perspective? Trade Unions Between Ideology and Social Action in the New Europe*, edited by Patrick Pasture, Johan Verberckmoes, and Hans De Witte (Brookfield, 1996).
61. The secularization of the labour movement – particularly in Europe – gathered momentum in the post-war years, and so one should not place too much weight on the residual influence of the church at this time. Patrick Pasture, 'Conclusion: reflections on the fate of ideologies and trade unions', in *The Lost Perspective? Trade Unions Between Ideology and Social Action in the New Europe*, edited by Patrick Pasture, Johan Verberckmoes, and Hans De Witte (Brookfield, 1996), pp. 379–80.

2 1945–72 – External Change: Incorporation and Statist Internationalism

62. Craig R. Littler and Gill Palmer, 'Communist and capitalist trade unionism: comparisons and contrasts', in *Trade Unions in Communist States*, edited by Alex Pravda and Blair A. Ruble (London, 1986), pp. 261–2.
63. Eliassen quoted in Rainer Deppe, Richard Herding, and Dietrich Hoss, 'The relationship between trade union action and political parties', in *The Resurgence of Class Conflict in Western Europe Since 1968*, edited by Colin Crouch and Alessandro Pizzorno (London, 1978), p. 180.
64. Enrique de la Garza, Javier Melgoza, and Marcia Campillo, 'Unions, Corporatism and the Industrial Relations System in Mexico', in *The State and Globalization: Comparative Studies of Labour and Capital in National Economies*, edited by Martin Upchurch (London, 1999), pp. 248–9. It is worth noting that the Mexican labour movement has not always been unified in its dealings with the state. Indeed, in 1947 a breakaway labour organization was formed by those seeking to distance labour from the state. Those behind the move were workers of the powerful industrial unions. The government response was to purge the affiliated unions of its leadership, thus undermining the whole project. For more on this episode of Mexican labour history, see Altha J. Cravey, 'Cowboys and dinosaurs: Mexican labor unionism and the state', in *Organizing the Landscape: Geographical Perspectives on Labor Unionism*, edited by Andrew Herod (Minneapolis, 1998).
65. The following were among the most notable examples of national trade union bodies gravitating towards government: Britain's Trade Union Congress, *via* the Labour Party; the Deutsche Gewerkschaftsbund (German Federation of Trade Unions), *via* the West German Social Democratic Party; and Sweden's Landorganisationen i Sverige (Swedish Trade Union Confederation), *via* that country's Social Democratic Party.
66. Crouch, 'The changing role of the state in industrial relations in Western Europe', p. 204. The relationship between labour leaders and government was very intimate, even though outward appearances sometimes suggested otherwise. See Peter Weiler, *British Labour and the Cold War* (Stanford, 1988), pp. 1–23.

67. For a thorough analysis of the way the productivist and nationalist value systems were imbibed by the American labour leaders in the post-war period see Rupert, *Producing Hegemony*, pp. 139–66.
68. See Pierre Dubois, 'New forms of industrial conflict: 1960–1974', in *The Resurgence of Class Conflict in Western Europe Since 1968*, edited by Colin Crouch and Alessandro Pizzorno (London, 1978), Frank Koscielski, *Divided Loyalties: American Unions and the Vietnam War* (New York, 1999), and Giovanni Arrighi, Terence K. Hopkins, and Immanuel Wallerstein, *Antisystemic Movements* (London, 1989), pp. 97–119.
69. For an excellent analysis of the fault lines existing between trade union leaderships and their constituents, as well as the steps taken by the latter to re-orientate leadership attitudes, see Deppe, Herding, and Hoss, 'The relationship between trade union action and political parties', p. 184.
70. Crouch, 'The changing role of the state in industrial relations in Western Europe', p. 216. Perhaps one of the most striking examples of turbulence resulting in integration is the case of post-war Japan. Throughout the late 1940s and early 1950s labour unions mounted a series of crippling strikes. Eventually the movement was subdued and then incorporated into what has subsequently become the quintessential corporatist relationship. Andrew J. Taylor, *Trade Unions and Politics* (London, 1989), pp. 15–16.
71. Classic *dualism* assumes a community of interest within socialist society so broad as to remove the very possibility of systemic industrial conflict, leaving only the most isolated, specific grievances open to debate and dispute. Alex Pravda, 'Trade unions in East European communist systems: toward corporatism?', *International Political Science Review* 4 (1983): 6.
72. Werner Reutter, 'Trade unions and politics in Eastern and Central Europe: tripartism without corporatism', in *The Lost Perspective? Trade Unions Between Ideology and Social Action in the New Europe*, edited by Patrick Pasture, Johan Verberckmoes, and Hans De Witte (Brookfield, 1996), p. 139.
73. This latitude came in the form of greater trade union decentralization, and was evident in the then Yugoslavia (1950), Hungary, Poland (1956–58), and in what was Czechoslovakia (1966–69). Pravda, 'Trade Unions in East European Communist Systems', pp. 9–10. Littler and Wilson also explore the various contexts of trade unionism. They reveal that in China, for example, the phenomenon of 'surplus labour' between the 1950s and 1970s in particular, mitigated the rise of shop-floor/trade union power, thus ensuring that such organizations were more or less emasculated. See Littler and Palmer, 'Communist and Capitalist Trade Unionism', and Jeanne L. Wilson, 'The People's Republic of China', in *Trade Unions in Communist States*, edited by Alex Pravda and Blair A. Ruble (London, 1986).
74. Chris Osakwe, *The Participation of the Soviet Union in Universal International Organizations* (Leiden, 1972), p. 56.
75. Forman, *Nationalism and the International Labor Movement*, p. 167.
76. For example, it is claimed that the American Institute of Free Labor Development – the AFL-CIO's foreign aid organization – received over 90 per cent of its funding from government. See Hobart A. Spalding, 'The two Latin american foreign policies of the U.S. Labor Movement: the AFL-CIO top brass vs. rank-and-file', *Science and Society* 56 (1992–93): 421. See also Beth Sims, *Workers of the World Undermined: American Labor's Role in U.S. Foreign Policy* (Boston, 1992), pp. 22–30.

77. Busch's research shows the extent of government sponsorship of the AIFLD which had, by the late 1970s, reached eight million dollars *per annum*. See Busch, *The Political Role of International Trade Unions*, p. 161. For more damning accounts of the activities of American labour see Hobart A. Spalding, 'Solidarity forever?: Latin American unions and the international labor network', *Latin American Research Review* XXIV (1989). Spalding provides a fascinating study of how the AIFLD in particular manipulated labour politics throughout Latin America between the 1960s and 1980s. He also provides details of the genuine assistance provided: this included the training of labour organizers, providing technical and material support, and supporting union-to-union programmes. See Spalding, 'The two Latin American foreign policies of the U.S. Labor Movement'.
78. See Robert W. Cox, 'Labor and hegemony (first published in 1977)', in *Approaches to World Order*, edited by Robert W. Cox (Cambridge, 1995), pp. 431–2, and Busch, *The Political Role of International Trade Unions*, pp. 146–8, 171–7 respectively.
79. This quote appears in Cox, 'Labor and hegemony (first published in 1977)', p. 432.
80. Spalding, 'The two Latin American foreign policies of the U.S. Labor Movement', pp. 423–4. The trade secretariat most implicated during this period was the International Ladies Garment Workers Union. See also Busch, *The Political Role of International Trade Unions*, pp. 161–2.
81. Cox, 'Labor and hegemony (first published in 1977)', p. 428.
82. Weiler, *British Labour and the Cold War*, pp. 47, 19.
83. It is estimated that the TUC received £75,000 per annum from this source. See Moody, *Workers in a Lean World*, p. 228. For more on this episode of British labour's involvement in foreign affairs see the following Heinz Richter, *British Intervention in Greece: From Varkiza to Civil War* (London, 1986), C.M. Woodhouse, *The Struggle for Greece, 1941–1949* (London, 1976).
84. Most notable among these were the 1956 invasion of Hungary and the Sino-Soviet split of 1960.
85. For an eyewitness account of events during this period see Bendiner, *International Labour Affairs*, p. 43, Waterman, A spectre is haunting labour internationalism.
86. As Busch points out, it was a sad irony that the All China Federation of Trade Unions was itself dissolved amid the turmoil of the Cultural Revolution. Busch, *The Political Role of International Trade Unions*, p. 105.
87. Busch, *The Political Role of International Trade Unions*, p. 103. Busch also provides a fascinating overview of the cleavages within the Indian labour movement in the years leading up to independence, and of how the Soviet Union and Chinese governments vied for the support of major Indian constituents. See pages 108–18.
88. As Busch argues, the pressure to affiliate also came from the American Federation of Labor-Congress of Industrial Organizations, a 'national' labour movement that was active in courting African labour organizations. This it did while acting as an agent on behalf of its own government in the latter's anti-communist campaign. See Ibid. Busch, *The Political Role of International Trade Unions*, pp. 88–93.
89. I believe the term 'labour–government nexus' was coined by Gary Busch. I adapt his phrase for my own purposes. Ibid.

90. As of 1914 there existed 33 such bodies. They increased from 132 in 1956, to 280 in 1972. Werner J. Feld, Robert S. Jordan, and Leon Hurwitz, *International Organizations: A Comparative Approach*, 3rd edn (London, 1994), p. 17. They included the International Monetary Fund, the General Agreement on Tariffs and Trade, the International Bank for Reconstruction and Development, the International Development Association, and the International Finance Corporation. There also emerged such organizations as the Organization for Economic Cooperation and Development, the Eastern bloc's Council for Mutual Economic Assistance, and the European Economic Community also functioned as an umbrella organization for 15 specialized agencies that together sustained the post-war liberal internationalist order.
91. This was the title given to a regular editorial column appearing in the ICFTU's journal, *Free Labour World*. See also J.H Oldenbroek, 'Communism and the ILO's work: statement by J.H. Oldenbroek, ICFTU General Secretary, at the 38th International Labour Conference', *Free Labour World* 62 (1955).
92. Thus, the ICFTU's Asian Regional Organization asserted its presence within the United Nations Economic Commission for Asia and the Far East; while ORIT, the ICFTU's Latin American regional organization, worked closely with the United Nations Economic Commission for Latin America. The following speech provides a good insight into ORIT's perspective on the United Nation's efforts to foster economic development in Latin America: see Rodolpho Echenique, 'The worker's contribution towards Latin American economic integrations: speech by Echenique of the ICFTU/ORIT office in Chile to the inaugural meeting of the Committee of the Whole of ECLA (UN Economic Commission for Latin America)', *Free Labour World* 95 (1958).
93. The Governing Body is the executive body of the ILO. It comprises 28 government representatives, 14 employers' representatives, and 14 employees' representatives.
94. Windmuller, *The International Trade Union Movement*, p. 78.
95. Houshang Ameri, *Politics and Process in the Specialized Agencies of the United Nations* (Aldershot, 1982), p. 65.
96. Ibid., p. 217.
97. One example of this form of manoeuvring was the (unsuccessful) attempt in 1972 to overcome the ICFTU's dominant position within the ILO's Governing Body. This move was made in concert with the World Confederation of Labour, the confederation hitherto representing Christian socialism within the ranks of cross-border labour organizations. Relations between the WFTU and the WCL warmed considerably in the early 1970s, with the ICFTU's prominence in such world fora proving a concern for both. See Windmuller, *The International Trade Union Movement*, p. 107.
98. Bendt, *One World, One Voice, Solidarity: The International Trade Secretariats*, p. 29. One such joint statement expressed the secretariats' 'unflinching support for the ILO Industrial Committees and assimilated bodies ... [as they] are an indispensable instrument for guiding governments and employers' and workers' organizations in their endeavours to implement the general principles embodied in ILO Constitution'. ITS, 'Extraordinary General Conference of the International Trade Secretariats: Resolution on ILO Problems', *Free Labour World* 106 (1959): 180.

99. Martin Peterson, *International Interest Organization and the Transformation of Postwar Society* (Stockholm, 1980), quoted in Murphy, *International Organization and Industrial Change*.

Part II 1972–89

100. The main factors at play here included the following: falling primary commodity prices, investment in heavy industry, and profits in general; under-consumption in the West; the American Federal Reserve's use of high interest rates to quell the growing inflation; the OPEC countries' decision to increase the price of oil; the emergence of currency markets beyond the control of any state; the increased competition for markets from 'newly industrializing'; and the tensions brought on by the displacement of Keynesian managerialism by neoliberal monetarist prescriptions. See Stephen Gill, *American hegemony and the Trilateral Commission* (Cambridge, 1990), pp. 100–5.
101. As Camilleri and Falk point out, between '… 1973 and 1978 European firms were involved in 4,612 mergers, and in the same period 623 US firms were taken over by Canadian, European and Japanese firms. In 1979 alone and again in 1980, more than 600 US firms were taken over by foreign transnationals'. Camilleri and Falk, *The End of Sovereignty?*, p. 73.
102. Glenn Adler provides a useful overview of the GDL literature in Glenn Adler, 'Global restructuring and labor: the case of the South African trade union movement', in *Globalization: Critical Reflections*, edited by James H. Mittelman (Boulder, 1996), pp. 117–24.
103. Marino Regini, 'The past and future of social studies of labour movements', in *The Future of Labour Movements*, edited by Marino Regini (London, 1992), pp. 5–8.
104. Carla Lipsig-Mummé, 'The politics of the new service economy', in *Work of the Future: Global Perspectives*, edited by Paul James, Walter F. Veit, and Steve Wright (St Leonards, 1997). This author distinguishes between services to consumers, and services to producers. Consumer services consist of social services – such as health, education, welfare and public administration – and also personal services, consisting of food, hotels, cleaning, dry-cleaning and retail trade. Producer services consist of those financial, legal, engineering, accounting, transport, and communication services that facilitate business or bureaucratic functions. See page 111 of this article.
105. One should not overstate the extent of the shift from traditional to manufacturing production methods in the developing countries. As Petras and Engbarth assert, the industrialization of the Third World is a far more complex phenomena than is often portrayed. James Petras and Dennis Engbarth, 'Third world industrialization and trade union struggles', in *Trade Unions and the New Industrialization of the Third World*, edited by Roger Southall (London, 1988).
106. David Held *et al.*, *Global Transformations: Politics, Economics and Culture* (Cambridge, 1999), pp. 363–9.
107. Approximate growth figures are as follows. INGOs: 1972–2100, 1977–3500, 1985–4300 and 1989–4600. IGOs: 1972–270, 1977–291, 1985–380, 1989–309.

Figures are taken from the Yearbook of International Organizations, 1996–97, as reproduced in Ibid., p. 54.

3 1972–89 – Internal Change: Expansion and Uneasy Integration

108. Throughout the 1980s, the ICFTU increased its support for the South African labour movement – and, most notably, of the Congress of South African Trade Unions – in that movement's struggle against apartheid. Admittedly, this was arms-length assistance, and took the form of ICFTU affiliates being granted tacit approval to provide material assistance. While still a member of the WFTU in 1989, the South African labour organization was gravitating towards the ICFTU. Peter Waterman, 'The ICFTU in SA: admissions, revelations, silences', *South African Labour Bulletin* 17 (1993).
109. Anthony Carew *et al.*, eds, *The International Confederation of Free Trade Unions* (Bern, 2000), p. 571.
110. Belgian Francs. This is the currency upon which affiliation fees are fixed.
111. Carew *et al.*, eds, *The International Confederation of Free Trade Unions*. pp. 566–7, 568–9.
112. One of the most telling setbacks for the WFTU was the defection in 1978 of Italy's Confederazione Generale Italiana del Lavoro, one of Europe's largest communist trade union confederations.
113. They showed membership increasing from 151 million in 1973, to 190 million in 1978, and 206 million in 1985. WFTU, *World Federation of Trade Unions: 1945–1985* (Prague, 1985), pp. 147, 158.
114. For a complete list of these Trade Union Internationals see Ibid. pp. 148–57.
115. This comment by the President of the TUI of Transport Workers, appeared in the WFTU's journal, *World Trade Union Movement*. Jean Brun, 'Answers to the international questionnaire', *World Trade Union Movement* (1981): 2.
116. J.P. Windmuller and S.K. Pursey, 'The international trade union movement', in *Comparative Labour Law and Industrial Relations in Industrial Market Economies*, edited by R. Blanpain and C. Engels (The Hague, 1998), p. 94.
117. Bob Reinalda, 'The ITF in the context of international trade unionism', in *The International Transport-workers Federation 1914–1945*, edited by Bob Reinalda (Amsterdam, 1997), p. 15.
118. For figures up to 1980, see Windmuller, *The International Trade Union Movement*, p. 164. Beyond that see Windmuller and Pursey, 'The International Trade Union Movement'.
119. Thus, from 1966 the International Metal Workers' Federation began to rely on its World Auto Council to oversee the activities of, among others, Ford, General Motors, Nissan and Toyota. Bendiner, *International Labour Affairs*, pp. 63–89.
120. The ICFTU's regional organizations included the Mexico City-based Organizacion Regional Interamericana de Trabajadores, the New Delhi-based Asian Regional Organization, the African Regional Organization, and European Regional Organization – known then by the acronyms ORIT, ARO, AFRO, and ERO. The WCL was represented in Asia by the Brotherhood of Asian Trade Unionists, in Latin America by the Central Latino Americana de Trabajordores, and in Africa by ODSTA.

121. Four of the seven pre-existing organizations were European-based. The seven consisted of the Caribbean Congress of Labour, the Permanent Congress of Trade Union Unity of Latin American Workers, the Economic and Social Committee of the European Communities, the European Civil Service Federation, the Federation of International Civil Servants' Associations, the International Confederation of Arab Trade Unions, and the World Confederation of Organizations of the Teaching Profession. For a comprehensive list of these new players, as well as for information about their political orientation, see Martin Upham, *Trade Unions and Employers' Organizations of the World* (London, 1993).
122. A thorough analysis of the issue of 'International Trade Union Gatherings' – seen from the viewpoint of the ICFTU – featured in the following Executive Board reports. ICFTU, 'Executive Board (report/document 75EB/15)', (Brussels, 1980), ICFTU, 'Executive Board (report/document 76EB/16)', (Brussels, 1980).
123. For example, refer to ICFTU, 'Executive Board (report/document 67EB/15)', (Brussels, 1976), ICFTU, 'Executive Board (report/document 75EB/15)'. In addition, see the following circulars: ICFTU, 'Circular (to affiliates #38)', (Brussels, 1988), ICFTU, 'Circular (to affiliates #46)', (Brussels, 1981).
124. See ICFTU, 'Circular (to affiliates #46)'. A similar warning also appears in the ICFTU's in-house periodical, *Free Labour World*. Unknown, 'Contacts with communists', *Free Labour World* 273 (1973).
125. ICFTU, 'Circular (to affiliates #50)', (Brussels, 1981). This circular cautions affiliates against attending the World Trade Union Conference on the Economic and Social Aspects of Disarmament (Paris 15–17 December 1981).
126. From its high point in the early 1970s this publication was cut back severely in 1985, and distributed only in eight-page broad-sheet format. Its coverage of labour affairs was thin, with passing references only to issues that would have hitherto warranted far greater column inches and 'analysis'. Some of this decline must be attributed to financial constraints forced on the ICFTU by the withdrawal, in 1969, of its American affiliate. Rebecca Gumbrell-McCormick, 'Facing new challenges: the International Confederation of Free Trade Unions (1972–1990s)', in *The International Confederation of Free Trade Unions*, edited by Anthony Carew, *et al.* (Bern, 2000), p. 343.
127. The first of these was a Swissair promotion in the February edition of 1987.
128. From this period I would contrast the excellent and weighty publications of the International Union of Food and Allied Workers' Associations, with the pamphlet-style circular of the International Federation of Building and Wood Workers. As for the World Confederation of Labour, the quality of its *Flash-flash WCL* was very poor indeed.
129. For examples, Waterman refers to the 'Emergency' (1975–77), and the 15-month strike by 200,000 textile workers in India (1981–83) as events that were ignored by most, if not all, the publications mentioned here. Peter Waterman, 'Needed: a new communications model for a new working-class internationalism', in *For a New Labour Internationalism: A Set of Reprints and Working Papers*, edited by Peter Waterman (The Hague, 1985), p. 235.
130. Radio had been employed in various national contexts by labour organizations since the 1930s. Cross-border transmissions were also commonplace during the early Cold War years. The ICFTU sponsored *The Voice of Free*

Trade Unions in an attempt to counter what it perceived as communist propaganda in Eastern Europe, while its Latin American regional organization, ORIT, also used the medium to reach anti-Peronist forces in Argentina and Costa Rica through the 1950s. ICFTU, 'Executive Board (report/document 7EB/7c)', (Brussels, 1952).

131. Rudi Breunung, 'The world federation of trade unions calling: a few words about the WFTU radio programme', *World Trade Union Movement* 9 (1985).
132. The series took a critical look at consumerism, and also covered subjects such as social justice, public initiative in industry, economic democracy, and trade unions' role in social transformation. unknown, 'Trade unionism on the air', *Syndicats* (2 March, 1974).
133. WFTU-Editorial, 'Direct broadcast satellites, cable TV and mass participation in television', *World Trade Union Movement* 9 (1990).
134. I refer here to such bodies as the International Labour Research and Information Group (South Africa), the Pakistan Institute of Labour Education and Research, and the Centre for Education and Communication (India). For examples of the use of this medium see Waterman, 'Needed', p. 242.
135. Gumbrell-McCormick, 'Facing new challenges', p. 351.
136. The most important such case was the application for membership by the Italian Confederazione Generale Italiana del Lavoro. Ultimately, the CGIL was accepted within the European confederation, in spite of the protestations of the ICFTU.
137. Gumbrell-McCormick, 'Facing new challenges', pp. 421–5. The ICFTU's own regional body in Africa, the African Regional Office (AFRO), had been dissolved in 1969. It was re-activated in 1973 with the aim of countering the growing pan-African appeal of the Organization of African Trade Union Unity.
138. Organizacion Regional Interamericana de Trabajadores or Inter-American Regional Organization of Workers.
139. This caused great consternation within the ICFTU, and especially among its European affiliates. For more detail on the withdrawal of the AFL-CIO from the ICFTU refer to Carew, 'Towards a free trade union Centre' pp. 323–8.
140. ORIT's mute response to the 1973 overthrow of the social-democrat administration of Salvador Allende in Chile was a case in point. Some accounts have it that ORIT distributed a press release congratulating the coup leader, General Pinochet. See Gumbrell-McCormick, 'Facing New Challenges' pp. 454–6. The most outspoken opponents of the American presence were the labour movements of Colombia, Argentina, Brazil's CNTI, and the Central Única de Trabajadores de Chile.
141. By 1979, the ICFTU Executive Board had managed to re-assert itself within ORIT. The pressure placed on them by not only the region's affiliates, but also by important European members – the Swedish and Danish labour leaders played important roles in this campaign – resulted in the expulsion of puppet labour confederations installed by the dictatorships of El Salvador, Uruguay, and Guatemala. See Gumbrell – McCormick, 'Facing new challenges', pp 458–60.
142. The Swedish trade union confederation, Landsorganisationen i Sverige (LO), took this stand in 1977–78. Gumbrell – McCormick, 'Facing new challenges', pp. 458–9.

143. While the ICFTU railed against 'dictatorships', it was mute in relation to the United State's sponsorship of such regimes. We search in vain for ICFTU condemnation of American support for the brutal regimes in place in El Salvador and Guatemala throughout the 1980s. We also note the WFTU's refusal to offer even token support for the beleaguered Polish Solidarity movement throughout 1980–81. An excellent analysis of this episode can be found in Alain Touraine *et al.*, *Solidarity: The Analysis of a Social Movement, Poland 1980–1981* (Cambridge, 1982). See also Busch, *The Political Role of International Trade Unions*, pp. 233–8.
144. ICFTU, 'Statements made and resolutions adopted by the Tenth World Congress of the ICFTU' (paper presented at The Tenth World Congress of the ICFTU, London, 1972), p. 9.
145. ICFTU, 'Programme for balanced world development: 1982 ICFTU World Economic Review', *Free Labour World* 379–80 (28 February, 1982): 15.
146. ICFTU, 'Circular (to affiliates #37) – Executive Board – North/South: A programme for Survival', (Brussels, 1980). For more on the ICFTU's view on development see ICFTU, 'Circular (to affiliates #24) – Preparations of the UN's new international development strategy: elements to be included', (Brussels, 1980), ICFTU, *Towards a New Economic and Social Order: ICFTU Development Charter* (Brussels, 1978), ICFTU, 'Unions' world development priorities: the New Delhi declaration', *Free Labour World* 369–70 (15 April, 1981), ICFTU-Statement, 'ICFTU statement to UNCTAD IV' (paper presented at the UNCTAD IV, Nairobi, 5–29 May 1976).
147. Ibrahim Zakaria, 'The unions must coordinate their efforts in the search for a solution to the development crisis (extracts from the introduction to the discussion)' (paper presented at the 36th Session of the WFTU General Council, 1984), p. 4.
148. WFTU-Editorial, 'Solidarity for development', *World Trade Union Movement* (3 March, 1980): 32.
149. Respectively: Ilie Frunza, 'We must struggle for a mutually advantageous commerce', *World Trade Union Movement* 8 (1981), WFTU, 'Trade unions and the challenges of the 1980s: 10th World Trade Union Congress' (paper presented at the 10th World Trade Union Congress, Havana, Cuba, 10–15 February 1982), p. 20.
150. This is suggestive of the ways in which the labour 'elite' were incorporated within the apparatus of state, and the ways in which these labour leaders imbibed the values of incumbent governments. Petras and Engbarth refer to this process when they claim that 'The ubiquitous state institutions ... penetrate and control trade unions at the apex – the leaders of federations and confederations frequently appear to be functionaries of government labour ministries'. Petras and Engbarth, 'Third world industrialization and trade union struggles', p. 103.

4 1972–89 – External Change: From Incorporation to Partial Disengagement

151. Marino Regini, ed., *The Future of Labour Movements* (London, 1992), p. 6.
152. Regini, 'The past and future of social studies of labour movements', p. 5.

153. de la Garza, Melgoza, and Campillo, 'Unions, corporatism and the industrial relations system in Mexico', p. 251.
154. For a more thorough account of the impact of contract system reforms see Ibid., pp. 252–6.
155. Coker's analysis of the Venezuelan setting also includes some interesting insights into the Mexican experience. See Trudie Coker, 'Globalization and corporatism: the growth and decay of organized labor in Venezuela, 1900–1998', *International Labor and Working-Class History* 60 (2001): pp. 194–5.
156. M. Victoria Murillo, 'From populism to neoliberalism: labor unions and market reforms in latin America', *World Politics* 52 (2000): 140.
157. Coker, 'Globalization and corporatism', pp. 190, 193.
158. Taylor, *Trade Unions and Politics*, p. 101.
159. Harry Katz and Owen Darbishire, *Converging Divergences: Worldwide Changes in Employment Systems* (New York, 2000), pp. 247–59. See also Marino Regini, 'The conditions for political exchange: how concertation emerged and collapsed in Italy and Great Britain', in *Order and Conflict in Contemporary Capitalism*, edited by John H. Goldthorpe (Oxford, 1984), pp. 139–42.
160. The first of these – Tjänstemännens Central organisation (TCO) – covered salaried workers; and the other – Sveriges Akademikers Central organisation (SACO) – covered professional workers. See Olle Hammarström and Tommy Nilsson, 'Employment relations in Sweden', in *International and Comparative Employment Relations*, edited by Greg J. Bamber and Russell D. Lansbury (London, 1998), pp. 229–30, Katz and Darbishire, *Converging Divergences*, pp. 242–3.
161. For a more comprehensive study of the German trade union reaction to the economic and political changes of the time, see Peter Gourevitch *et al.*, *Unions and Economic Crisis: Britain, West Germany and Sweden* (London, 1984).
162. Taylor, *Trade Unions and Politics*, pp. 159–61.
163. Ibid., p. 120. See also pp. 116–17.
164. The erosion of the Basic Steel Agreement, concession bargaining in the auto industry, and reduction of pattern bargaining across industry were significant events in 1982. See Bruce Western, *Between Class and Market: Postwar Unionization in the Capitalist Democracies* (New Jersey, 1997), pp. 173–4.
165. There were two national trade union confederations: the Canadian Labour Congress was the largest, but also the weakest; and the Quebec-based, left-leaning, Confederation of National Trade Unions.
166. This was formed in 1983 by business groups, the ruling Australian Labor Party, and the Australian Council of Trade Unions.
167. Moody notes that 'In the late 1970s, twelve of Western Europe's eighteen governments were held by social-democratic or labor-based parties. In the US, the Democrats dominated Washington; in Canada, the Liberals sat in Ottawa ... A decade later, the majority of Western governments were conservative'. Moody, *Workers in a Lean World*, p. 117.
168. Western, *Between Class and Market: Postwar Unionization in the Capitalist Democracies*, p. 176.
169. This was a pattern evident in numerous other settings. Western provides a table of *Bargaining Decentralization Trends in the 1980s*. The following excerpts emphasize how widespread this trend was. Belgium: Suspension of

national bargaining from 1975 to 1986, with rapid growth in local bargaining through the late 1970s and 1980s. Denmark: Industry bargaining from 1981, following breakdown of central negotiations in 1975, 1977, and 1979. Finland: Failed attempts at central bargains common through the 1970s and 1980s. France: Aroux legislation establishes compulsory local negotiations in 1982. Ireland: Breakdown of centralized bargaining experiments in 1981, following locally organized strike activity. Ibid., p. 161.

170. Peter Lange, Michael Wallerstein, and Miriam Golden, 'The end of corporatism? Wage setting in the Nordic and Germanic Countries', in *The Workers of Nations: Industrial Relations in a Global Economy*, edited by Sanford M. Jacoby (Oxford, 1995). See also Lonny E. Carlile, 'Party politics and the Japanese labor movement: RENGO's "New Political Force" ', *Asian Survey* 34 (1994): 606. Peter Wad, 'The Japanization of the Malaysian trade union movement', in *Trade Unions and the New Industrialization of the Third World*, edited by Roger Southall (London, 1988), Hugh Williamson, 'Japanese enterprise unions in transnational companies: prospects for international co-operation', *Capital and Class* 45 (1991).

171. Jolanta Kulpinska, 'Introrganizational determinants of workers' self-management activity', in *Labour Relations in Transition in Eastern Europe*, edited by György Széll (Berlin, 1992), p. 201.

172. Alex Pravda and Blair A. Ruble, 'Communist trade unions: varieties of dualism', in *Trade Unions in Communist States*, edited by Alex Pravda and Blair A. Ruble (London, 1986), p. 16.

173. Severyn Bruyn, 'Toward a social market in communist nations', in *Labour Relations in Transition in Eastern Europe*, edited by György Széll (Berlin, 1992), p. 275.

174. Ludovit Czíria, 'Collective forms of work organization in Czechoslovak economic practice', in *Labour Relations in Transition in Eastern Europe*, edited György Széll (Berlin, 1992).

175. Natalia Chernina, 'Perspectives of self-government and de-alienation in business in the USSR', in *Labour Relations in Transition in Eastern Europe*, edited by György Széll (Berlin, 1992), Vladimir Gershikov, 'Business democracy: work collective councils and trade unions', in *Labour Relations in Transition in Eastern Europe*, edited by György Széll (Berlin, 1992).

176. Volkmar Kreißig and Erhard Schreiber, 'Participation and technological alternatives in the German Democratic Republic: the dilemma of scientific prediction and co-management by trade unions in the past and present', in *Labour Relations in Transition in Eastern Europe*, edited by György Széll (Berlin, 1992).

177. Lajos Héthy, 'Hungary's changing labour relations system', in *Labour Relations in Transition in Eastern Europe*, edited by György Széll (Berlin, 1992), p. 178.

178. Nigel Harris, *The End of the Third World: New Industrializing Countries and the Decline of an Ideology* (London, 1986), p. 196.

179. Ronnie Munck, *The New International Labour Studies* (London, 1988), pp. 125–6.

180. Frederic C. Deyo, *Beneath the Miracle: Labor Subordination in the New Asian Industrialism* (Berkeley, 1989), p. 110. Using case studies set in Hong Kong, Taiwan, South Korea, and Singapore, Deyo concludes that government policies in relation to labour changed according to the degree of militancy

confronted. Where the trade unions were weak (Hong Kong and Taiwan) governments would incorporate or exclude altogether the organizations representing labour. Where trade unions were militant (South Korea and Singapore) more coercive and repressive measures were employed. In each scenario, labour was estranged from the centre of power.

181. Petras and Engbarth, 'Third world industrialization and trade union struggles', p. 103.
182. Deyo, *Beneath the Miracle: Labor Subordination in the New Asian Industrialism*, pp. 144–7.
183. Here Mike Press cites the work of a colleague – Don Thomson – pointing out that from 1977 the TUC was payed £75,000 annually by the government for its Third World programmes. Press also points out that staff at the TUC's International Department had been seconded to the Foreign Office. It should be noted (as Press does) that these claims, and the inferences that flow, have been strenuously denied by the leadership of the TUC. Mike Press, 'The People's Movement', in *Solidarity for Survival: The Don Thomson Reader on Trade Union Internationalism*, edited by Mike Press and Don Thomson (Nottingham, 1989), p. 34.
184. For more on the ways in which the British and American labour movements differed in their orientation to important *isms* of the day – in this instance, colonialism and communism – see Anthony Carew, 'Conflict within the ICFTU: anti-communism and anti-colonialism in the 1950s', *International Review of Social History* 41 (1996).
185. The most important of these offshoots was the American Institute for Free Labor Development. Others included the African-American Labor Center, the Asian-American Free Labor Institute, and the Free Trade Union Institute. For more see Sims, *Workers of the World Undermined*, pp. 22–5.
186. Hobart Spalding notes the role played by the American Institute for Free Labor Development in the wake of the United States' 1983 invasion of Grenada. There, the Institute was enlisted to restructure the Grenadian labour movement, with its first task being to mobilize the remnants of 'friendly' trade unions to paint over the slogans of the ousted New Jewell movement. In addition, Spalding notes the manner in which the Institute created its own puppet trade union federation in El Salvador, thus orchestrating a split in that country's labour ranks in order to undermine opposition to the American-backed junta. Spalding is worth quoting here in order to gain a more complete understanding of the Institute's orientation. He has stated that it '... refuses to help jailed unionists if it disagrees with their activities. It usually calls strikes conducted by those workers 'political' and thus fair game for state repression. [The Institute] has even run special training courses for management on how to deal with "political strikes" '. Spalding, 'The two Latin American foreign policies of the U.S. labor movement', pp. 425–30, 435.
187. For more see Tom Barry and Deb Preusch, *AIFLD in Central America: Agents as Organizers* (Albuquerque, 1986), Paul Buhle, *Taking Care of Business: Samuel Gompers, George Meany, Lane Kirkland, and the Tragedy of American Labor* (New York, 1999), Dave Slaney, 'Solidarity and self-Interest', *NACLA: Report on the Americas* 22 (1988).
188. Sims, *Workers of the World Undermined*, p. 71.

189. In 1987 alone, the Agency contributed over 27 million dollars for AFL-CIO projects in countries in Africa, Central and Latin America, as well as in the Philippines. Ibid., pp. 24–5. The National Endowment for Democracy channelled 4.8 million dollars to the AFL-CIO's Free Trade Union Institute in the same year. That labour institute had received some 35 million dollars from the Endowment between 1984 and 1988. See Spalding, 'The two Latin American foreign policies of the U.S. labor movement' p. 424.
190. One example of this challenge to the status quo came in 1987. In Washington DC 45,000 trade unionists (leading a rally of more than 90,000) supported leaders of dissenting unions who condemned the policies of their government and the AFL-CIO executive. See Slaney, 'Solidarity and self-interest'.
191. Sims, *Workers of the World Undermined*, p. 92.
192. For a thorough account of the relationship between labour and government in Japan see Carlile, 'Party politics and the Japanese labor movement'.
193. Asian and Pacific Regional Organization. Robert Q. Hanham and Shawn Banasick, 'Japanese labor and the production of the space-economy in an era of globalization', in *Organizing the Landscape: Geographical Perspectives on Labor Unionism*, edited by Andrew Herod (Minneapolis, 1998), p. 110.
194. This follows similar policies adopted by Domei, one of RENGO's earlier incarnations. It had promoted overseas investment of Japanese capital and the revaluation of the yen. Ibid., pp. 110–11.
195. Blair A. Ruble, *Soviet Trade Unions: Their development in the 1970s* (Cambridge, 1981), pp. 130–6.
196. Ibid., p. 132.
197. Tom Keenoy, 'Solidarity: the anti-trade union', in *Trade Unions in Communist States*, edited by Alex Pravda and Blair A. Ruble (London, 1986), pp. 155–6.
198. Bendiner notes the hostile reaction to Solidarność by key figures within the WFTU and the Communist Party's Central Committee. Bendiner, *International Labour Affairs*, pp. 34–44.
199. It was felt by many that this decline had already begun when, in 1973, the ICFTU was excluded from a 'Group of Eminent Persons' working party set up to formulate the United Nation's actions on multinationals. Gumbrell-McCormick, 'Facing New Challenges', p. 388.
200. There are too many of these to list here, but for 1980 alone they included the World Conference on the UN Decade of Women, the Sixth UN Conference on the Prevention of Crime and the Treatment of Offenders, the Eleventh Special Session of the General Assembly, and the UN Conference on the Law of the Sea. Refer to ICFTU, 'Executive Board (report/document 76EB/11(a,b,c)', (Brussels, 1980).
201. In these United Nations and associated bodies the ICFTU waged a number of campaigns. One of the most important in this period was the campaign aimed at restricting the influence of the multinationals. This was crucial, for it had implications for many other areas of concern for labour. It complemented the prolonged campaign for the incorporation of a social clause in the General Agreement on Tariffs and Trade (GATT) treaties. The focus on multinationals also dovetailed with the ICFTU's campaign against apartheid. Here the ICFTU published material exposing corporate investors in South Africa known to have overtly racist employment regimes. ICFTU, 'Circular (to affiliates #72)', (Brussels, 1974). This circular to affiliates is one of many

that listed companies with interests in South Africa. Likewise, the focus on multinationals featured prominently in the ICFTU's contribution to the ILO's World Employment Conference in 1976.
202. The UNESCO remained a site of great discord between the member states of all political disposition and, by extension, the delegates of antagonistic trade union confederations. Government representatives from communist, developing, and Third World countries expressed fierce opposition to Western economic and strategic interests in this forum. The United States was the target of much of this criticism. This conflict of member states' interests within the UNESCO necessarily implicated the labour representatives in the politics of state. Eventually, this discord precipitated the withdrawal of the American government from the United Nations in 1984. The ICFTU's sympathy for the American position was restrained but evident nonetheless. ICFTU, 'Executive Board (report/document 67EB/15).', ICFTU-Editorial, 'World Trade Union Unity?', *Free Labour World* 281 (1973).
203. ICFTU supporters would no doubt consider the formation in 1974 of the UN Centre and Commission on Transnational Corporations as one such gain. Likewise, they might point to the 1977 adoption by the ILO of a Tripartite Declaration of Principles Concerning Multinational Enterprises and Social Policy as representing another. Certainly, the ICFTU's support for the international commission headed by the former German Chancellor, Willy Brandt, was crucial to the United Nation's adoption of his watershed 1980 report, *North, South: A Programme for Survival* (or, *The Brandt Report*). ICFTU, 'Circular (to affiliates #37) – Executive Board – North/South: A programme for Survival'. And finally, the ICFTU's important contributions to the worldwide anti-apartheid struggle would have been much diminished without access to intergovernmental fora throughout the 1970s and 1980s.
204. Once again, I have chosen to overlook the World Confederation of Labour. Though still active throughout this period, we find very little primary or secondary material that might help assess the extent to which it too engaged with intergovernmental organizations. Indeed, its published 'manifesto' of 1977 scarcely refers to the United Nations at all. World Confederation of Labour (WCL), *The World Confederation of Labour (WCL)* (Brussels, 1977), p. 21. However, fleeting mentions of the WCL in many of the other confederations' material suggest that it was also eager to interact with organizations on this global plane. See, for example, Johan Verstraeste, 'World Confederation of Labour on the Threshold of the 1990s', *World Trade Union Movement* 1 (1989), WFTU-Editorial, 'With the WCL we are ready', *World Trade Union Movement* 2 (1978).
205. The following supplement to the WFTU's periodical provides a good summation of that organization's very positive approach to the United Nations. WFTU-Dossier, 'The World Federation of Trade Unions and the United Nations Organisation', *World Trade Union Movement* 11 (1972).
206. These were too numerous to list, but included such events as the World Trade Union Conferences against apartheid (1972, 1977, and 1983), and the ILO organized Tripartite Conference on Employment (1976).
207. WFTU-Editorial, 'Transnational corporations and their loot of developing countries', *World Trade Union Movement* (1983).

208. WFTU-Editorial, 'Defenders of the old order', *World Trade Union Movement* 12 (1981), WFTU-Editorial, 'U.S.-led opposition rejects international economic action', *World Trade Union Movement* 3 (1984).
209. The following contain typical denunciations. WFTU-Editorial, 'Transnational corporations and their loot of developing countries'. WFTU-Editorial, 'The trilateral – its philosophy and objectives', *World Trade Union Movement* 9 (1980).
210. Trade secretariats gained access to the OECD through the nation-based confederation, the Trade Union Advisory Committee; and to the European Economic Community *via* the European Trade Union Confederation.
211. For example, direct IUF (The International Union of Food, Agricultural, Hotel, Restaurant, Catering, Tobacco and Allied Workers' Associations) engagement with the ILO industrial activities section intensified further after that United Nations agency established permanent industry committees for the food, hotels, and tourism sectors. For more see section 6(b), *Relations with other organizations: other inter-governmental institutions*. IUF, 'Executive Committee Report' (paper presented at the 19th Congress, München, 25–31 May 1981). The IUF also engaged in a campaign to limit the influence of multinationals *within* such intergovernmental organizations. See Item 8(a): *The World Food Situation: The FAO and the Food Crisis*. IUF, 'Executive Committee Report' (paper presented at the 18th Congress, Geneva, 23–28 January 1977).
212. See ICFTU, 'Statements made and resolutions adopted by the Twelfth World Congress of the ICFTU' (paper presented at The Twelfth World Congress of the ICFTU, Madrid, 1979), p. 3.

Part III   1989–2005

213. By the late 1990s it was estimated that around 53,000 such corporations existed, accounting for up to 70 per cent of world trade. Held *et al.*, *Global Transformations: Politics, Economics and Culture*, p. 282. Of these, a very small number – the largest 100 – controlled approximately 20 per cent of foreign global assets, and 30 per cent of all multinational corporations' total world sales. UNCTAD, 'World Investment Report 1997: Transnational Corporations, Market Structure and Competition Policy' (New York, 1997), p. 8.
214. While debate continues on the overall rate of development and wealth accumulation, there is consensus on the question of disparity: 2.8 billion people continue to live on just 2 dollars per day; the richest twenty-five million Americans have an income equivalent to almost 2-billion people; the assets of the world's 3 richest men are equal to the combined income of the world's least developed countries. UNDP, *'UNDP: The Human Development Report'* (New York, 2002).
215. Peter McMahon, 'Technology and globalization: an overview', *Prometheus* 19 (2001): 218.
216. One can refer, for example, to the following: the increased integration within the framework of the European Economic and Monetary Union (with the 1991 Maastricht, and 1997 Amsterdam Treaties facilitating still

greater integration); the formation of the forum of Asia-Pacific Economic Cooperation (1989); the Southern Cone Common Market (or MERCOSUR, established in 1991); the North American Free Trade Agreement (1996); and the Gulf Cooperation Council. She cites the example of the growing network of such bodies in the Asia-Pacific region. These now include the Pacific Economic Cooperation Council, the Pacific Trade and Development Conference, the Council for Security Cooperation in the Asia Pacific, and the APEC Business Advisory Council. Margaret P. Karns, 'Postinternational politics and the growing glomerations of global governance', in *Pondering Postinternationalism: A Paradigm for the Twenty-First Century*, edited by Heidi H. Hobbs (Albany, 2000), pp. 43–4.
217. Since the previous review of such growth in the numbers of intergovernmental organization there have emerged still more, with most concerned with the 'management' of free trade. Among these have been the following organizations within the Americas: the North American Free Trade Agreement (1994), the Southern Cone Common Market (1991), and the System of Central American Integration (1993). Since 1992, states in the Asia-Pacific region established the ASEAN Free Trade Area, and then implemented the South Asian Preferential Trading Arrangement. At the same time, the Southern African Development Community was formed. Expansion of existing regimes is exemplified by the European Union's acceptance of new members throughout the 1990s (Austria, Sweden, Finland, and, more recently, Poland, Hungary, and the Czech Republic). Such examples of expansion can also be found across regions, from the Americas, the Caribbean, and Asia. For more detail on the emerging layers of governance see ILO, Globalization [Internet] (International Labour Organization: ACTRAV Bureau for Workers' Activities, 1998 [cited 18 January 2003]); available from http://www.ilo.org/public/english/230actra/index.htm.
218. By 1996, these international non-governmental organizations numbered approximately 5400, an increase of 800 in the space of just 7 years. Held et al., *Global Transformations: Politics, Economics and Culture*, pp. 52–5.

5 1989–2005 – Internal Change: Consolidation and Integration

219. Outlined in the Congress report: http://www.icftu.org/www/pdf/Globalising%20Solidarity.pdf
220. While the World Federation of Trade Unions survives, it is moribund. At the time of writing, its principal affiliates were the Central de Trabajadores de Cuba, the Vietnam Federation of Trade Unions, and the All India Trades Union Congress.
221. According to the ICFTU's homepage, the confederation comprises 225 affiliates, representing 157 million workers in 148 countries. ICFTU, The ICFTU: What it is, What it does ... [web] (International Confederation of Free Trade Unions, 2002 [cited 18 November 2002]); available from http://www.icftu.org/displaydocument.asp?Index=990916422.
222. The World Confederation of Labour lays claim to 144 affiliate trade unions, representing some 26 million workers. See WCL, What's the WCL? [Web]

(World Confederation of Labour, 2002 [cited 20 November 2002]); available from http://www.cmt-wcl.org/1cmt-wcl/cmt-en/01whatis.htm. However, these figures should be treated with suspicion, not least because this organization counts among its affiliates both individual unions, and national organizations.
223. This process of consolidation also entailed name changes. Indeed, the generic label of 'International Trade Secretariat' was itself altered to 'Global Union Federations' in 2001. I am very mindful of the difficulties many people experience when trying to comprehend the labyrinth-like world of international labour politics. One of the obstacles is the number of sound-alike confederations. I do not wish to burden the reader more than is necessary in this regard, and for this reason I choose not – at this late point in the book – to adopt the new label of Global Union Federation.
224. Joining together in this cyber alliance are the International Confederation of Free Trade Unions, the Trade Union Advisory Committee to the OECD, and the following trade secretariats: Education International, International Federation of Building and Wood Workers, International Federation of Chemical, Energy, Mine and General Workers' Union, International Federation of Journalists, International Metalworkers' Federation, International Textile, Garment and Leather Workers' Federation, International Transport Workers' Federation, International Union of Food, Agricultural, Hotel, Restaurant, Catering, Tobacco and Allied Workers' Association, Public Services International, and the Union Network International.
225. These bodies proliferated throughout the 1990s in areas of Europe that witnessed high levels of cross-border labour migration and economic integration. By the end of the decade their number had swelled to 30.
226. The following trade secretariats serve as examples of this trend. The International Transport Workers' Federation has now established ITF Japan, ITF Russia, and ITF Americas. Union Network International – itself launched in 1999 after the amalgamation of four secretariats – has established UNI-Europe, UNI-Africa, and UNI-Asia-Pacific. Finally, the International Federation of Chemical, Energy, Mine and General Workers' Unions has established ICEM Asia Pacific, ICEM North America Regional Office, ICEM Latin America and Caribbean, and ICEM Russia, Eastern Europe and the Transcaucasus.
227. Wills, 'Taking on the cosmocorps: experiments in transnational labor organization', pp. 122–3.
228. Dan Gallin, 'Labour as a global social force: past divisions and new tasks', in *Global Unions? Theory and Strategies of Organized Labour in the Global Political Economy*, edited by Jeffrey Harrod and Robert O'Brien, RIPE Series in Global Political Economy (London, 2002), p. 240.
229. Wayne J. Diamond and Richard B. Freeman, Will unionism prosper in cyber-space? The promise of the internet for employee organization [Web] (National Bureau of Economic Research, 2001 [cited 22 November 2002]); available from http://www.nber.org/papers/w8483, Stuart Hodkinson, 'Problems@labour: towards a net-internationalism?' (paper presented at the International Labour (and other) Networking Panel, GSA Conference, Manchester, 3–5 July 2001), p. 7. The latter cites statistics showing that in just 2 years – from 1999 to 2001 – trade union organization websites increased in number from 1500 to 2700.

230. Hodkinson, 'Problems@labour', p. 7.
231. Following a 1995 amalgamation with the International Miners' Federation, this secretariat later adopted the name International of Chemical, Energy, Mining and General Workers.
232. Energy and General Workers' Unions (ICEF) International Federation of Chemical, 'Computers of the world unite: the ICEF is networking', *ICEF INFO* 4 (1993): 6. For an account of the ICEF's early use of e-mail and databases see Peter Waterman, *International Labour Communication by Computer: The Fifth International?*, Working Paper Series number 129, July 1992 (The Hague, 1992), pp. 25–8.
233. The significance of the databases cannot be understated, for these were the same repositories of information that the business world relied upon, and that were now available to all by subscription. The databases utilized by the ICEF were specifically related to occupational health, industry news, and stock-brokers' reports. Energy and General Workers' Unions (ICEF) International Federation of Chemical, 'Yearbook,' (Brussels, 1994). Other instances of such utilization of modern communications technology include the Public Service International's use of a multilingual database on privatization and multinationals. This includes files on over 2000 companies, their activities, management strategies, and performance. Hodkinson, 'Problems@labour, p. 8.
234. Global-unions, about global unions [internet] (The ICFTU, Global Unions federations, and the Trade Union Advisory Committee to the OECD, 2002 [cited 2 December 2002]); available from http://www.global-unions.org/default.asp.
235. Diamond and Freeman explore how this is happening within the British and American contexts. Diamond and Freeman, Will unionism prosper in cyber-space?.
236. Eric Lee, 'Trade unions, computer communications and the new world order', in *Labour Worldwide in the Era of Globalization: Alternative Union Models in the New World Order*, edited by Ronaldo Munck and Peter Waterman (London, 1999), p. 240.
237. Perhaps the most noteworthy instances of this sort came during the 1995–98 Liverpool dockers' lock-out, and in the 1997 dispute between the United Steelworkers of America and Bridgestone/Firestone. In the former, computer-mediated communications gave worldwide prominence to the dispute and led to joint action by American, Australian, Spanish, and Israeli dockworkers. In the latter, unionists were shown how to inundate the corporation, and its major clients, with protest messages sent *via* e-mail. An excellent account of such computer-mediated campaigns can be found in Andreas Breitenfellner, 'Global unionism: a potential player,' *International Labour Review* 136 (1997). See also Jeff Rechenbach and Larry Cohen, 'Union global alliances at multinational corporations: a case study of the American alliance', in *Unions in a Globalized Environment: Changing Borders, Organizational Boundaries, and Social Roles*, edited by Bruce Nissen (New York, 2002).
238. Some were surprisingly slow. Indeed, the prominent trade secretariat, the International Metalworkers' Federation established its website in 1999. See Stig Jutterstöm, 'Help us improve the IMF News', *IMF News* 4 (1999).

For a similar example see International Federation of Building and Wood Workers (IFBWW), 'IFBWW Action Programme 1997–2001', *Building and Wood: Bulletin of the International Federation of Building and Wood Workers* 2 (1997): 7. Diamond and Freeman highlight the unevenness of union modernization at the national level. Diamond and Freeman, Will Unionism Prosper in Cyber-Space?.

239. Hodkinson, 'Problems@labour, p. 12. There are many reasons why the prevailing communications regime has not yet fulfilled the hopes of labour internationalists. Lee highlights many obstacles, including the lack of accessibility to new technologies – particularly given the prevailing North–South divide – along with the problems of cultural, political, and economic control that the technologies are subject to. Lee, 'Trade unions, computer communications and the new world order', pp. 230–4.
240. W. Form, quoted in Daniel B. Cornfield, 'Labor transnationalism?', *Work and Occupations* 24 (1997): 284.
241. While I emphasize the tensions here, it must be acknowledged that the cross-border alliance that emerged between these three protagonists represented a watershed for those concerned with recent instances of labour internationalism. See Carr, 'Labour internationalism and the North American Free Trade Agreement', Cornfield, 'Labor Transnationalism'?.
242. The response of the Mexican trade union movement should not be attributed solely to a compliant disposition. An important consideration was also a wariness of American labour interference, and a form of trade union imperialism with which they were all too familiar. See Terry Boswell and Dimitris Stevis, 'Globalization and international labor organizing', *Work and Occupations* 24 (1997): 297–8.
243. Gordon Laxer, 'The movement that dare not speak its name: the return of left nationalism/internationalism', *Alternatives* 26 (2001).
244. James Goodman and Patricia Ranald, eds, *Stopping the Juggernaut: Public Interest versus the Multilateral Agreement on Investment* (Annandale, 2000), p. ix.
245. TUAC acted as the ICFTU's proxy by insinuating itself into the negotiation process – such as there was – and by proposing the incorporation of clauses that would guarantee workers' rights. It would thus be wrong to claim that the ICFTU–TUAC approach amounted to uncritical acceptance of the MAI in its original form. Furthermore, I do not wish to characterize this episode as a major cleavage within the movement. However, the national affiliates were far more sensitive to the dangers inherent in the MAI – pro-labour clauses notwithstanding – than were their peak confederations. Tim Harcourt provides an excellent analysis from an Australian perspective, as well as an outline of the nature of the ameliorating measures proposed by the TUAC. Tim Harcourt, 'Australian perspectives on the MAI: Australian Council of Trade Unions', in *Stopping the Juggernaut: Public Interest versus the Multilateral Agreement on Investment*, edited by James Goodman and Patricia Ranald (Annandale, 2000).
246. The best example of this sort of campaign is that mounted by the ICFTU. It continues to lobby for a social clause to be inserted into the regulatory regime of the World Trade Organization. The social clause favoured by the ICFTU identifies seven ILO 'core conventions' that provided the minimum standards for workers' rights. These were conventions 29 and 105 on the

abolition of forced labour; 87 and 98 on freedom of association and collective bargaining; 111 and 100 on discrimination in employment and equal pay for work of equal value; and 138 on the minimum age for employment.
247. Robert O'Brien, 'Workers and world order: the tentative transformation of the international union movement', *Review of International Studies* 26 (2000): 544.
248. The following provide a good account of the ICFTU's position (the November 1994 citation is of particular interest because it stresses the *anti*protectionist nature of the proposed social clause). ICFTU-Editorial, 'ICFTU presses for a social clause,' *Free Labour World* (1994), ICFTU-Editorial, 'Social clause debate reaches the ILO', *Free Labour World* (1994), ICFTU-Editorial, 'The social clause remains firmly on the agenda', *Free Labour World* (1994). For reference to the Indian labour movement's resistance to the social clause see Gumbrell-McCormick, 'Facing New Challenges, pp. 509–10. According to O'Brien, the Malaysian delegates' concerns were voiced at the ICFTU's Sixteenth World Congress, June 1996. O'Brien, 'Workers and world order: the tentative transformation of the international union movement', p. 544.
249. The following editorial accuses the ICFTU of harbouring collaborationist national trade union bodies throughout Asia. The editorial claims that the Trade Union Council of the Philippines, the Malaysian Trade Union Congress, and Indonesia's SPSI were all, in one way or another, the product of dictatorial regimes. According to this perspective, one of the most objectionable features of this form of unionism is that it facilitates the establishment throughout Asia of Export Processing Zones, thus providing multinational corporations with even greater leverage over labour. SALB-Editorial, 'COSATU, the ICFTU and dictatorships in Asia', *South African Labour Bulletin* 17 (1993).
250. In the *South African Labour Bulletin* in the early 1990s we read accounts by those imploring COSATU to reject the ICFTU's offers of affiliation, and also by those pointing to the ICFTU's redeeming features. See Mike Allen, 'New internationalism ... or old rhetoric?', *SA Labour Bulletin* 16 (1991), SALB-Editorial, 'COSATU, the ICFTU and dictatorships in Asia', Waterman, 'The ICFTU in SA'.
251. Andrew Herod, 'The geostrategics of labor in post-Cold War Eastern Europe: an examination of the activities of the International Metalworkers' Federation', in *Organizing the Landscape: Geographical Perspectives on Labor Unionism*, edited by Andrew Herod (Minneapolis, 1998), pp. 51–8.
252. Sarah Ashwin, 'International labour solidarity after the Cold War', in *Global Social Movements*, edited by Robin Cohen and Shirin M. Rai (London, 2000), pp. 103–7. See also ICFTU-Editorial, 'Transformation of trade unions in Central and Eastern Europe', *Free Labour World* 14 (31 August, 1990).
253. Ashwin, 'International Labour Solidarity After the Cold War', p. 104.
254. Gumbrell-McCormick's overview of this period is more sympathetic to the ICFTU, stressing that the confusion and uncertainty that prevailed throughout the region at the time ought to be seen as an important mitigating factor. Gumbrell-McCormick, 'Facing New Challenges, pp. 499–503.
255. Ashwin, 'International Labour Solidarity After the Cold War', p. 105. Social dumping refers to the attraction of investment using as enticements the existing low wages and poor conditions.

256. Ibid., pp. 114–15. For more on the ways in which the trade secretariats approached this transition see ICFTU-Editorial, 'ITS develop contacts in the East', *Free Labour World* 14 (31 August, 1990). Herod also provides a good account of the International Metalworkers' Federation's attempts to establish relationships in Central and Eastern Europe. See Herod, 'The geostrategics of labor in post-Cold War Eastern Europe', pp. 51–8.
257. Bill Jordan, ICFTU, 'The global market – trade unionism's greatest challenge' (paper presented at the International Confederation of Free Trade Unions, Sixteenth World Congress of the ICFTU, 1996), p. 1.
258. ICFTU-Editorial, 'Delegates unanimous on social clause', *Free Labour World* (1996): 5, ICFTU-Editorial, 'ILO, ETUC, TUAC and WCL ... all fighting on the same side', *Free Labour World* (1996): 2. The emphasis on collaboration with other trade union organizations is also articulated in the following congress summary. ICFTU-Editorial, 'ICFTU aims to be at the centre of a worldwide social movement', *Free Labour World* (1996).
259. ICFTU, 'The future shape of the trade union movement', *Trade Union World* 5 (2000): 34–5. See also ICFTU, 'End discrimination: equality for women now! decision adopted by the Seventeenth World Congress of the ICFTU' (paper presented at the Seventeenth World Congress of the ICFTU, Durban, 25–29 June 2000).
260. For background on the ICFTU's campaign against child labour see ICFTU, 'Campaigning for an end to child labour' (paper presented at the 17th World Congress of the ICFTU, Durban, 25–29 June 2000), ICFTU, 'Eradicating child labour: a strategy to deal with the causes of child labour: Congress Resolutions' (paper presented at the 16th World Congress of the ICFTU, Brussels, 25–29 June 1996), ICFTU-Editorial, 'The world's best kept secret', *Free Labour World* 6 (1994). For more on the question of violence directed against trade unionists see ICFTU, 'An ICFTU strategy to defend trade union rights: decisions adopted by the 17th World Congress of the ICFTU' (paper presented at the 17th World Congress of the ICFTU, Durban, 25–29 June 2000), ICFTU-Editorial, 'Being a trade unionist is a dangerous occupation', *Free Labour World* (1994), ICFTU-Editorial, 'Union rights abuses "still alarming", says ICFTU', *Free Labour World* (1990).
261. The following record of the WCL's 25th Congress gives a good overview of that confederation's position on the role of women, multinational corporations, and development. The following page numbers refer to these topics in the sequence listed. World Confederation of Labour (WCL), 'The policy resolution and the topical resolutions of the WCL' (paper presented at the 25th Congress of the WCL, Romania, October 2001), pp. 36, 38, 9, 8. For more on its position on child labour and the social clause see Delphine Sanglan, 'Child Labour: Ratify Convention 182', *Labor Magazine* (2000/1), World Confederation of Labour (WCL), Social clauses – Reciprocal Social Commitments (RSCs) as levers [Internet] (World Confederation of Labour, 2000 [cited 18 December 2002]); available from http://www.cmt-wcl.org, WCL-Editorial, 'Women – marching to be respected', *Labor Magazine* (2000/1).
262. From Willy Peirens, the WCL's President, quoted in the following. ICFTU-Editorial, 'ILO, ETUC, TUAC and WCL ... all fighting on the same side', p. 2.
263. European Trade Union Confederation, Activity Report: 1995–1998 (European Trade Union Confederation-ETUC, 1999 [cited 18 December,

2002); available from http://www.etuc.org/. For reference to the ETUC's campaigns on discrimination and the social clause, see pages 11, 17–18 respectively. The trend towards greater cooperation is in the context of campaigning for greater European aid to African states, though it also extends beyond this issue. See page 18 in this Activity Report.
264. Trade Union Advisory Committee to the OECD (TUAC), 'Trade and labour standards: TUAC Briefing Note for OECD Workshop', (Paris, 1996), Trade Union Advisory Committee to the OECD (TUAC), 'The trade union view on International labour standards' (paper presented at the ITGLWF Conference on International Trade, Copenhagen, 5–6 October 1995).
265. Sources are listed here in the same order in which the quotations appear. Global-Unions, Global Union proposes measures to prevent economic slowdown [Internet] (International Confederation of Free Trade Unions, 2001 [cited 19 November 2002]); available from http://www.icftu.org/. Global-Unions, Global Union demand boost to world economy: 16 November, 2001 [Internet] (International Confederation of Free Trade Unions, 2001 [cited 19 November 2002]); available from http://www.icftu.org/. Global-Unions, 'Global Unions Statement to International Conference on Financing for Development' (paper presented at The 4th Prepcom of the International Conference on Financing for Development, New York, 14–25 January 2001), p. 3. Bill, Jordan, ICFTU, 'The global market – trade unionism's greatest challenge', p. 22, Trade Union Advisory Committee to the OECD (TUAC), 'Now is the time to reflate the global economy' (Paris, 2002).
266. The precise nature of these social clauses and compacts will be outlined in subsequent discussion of the network's external dimensions of change.
267. TUAC and ITS Global-Unions: Statement by the ICFTU, 'The role of the international financial institutions in a globalized economy' (paper presented at the 2001 Annual Meetings of the IMF and World Bank, Washington, 29–30 September 2001), ICFTU, 'Employment, sustainable development and social justice: ICFTU programme for sustainable economic growth' (paper presented at the 17th World Congress of the ICFTU, Durban, 25–29 June 2000).
268. All this is not to say that radical collectivist creeds are nowhere evident. Indeed, in subsequent discussion we will note the emergence in some parts of the network of an orientation that may have fused traditional anarcho-syndicalism with gender and environment-sensitive tendencies.

6 1989–2005 – External Change: Eviction and Insinuation

269. Philip G. Cerny, 'Restructuring the political arena: globalization and the paradox of the competition state', in *Globalization and its Critics: Perspectives from Political Economy*, edited by Randall D. Germain (New York, 2000), Clark, *Globalization and International Relations Theory*.
270. Oliver Clarke, Greg J. Bamber, and Russell D. Lansbury, 'Conclusions: towards a synthesis of international and comparative experience in employment relations', in *International and Comparative Employment Relations*, edited by Greg J. Bamber and Russell D. Lansbury (London, 1998), p. 309, Katz and Darbishire, *Converging Divergences*, pp. 265–6, 280–4.

271. Sven Bislev, Dorte Salskov-Iversen, and Hans Krause Hansen, 'The global diffusion of managerialism: transnational discourse communities at work', *Global Society* 16 (2002).
272. For more see Duncan Macdonald, Rachid Zeffane, and Roy Green, 'Managerial ideologies: do they matter?' (paper presented at the 12th Association of Industrial Relations Academics of Australia and New Zealand, Wellington, New Zealand, 3–5 February 1998), Nigel Thrift, 'The rise of soft capitalism', in *An Unruly World? Globalization, Governance and Geography*, edited by Andrew Herod, Gearóid O Tuathail, and Susan M. Roberts (London, 1998).
273. Membership in trade unions fell in 72 of the 92 countries surveyed by the ILO in its World Labour Report 1997–98. The most alarming falls came in former communist countries: by 50.6 per cent in Russia, 50 per cent in the Czech Republic, 45.7 per cent in Poland, 38 per cent in Hungary, and 22.8 per cent in Belarus. Membership also declined dramatically elsewhere: by 75.7 per cent in Israel, 38.3 per cent in Uganda, 32.2 per cent in Venezuela, 55.1 per cent in New Zealand, 31.2 per cent in France, 25.2 per cent in the United Kingdom, 20.3 per cent in Germany, and 29.6 per cent in Australia. ILO, 'World Labour Report 1997–1998,' (Geneva, 1997).
274. Kathryn Hodder, 'The ICFTU Annual Survey of Violations of Trade Union Rights', *International Union Rights* 5 (1998): 3. This report shows that 299 trade unionists were murdered in 1998, over 2300 were arrested or detained for union activities, 1681 ill-treated or tortured, over 290 received death threats, 3000 placed under police surveillance, and 450 strikes violently suppressed.
275. For more on the question of whether systems of industrial relations are converging or diverging see the following. Richard Hyman, 'National industrial relations systems and transnational challenges: an essay in review', *European Journal of International Relations* 5 (1999), Katz and Darbishire, *Converging Divergences*, pp. 263–84.
276. Reutter, 'Trade unions and politics in Eastern and Central Europe.'
277. Ibid., p. 147.
278. Thirkell, Scase, and Vickerstaff also reflect on emerging post-corporatist relationships, observing that 'governments of an avowedly neoliberal persuasion are prepared to enter into tripartite negotiation to avoid confrontation and in order to maintain the pace of economic reform'. See John Thirkell, Richard Scase, and Sarah Vickerstaff, 'Models of labour relations: trends and prospects', in *Labour Relations and Political Change in Eastern Europe: A Comparative Perspective*, edited by John Thirkell, Richard Scase, and Sarah Vickerstaff (London, 1995), p. 182.
279. Greg J. Bamber and Russell D. Lansbury, 'An introduction to international and comparative employment relations', in *International and Comparative Employment Relations*, edited by Greg J. Bamber and Russell D. Lansbury (London, 1998), pp. 24–5.
280. Respectively: F. Traxler in Gerda Falkner, 'Corporatist governance and Europeanisation: no future in the multi-level game?' [Internet] (European Integration online Papers, 1997 [cited 15 July 2000]); available from http://eiop.or.at/eiop/texte/1997-011a.htm.
281. Laxer, 'The movement that dare not speak its name: The Return of Left Nationalism/Internationalism,' pp. 21–2.

282. In addition to intergovernmental organizations such as the OECD, the ILO, the World Bank and the International Monetary Fund, other important regimes for labour included the G8 Summits (of May 1998 and July 2000), the UN Conference on Environment and Development (1992), the UN Fourth World Women's Conference (1995), the series of UN Social Summits (1995, 2000), the UN Commission on Trade and Development (2000), the UN Environmental Programme. and the UN Cairo Conference on Population. Trade Union Advisory Committee to the OECD (TUAC), 'Transforming the global economy: a stocktaking of trade union action with international and regional institutions' (Paris, 2000), pp. 38–55.
283. Ashwin, 'International Labour Solidarity After the Cold War', p. 110.
284. For more on the ways in which the peak confederations have sought to influence the World Bank and the International Monetary Fund see (TUAC), 'Transforming the global economy' pp. 13–29.
285. For instance, the World Confederation of Labour continues to engage with – and lobby for reform to – a range of intergovernmental organizations. See, for example, the following proposals for reform to intergovernmental organizations. (WCL), 'The policy resolution and the topical resolutions of the WCL', pp. 7–10. In addition, trade secretariats try to influence major intergovernmental organizations. Most of their campaigns are directed towards the IMF and World Bank, as well as towards the more established United Nations bodies. A concise summary of all secretariat involvement can be found in (TUAC), 'Transforming the global economy: a stocktaking of trade union action with international and regional institutions', pp. 22–9. Common to all is an imperative to not only respond to, but also establish formal liaison mechanisms with, the World Bank, the International Monetary Fund, the OECD, and a host of second-tier bodies such as investment banks. And, finally, we might also include here the activities of some of the major national and regional trade union organizations. Organizations such as Japan's Confederation of Public Sector Trade Unions, the Nordic Trade Union Council, and the American Federation of Labor-Congress of Industrial Organizations, also devote significant resources to engagement with political realm actors on this global plane. (TUAC), 'Transforming the global economy', p. 29.
286. Numerous 'joint statements' and submissions issued by labour within intergovernmental regimes can be cited to illustrate the nature of this form of engagement. The following are typical: Global-Unions, 'Global Unions Statement to International Conference on Financing for Development', Global-Unions, 'Global Unions Statement: The Role of the IMF and the World Bank' (paper presented at the Fall 2001 Meetings of the IMF (International Monetary and Financial Committee) and World Bank (Development Committee), Ottawa, 17–18 November 2001), Global-Unions: Statement by the ICFTU, 'The role of the international financial institutions in a globalized economy'. For another example of coordination of this sort see European Trade Union Confederation, Activity Report: 1995–1998 (cited).
287. (TUAC), 'Transforming the global economy' p. 58, 64.
288. The Central Latinoamericana de Trabajadores.
289. These have included the following: the Trade Union Educators Conference (October, 1993, Kampala); the ILO/ICFTU-AFRO Workshop on Employment

Creation and the Informal Sector: The Trade Union Role (May, 1999, Johannesburg); a regional educators' gathering on the Role of Trade Union Education in Employment Creation in Africa (September, 1999, Nairobi); and the high-level symposium on the Role of Trade Unions in Poverty Alleviation and Employment Creation in Africa (May, 2001, Nairobi). (TUAC), 'Transforming the global economy' pp. 69–70.
290. O'Brien et al., Contesting Global Governance, p. 100.
291. Ibid. O'Brien and his colleagues stress that the few gains made in labour's 'most successful' foray into the World Trade Organization (WTO Ministerial Meeting, Singapore 1996) accrued only when governments relented and provided greater access to briefings and officials. O'Brien et al., Contesting Global Governance, p. 89. The importance of access to individual governments, and of the latter's role as facilitator, is also emphasized in TUAC's Millennium Report. See (TUAC), 'Transforming the global economy', pp. 44–5.

Conclusion

292. Fred van Leeuwen, General Secretary of Education International at the ICFTU World Congress in Brussels, in 1996. Cited in O'Brien, 'Workers and world order', p. 553.
293. ICFTU-Editorial, 'ICFTU aims to be at the centre of a worldwide social movement', p. 1.
294. ICFTU, 'Trade unions, NGOs and tripartism: Decisions adopted by the Seventeenth World Congress of the ICFTU' (paper presented at the Seventeenth World Congress of the ICFTU, Durban, 3–7 April 2000), p. 2.
295. ICFTU, 'An ICFTU strategy to defend trade union rights: decisions adopted by the Seventeenth World Congress of the ICFTU', p. 7.
296. Other participants include the OECD, the International Chamber of Commerce, and a range of multinational corporations. For a more complete list see the Eliminating Child Labour Foundation web-site at http://www.endchildlabour.org/links/
297. World Confederation of Labour (WCL), 'World Confederation of Labour: Activities Report 1998–2001', (Brussels, 2001), p. 19.
298. (WCL), 'The Policy Resolution and the Topical Resolutions of the WCL', pp. 15, 16, 17, and 19, (WCL), 'World Confederation of Labour: Activities Report 1998–2001', p. 47. Other references of this sort can be found on pages 14, 25, and 37.
299. The trade secretariats and their campaigns are too numerous to list. Among the most active secretariats in this regard are the International Federation of Chemical, Energy, Mine and General Workers' Unions, the Union Network International, Education International, the International Union of Food, Agriculture, Hotel, Restaurant, Catering, Tobacco and Allied Workers Association (IUF), and the International Textile, Garment and Leather Workers' Federation.
300. The worldwide web hosts numerous sites, discussion groups, and mailing lists that facilitate labour and oppositional civil realm actor engagement. Examples include LabourStart (at http://www.labourstart, and maintained by Eric Lee), and Unionists Against Corporate Tyranny (at uactsolidarity@yahoogroups.com).

301. Peter Waterman coined the terms *social movement unionism*, and *new social unionism*. The following article by Waterman is considered a seminal work in this area of labour studies. Peter Waterman, 'Social movement unionism: a new model for a new world order', *Review* 16 (1993). See also Munck, *Globalisation and Labour*, pp. 99–102.
302. Philip Hirschsohn, 'From grassroots democracy to national mobilization: COSATU as a model of social movement unionism', *Economic and Industrial Democracy* 19 (1998): 655.
303. Ibid., p. 643.
304. Patricia Ranald, 'Korean unions resisting the International Monetary Fund', in *Protest and Globalisation*, edited by James Goodman (Sydney, 2002).
305. Helen Trinca and Anne Davies, *Waterfront: The Battle That Changed Australia* (Milsons Point, 2000), pp. 211–23, John Wiseman, 'Trade union solidarity: the Australian waterfront, 1998', in *Protest and Globalisation*, edited by James Goodman (Sydney, 2002), p. 180.
306. WTO Secretariat (http://www.wto.org/english/tratop_e/region_e/regfac_e.htm) accessed 20 March 2004. See also Arne Melchior, 'A global race for free trade agreements', (Oslo, 2003).
307. Barry Carr, 'Globalisation from below: labour internationalism under NAFTA', *International Social Science Journal* 159 (1999): 53–4.
308. Hunter, 'Globalization from below?', pp. 2–3.

Bibliography

Adler, Glenn. 'Global restructuring and labor: the case of the south african trade union movement'. In *Globalization: Critical Reflections*, edited by James H. Mittelman, 117–44. Boulder: Lynne Rienner Press, 1996.
Allen, Mike. 'New internationalism ... or old rhetoric?' *SA Labour Bulletin* 16, no. 2 (1991): 61–9.
Ameri, Houshang. *Politics and Process in the Specialized Agencies of the United Nations*. Aldershot: Gower, 1982.
Arrighi, Giovanni, Terence K. Hopkins, and Immanuel Wallerstein. *Antisystemic Movements*. London: Verso, 1989.
Ashwin, Sarah. 'International labour solidarity after the cold war'. In *Global Social Movements*, edited by Robin Cohen and Shirin M. Rai, 101–16. London: The Athlone Press, 2000.
Bamber, Greg J. and Russell D. Lansbury. 'An introduction to international and comparative employment relations'. In *International and Comparative Employment Relations*, edited by Greg J. Bamber and Russell D. Lansbury, 1–33. London: Sage, 1998.
Barry, Tom and Deb Preusch. *AIFLD in Central America: Agents as Organizers*. Albuquerque: The Resource Center, 1986.
Bendiner, Burton. *International Labour Affairs: The World Trade Unions and the Multinational Companies*. Oxford: Clarendon Press, 1987.
Bendt, Heinz. *One World, One Voice, Solidarity: The International Trade Secretariats*. Bonn: Friedrich-Ebert-Stiftung, 1996.
Bislev, Sven, Dorte Salskov-Iversen, and Hans Krause Hansen. 'The global diffusion of managerialism: Transnational discourse communities at work'. *Global Society* 16, no. 2 (2002): 199–212.
Boli, John. 'Conclusion: world authority structures and legitimations'. In *Constructing World Culture: International Non-Governmental Organizations Since 1875*, edited by John Boli and George M. Thomas, 267–302. Stanford: Stanford University Press, 1999.
Boswell, Terry and Dimitris Stevis. 'Globalization and international labor organizing'. *Work and Occupations* 24, no. 3 (1997): 288–308.
Breitenfellner, Andreas. 'Global unionism: A potential player'. *International Labour Review* 136, no. 4 (1997): 531–55.
Breunung, Rudi. 'The world federation of trade unions calling: A few words about the WFTU radio programme'. *World Trade Union Movement* 9 (1985): 5–6.
Brun, Jean. 'Answers to the international questionnaire'. *World Trade Union Movement*, no. 12 (1981): 2.
Bruyn, Severyn. 'Toward a social market in communist nations'. In *Labour Relations in Transition in Eastern Europe*, edited by György Széll, 263–79. Berlin: Walter de Gruyter, 1992.
Buhle, Paul. *Taking Care of Business: Samuel Gompers, George Meany, Lane Kirkland, and the Tragedy of American labor*. New York: Monthly Review Press, 1999.

Busch, Gary K. *The Political Role of International Trade Unions*. London: The MacMillan, 1983.
Camilleri, Joseph A. and Jim Falk. *The End of Sovereignty?* Aldershot: Edward Elgar, 1992.
Carew, Anthony. 'Conflict within the ICFTU: Anti-communism and anti-colonialism in the 1950s'. *International Review of Social History* 41 (1996): 147–81.
———. 'Towards a free trade union centre: The International Confederation of Free Trade Unions (1949–1972)'. In *The International Confederation of Free Trade Unions*, edited by Anthony Carew, Michel Dreyfus, Geert van Goethem, Rebecca Gumbrell-McCormick and Marcel Van der Linden, 187–99. Bern: Peter Lang, 2000.
Carew, Anthony, Michel Dreyfus, Geert van Goethem, Rebecca Gumbrell-McCormick, and Marcel Van der Linden, eds. *The International Confederation of Free Trade Unions*. Bern: Peter Lang, 2000.
Carlile, Lonny E. 'Party politics and the Japanese labor movement: Rengo's "New Political Force" '. *Asian Survey* 34, no. 7 (1994): 606–20.
Carr, Barry. 'Globalisation from below: Labour internationalism under NAFTA'. *International Social Science Journal* 159, no. March (1999): 49–59.
———. 'Labour internationalism and the North American Free Trade Agreement'. In *Protest and Globalisation*, edited by James Goodman, 203–15. Sydney: Pluto, 2002.
Castles, Stephen. 'Globalization from below'. *Arena Magazine* 2000, 45–7.
Cerny, Philip G. 'Globalization and the changing logic of collective action'. *International Organization* 49, no. 4 (1995): 595–625.
———. 'Restructuring the political arena: Globalization and the paradox of the competition state'. In *Globalization and its Critics: Perspectives from Political Economy*, edited by Randall D. Germain, 117–38. New York: St. Martins Press, 2000.
Chernina, Natalia. 'Perspectives of self-government and de-alienation in business in the USSR'. In *Labour Relations in Transition in Eastern Europe*, edited by György Széll, 335–42. Berlin: Walter de Gruyter, 1992.
Clark, Ian. *Globalization and International Relations Theory*. Oxford: Oxford University Press, 1999.
Clarke, Oliver, Greg J. Bamber, and Russell D. Lansbury. 'Conclusions: Towards a synthesis of international and comparative experience in employment relations'. In *International and Comparative Employment Relations*, edited by Greg J. Bamber and Russell D. Lansbury, 294–327. London: Sage, 1998.
Coker, Trudie. 'Globalization and corporatism: The growth and decay of organized labor in Venezuela, 1900–1998'. *International Labor and Working-Class History* 60, no. Fall (2001): 180–202.
Cornfield, Daniel B. 'Labor transnationalism?' *Work and Occupations* 24, no. 3 (1997): 278–287.
Cox, Robert W. 'Labor and hegemony (first published in 1977)'. In *Approaches to World Order*, edited by Robert W. Cox, 420–70. Cambridge: Cambridge University Press, 1995.
Cravey, Altha J. 'Cowboys and dinosaurs: Mexican labor unionism and the state'. In *Organizing the Landscape: Geographical Perspectives on Labor Unionism*, edited by Andrew Herod, 75–98. Minneapolis: University of Minnesota Press, 1998.

Crouch, Colin. 'The changing role of the state in industrial relations in Western Europe'. In *The Resurgence of Class Conflict in Western Europe Since 1968*, edited by Colin Crouch and Alessandro Pizzorno, 197–220. London: Macmillan, 1978.

Czíria, Ludovit. 'Collective forms of work organization in czechoslovak economic practice'. In *Labour Relations in Transition in Eastern Europe*, edited by György Széll, 187–200. Berlin: Walter de Gruyter, 1992.

de la Garza, Enrique, Javier Melgoza, and Marcia Campillo. 'Unions, corporatism and the industrial relations system in Mexico'. In *The State and Globalization: Comparative Studies of Labour and Capital in National Economies*, edited by Martin Upchurch, 248–68. London: Mansell Publishing, 1999.

Deppe, Rainer, Richard Herding, and Dietrich Hoss. 'The relationship between trade union action and political parties'. In *The Resurgence of Class Conflict in Western Europe Since 1968*, edited by Colin Crouch and Alessandro Pizzorno, 177–96. London: Macmillan, 1978.

Deyo, Frederic C. *Beneath the Miracle: Labor Subordination in the New Asian Industrialism*. Berkeley: University of California Press, 1989.

Diamond, Wayne J. and Richard B. Freeman. *Will Unionism Prosper in Cyber-Space? The Promise of the Internet for Employee Organization* [Web]. National Bureau of Economic Research, 2001 [cited 22 November 2002]. Available from http://www.nber.org/papers/w8483.

Douglas, Ian R. 'Globalization and the retreat of the state'. In *Globalization and the Politics of Resistance*, edited by Barry K. Gills, 110–32. London: MacMillan, 2000.

Drainville, André C. 'Left internationalism and the politics of resistance in the new world order'. In *A New World Order: Global Transformations in the Late Twentieth Century*, edited by David A. Smith and József Böröcz, 217–37. London: Greenwood Press, 1995.

Dubois, Pierre. 'New forms of industrial conflict: 1960–1974'. In *The Resurgence of Class Conflict in Western Europe Since 1968*, edited by Colin Crouch and Alessandro Pizzorno, 1–34. London: Macmillan, 1978.

Eagleton, Terry. *Ideology: An Introduction*. London: Verso, 1991.

Echenique, Rodolpho. 'The worker's contribution towards Latin American economic integrations: Speech by Echenique of the ICFTU/ORIT office in Chile to the inaugural meeting of the Committee of the Whole of ECLA (UN Economic Commission for Latin America)'. *Free Labour World* 95, no. May (1958): 48.

European Trade Union Confederation. *Activity Report: 1995–1998* European Trade Union Confederation-ETUC, 1999 [cited 18 December 2002]. Available from http://www.etuc.org/.

Falk, Richard. 'Resisting "globalization-from-above" through "globalization-from-below" '. In *Globalization and the Politics of Resistance*, edited by Barry K. Gills, 46–56. London: MacMillan, 2000.

Falkner, Gerda. *Corporatist Governance and Europeanisation: No Future in the Multi-level Game?* [Internet]. European Integration online Papers, 1997 [cited 15 July 2000]. Available from http://eiop.or.at/eiop/texte/1997-011a.htm.

Feld, Werner J., Robert S. Jordan, and Leon Hurwitz. *International Organizations: A Comparative Approach*. 3rd edn. London: Praeger, 1994.

Forman, Michael. *Nationalism and the International Labor Movement*. University Park: The Pennsylvania State University Press, 1998.

Frunza, Ilie. 'We must struggle for a mutually advantageous commerce'. *World Trade Union Movement* 8 (1981): 13–14.

Gallin, Dan. 'Labour as a global social force: past divisions and new tasks'. In *Global Unions? Theory and Strategies of Organized Labour in the Global Political Economy*, edited by Jeffrey Harrod and Robert O'Brien, 235–50. London: Routledge, 2002.

Gensous, Pierre. 'Concluding Speech (of the 22nd Session of the WFTU General Council)'. *World Trade Union Movement* 11, November (1972): 3–6.

——. 'The role, tasks and responsibilities of the unions (extracts from a report presented by Assistant General Secretary of the WFTU at the Seventh World Trade Union Congress)'. *World Trade Union Movement* 11, November (1969): 7–19.

Gershikov, Vladimir. 'Business democracy: Work collective councils and trade unions'. In *Labour Relations in Transition in Eastern Europe*, edited by György Széll, 219–29. Berlin: Walter de Gruyter, 1992.

Gill, Stephen. *American Hegemony and the Trilateral Commission*. Cambridge: Cambridge University Press, 1990.

Global-Unions. *About Global Unions* [internet]. The ICFTU, Global Unions federations, and the Trade Union Advisory Committee to the OECD, 2002 [cited 2 Deccember 2002]. Available from http://www.global-unions.org/default.asp.

——. *Global Union Demand Boost to World Economy: 16 November, 2001* [Internet]. International Confederation of Free Trade Unions, 2001 [cited 19 November 2002]. Available from http://www.icftu.org/.

——. *Global Union Proposes Measures to Prevent Economic Slowdown* [Internet]. International Confederation of Free Trade Unions, 2001 [cited 19 November 2002]. Available from http://www.icftu.org/.

——. 'Global Unions Statement to International Conference on Financing for Development'. Paper presented at The 4th Prepcom of the International Conference on Financing for Development, New York, 14–25 January 2001.

——. 'Global Unions Statement: The Role of the IMF and the World Bank'. Paper presented at the Fall 2001 Meetings of the IMF (International Monetary and Financial Committee) and World Bank (Development Committee), Ottawa, 17–18 November 2001.

Global-Unions: Statement by the ICFTU, TUAC and ITS. 'The Role of the International Financial Institutions in a Globalized Economy'. Paper presented at the 2001 Annual Meetings of the IMF and World Bank, Washington, 29–30 September 2001.

Goodman, James, and Patricia Ranald, eds. *Stopping the Juggernaut: Public Interest versus the Multilateral Agreement on Investment*. Annandale: Pluto, 2000.

Gourevitch, Peter, Andrew Martin, George Ross, Christopher Allen, Stephen Bornstein, and Andrei Markovits. *Unions and Economic Crisis: Britain, West Germany and Sweden*. London: George Allen and Unwin, 1984.

Gramsci, Antonio. *Selections from the Prison Notebooks of Antonio Gramsci*. Edited by Quintin Hoare and Geoffrey Nowell (eds and translators) Smith. tenth printing 1989 edn. New York: International Publishers, 1971.

Gumbrell-McCormick, Rebecca. 'Facing new challenges: The International Confederation of Free Trade Unions (1972–1990s)'. In *The International Confederation of Free Trade Unions*, edited by Anthony Carew, Michel Dreyfus, Geert van Goethem, Rebecca Gumbrell-McCormick and Marcel Van der Linden, 341–518. Bern: Peter Lang, 2000.

Hammarström, Olle and Tommy Nilsson. 'Employment relations in Sweden'. In *International and Comparative Employment Relations*, edited by Greg J. Bamber and Russell D. Lansbury, 224–48. London: Sage, 1998.

Hanham, Robert Q. and Shawn Banasick. 'Japanese labor and the production of the space-economy in an era of globalization'. In *Organizing the Landscape: Geographical Perspectives on Labor Unionism*, edited by Andrew Herod, 99–122. Minneapolis: University of Minnesota Press, 1998.
Harcourt, Tim. 'Australian perspectives on the MAI: Australian Council of Trade Unions'. In *Stopping the Juggernaut: Public Interest versus the Multilateral Agreement on Investment*, edited by James Goodman and Patricia Ranald, 132–51. Annandale: Pluto, 2000.
Harris, Nigel. *The End of the Third World: New Industrializing Countries and the Decline of an Ideology*. London: Penguin, 1986.
Harrod, Jeffrey, and Robert O'Brien, eds. *Global Unions? Theory and Strategies of Organized Labour in the Global Political Economy*. Edited by Otto Holman, Marianne Marchand, H., Henk Overbeek, and Marianne Franklin, *RIPE Series in Global Political Economy*. London: Routledge, 2002.
Held, David, Anthony McGrew, David Goldblatt, and Jonathan Perraton. *Global Transformations: Politics, Economics and Culture*. Cambridge: Polity Press, 1999.
Herod, Andrew. 'The geostrategics of labor in post-cold war Eastern Europe: An examination of the activities of the International Metalworkers' Federation'. In *Organizing the Landscape: Geographical Perspectives on Labor Unionism*, edited by Andrew Herod, 45–74. Minneapolis: University of Minnesota Press, 1998.
———. 'Labor unions and the making of economic geographies'. In *Organizing the Landscape: Geographical Perspectives on Labor Unionism*, edited by Andrew Herod, 255–62. Minneapolis: University of Minnesota Press, 1998.
———. *Organizing the Landscape: Geographical Perspectives on Labor Unionism*. Minneapolis: University of Minnesota Press, 1998.
Héthy, Lajos. 'Hungary's changing labour relations system'. In *Labour Relations in Transition in Eastern Europe*, edited by György Széll, 175–82. Berlin: Walter de Gruyter, 1992.
Hirschsohn, Philip. 'From grassroots democracy to national mobilization: COSATU as a model of social movement unionism'. *Economic and Industrial Democracy* 19 (1998): 633–66.
Hodder, Kathryn. 'The ICFTU annual survey of violations of trade union rights'. *International Union Rights* 5, no. 3 (1998): 3–4.
Hodkinson, Stuart. 'Problems @ labour: towards a net-internationalism?' Paper presented at the International Labour (and other) Networking Panel, GSA Conference, Manchester, 3–5 July 2001, 2001.
Hoffmann, Karel. 'The role of trade unions in the socialist countries'. *World Trade Union Movement* 12, December (1980): 5–7.
Horsman, Mathew and Andrew Marshall. *After the Nation-State: Citizens, Tribalism and the New World Disorder*. London: HarperCollins, 1995.
Hunter, Allen. 'Globalization from below? Promises and perils of the new internationalism'. *Social Policy* 25, no. 4 (1995): 6–13.
Hyman, Richard. 'National industrial relations systems and transnational challenges: An essay in review'. *European Journal of International Relations* 5, no. 1 (1999): 89–110.
(ICEF) International Federation of Chemical, Energy and General Workers' Unions. 'Computers of the World Unite: the ICEF is Networking'. *ICEF INFO* 4 (1993).
———. 'Yearbook'. Brussels: ICEF, 1994.
ICFTU. 'Campaigning for an end to child labour'. Paper presented at the 17th World Congress of the ICFTU, Durban, 25–29 June 2000.

ICFTU. 'Circular (to affiliates #24) – Preparations of the UN's New International Development Strategy: Elements to be included'. Brussels: From the archives of the International Institute of Social History (hereafter, the 'IISH'), Amsterdam, 1980.
——. 'Circular (to affiliates #37) – Executive Board – North/South: A programme for Survival'. Brussels: From the IISH, Amsterdam, 1980.
——. 'Circular (to affiliates #38)'. Brussels: From the IISH, Amsterdam, 1988.
——. 'Circular (to affiliates #46)'. Brussels: From the IISH, Amsterdam, 1981.
——. 'Circular (to affiliates #50)'. Brussels: From the IISH, Amsterdam, 1981.
——. 'Circular (to affiliates #72)'. Brussels: From the IISH, Amsterdam, 1974.
——. 'Employment, sustainable development and social justice: ICFTU Programme for Sustainable Economic Growth'. Paper presented at the 17th World Congress of the ICFTU, Durban, 25–29 June 2000.
——. 'End discrimination: Equality for women now! decision adopted by the 17th World Congress of the ICFTU'. Paper presented at the 17th World Congress of the ICFTU, Durban, 25–29 June 2000.
——. 'Eradicating child labour: A strategy to deal with the causes of child labour: Congress Resolutions'. Paper presented at the 16th World Congress of the ICFTU, Brussels, 25–29 June 1996.
——. 'Executive Board (report/document 7EB/7)'. Brussels: From the IISH, Amsterdam, 1952.
——. 'Executive Board (report/document 7EB/7c)'. Brussels: From the IISH, Amsterdam, 1952.
——. 'Executive Board (report/document 9EB/8)'. Brussels: From the IISH, Amsterdam, 1952.
——. 'Executive Board (report/document 39EB/23)'. Brussels: From the IISH, Amsterdam, 1966.
——. 'Executive Board (report/document 67EB/15)'. Brussels: From the IISH, Amsterdam, 1976.
——. 'Executive Board (report/document 75EB/15)'. Brussels: From the IISH, Amsterdam, 1980.
——. 'Executive Board (report/document 76EB/11(a,b,c)'. Brussels: From the IISH, Amsterdam, 1980.
——. 'Executive Board (report/document 76EB/16)'. Brussels: From the IISH, Amsterdam, 1980.
——. 'For economic equality: notes on the ICFTU World Economic Conference'. Paper presented at the ICFTU World Economic Conference, Geneva, 24–26 June 1971.
——. 'The future shape of the trade union movement'. *Trade Union World* 5 (2000): 1–39.
——. 'An ICFTU strategy to defend trade union rights: Decisions adopted by the 17th World Congress of the ICFTU'. Paper presented at the 17th World Congress of the ICFTU, Durban, 25–29 June 2000.
——. *ICFTU Viewpoints: A Selection of Editorials from Free Labour World*. Brussels: ICFTU, 1970.
——. *The ICFTU: What it is, What it does* ... [web]. International Confederation of Free Trade Unions, 2002 [cited 18 November 2002]. Available from http://www.icftu.org/displaydocument.asp?Index = 990916422.
——. 'Programme for balanced world development: 1982 ICFTU World Economic Review'. *Free Labour World* 379–80, February (1982): 14–16.

——. 'Report of the Asian Regional Secretary to the ICFTU Executive Board (report/document 7EB/7d)'. Brussels: From the IISH, Amsterdam, 1952.
——. 'Resolutions adopted by the ICFTU Sixth World Congress'. Paper presented at The Sixth World Congress of the ICFTU, Brussels, 1–3, December 1960.
——. 'Statements made and resolutions adopted by the Tenth World Congress of the ICFTU'. Paper presented at The Tenth World Congress of the ICFTU, London 1972.
——. 'Statements made and resolutions adopted by the Twelfth World Congress of the ICFTU'. Paper presented at The Twelfth World Congress of the ICFTU, Madrid 1979.
——. *Towards a New Economic and Social Order: ICFTU Development Charter*. Brussels: ICFTU, 1978.
——. 'Trade Unions, NGOs and Tripartism: Decisions adopted by the 17th World Congress of the ICFTU'. Paper presented at the 17th World Congress of the ICFTU, Durban, 3–7 April 2000.
——. 'Unions' world development priorities: The New Delhi Declaration'. *Free Labour World* 369–70 (1981).
ICFTU-Editorial. 'Being a trade unionist is a dangerous occupation'. *Free Labour World*, May (1994): 2.
——. 'The decolonization of trade'. *Free Labour World* 173, no. November (1964): 2.
——. 'Delegates unanimous on social clause'. *Free Labour World*, July/August (1996): 5.
——. 'ICFTU aims to be at the centre of a worldwide social movement'. *Free Labour World*, July/August (1996): 1.
——. 'ICFTU presses for a social clause'. *Free Labour World*, no. March (1994): 1.
——. 'ILO, ETUC, TUAC and WCL ... all fighting on the same side'. *Free Labour World*, July/August (1996): 2.
——. 'ITS develop contacts in the East'. *Free Labour World* 14, no. August (1990): 4.
——. 'Labour's plan for trade and aid'. *Free Labour World* 166, April (1964): 1–2.
——. 'Moscow's Agents in the Tribunes of the Free World'. *Free Labour World* 59, May (1959): 3–6.
——. 'Social clause debate reaches the ILO'. *Free Labour World*, no. June (1994): 8.
——. 'The social clause remains firmly on the agenda'. *Free Labour World*, November (1994): 3.
——. 'Transformation of trade unions in central and eastern Europe'. *Free Labour World* 14, August (1990): 6–7.
——. 'Union rights abuses "still alarming"', says ICFTU'. *Free Labour World*, October (1990): 1–2.
——. 'The WFTU in the service of the Kremlin's foreign policy'. *Free Labour World* 64, October (1955): 7–8.
——. 'Where "unions" stay silent'. *Free Labour World* 193–4, July–August (1966): 33.
——. 'World trade union unity?' *Free Labour World* 281, no. November (1973): 1.
——. 'The world's best kept secret'. *Free Labour World* 6, June (1994): 2–3.
Jordan, Bill, ICFTU. 'The Global Market – trade unionism's greatest challenge'. Paper presented at the International Confederation of Free Trade Unions, Sixteenth World Congress of the ICFTU 1996.
ICFTU-Statement. 'ICFTU Statement to UNCTAD IV'. Paper presented at the UNCTAD IV, Nairobi, 5–29 May 1976.

(IFBWW), International Federation of Building and Wood Workers. 'IFBWW Action Programme 1997–2001'. *Building and Wood: Bulletin of the International Federation of Building and Wood Workers* 2 (1997).
ILO. *Globalization* [Internet]. International Labour Organization: ACTRAV Bureau for Workers' Activities, 1998 [cited 18 January 2003]. Available from http://www.ilo.org/public/english/230actra/index.htm.
——. 'World Labour Report 1997–1998'. Geneva: International Labour Organization, 1997.
ITS. 'Extraordinary General Conference of the International Trade Secretariats: Resolution on ILO problems'. *Free Labour World* 106, no. April (1959): 179–80.
IUF. 'Executive Committee Report'. Paper presented at the 19th Congress, München, 25–31 May 1981.
——. 'Executive Committee Report'. Paper presented at the 18th Congress, Geneva, 23–28 January 1977.
James, Paul. *Nation Formation: Towards a Theory of Abstract Community*. London: Sage, 1996.
Jones, Barry R.J. 'Globalization in Perspective'. In *Globalization and its Critics: Perspectives from Political Economy*, edited by Randall D. Germain, 245–66. New York: St. Martins Press, 2000.
Jutterstöm, Stig. 'Help us improve the IMF News'. *IMF News* 4 (1999).
Karns, Margaret P. 'Postinternational politics and the growing glomerations of global governance'. In *Pondering Postinternationalism: A Paradigm for the Twenty-First Century*, edited by Heidi H. Hobbs, 39–60. Albany: State University of New York Press, 2000.
Katz, Harry and Owen Darbishire. *Converging Divergences: Worldwide Changes in Employment Systems*. New York: Cornell University Press, 2000.
Keenoy, Tom. 'Solidarity: The anti-trade union'. In *Trade Unions in Communist States*, edited by Alex Pravda and Blair A. Ruble, 149–72. London: Allen and Unwin, 1986.
Koscielski, Frank. *Divided Loyalties: American Unions and the Vietnam War*. New York: Garland Publishing, 1999.
Kreißig, Volkmar, and Erhard Schreiber. 'Participation and technological alternatives in the German Democratic Republic: The dilemma of scientific prediction and co-management by trade unions in the past and present'. In *Labour Relations in Transition in Eastern Europe*, edited by György Széll, 249–60. Berlin: Walter de Gruyter, 1992.
Kulpinska, Jolanta. 'Introrganizational determinants of workers' self-management activity'. In *Labour Relations in Transition in Eastern Europe*, edited by György Széll, 201–18. Berlin: Walter de Gruyter, 1992.
Lange, Peter, Michael Wallerstein, and Miriam Golden. 'The end of corporatism? Wage setting in the Nordic and Germanic countries'. In *The Workers of Nations: Industrial Relations in a Global Economy*, edited by Sanford M. Jacoby, 76–100. Oxford: Oxford University Press, 1995.
Laxer, Gordon. 'The movement that dare not speak its name: The return of left nationalism/internationalism'. *Alternatives* 26 (2001): 1–32.
Lee, Eric. 'Trade unions, computer communications and the new world order'. In *Labour Worldwide in the Era of Globalization: Alternative Union Models in the New World Order*, edited by Ronaldo Munck and Peter Waterman, 229–45. London: MacMillan, 1999.

Lipsig-Mummé, Carla. 'The politics of the new service economy'. In *Work of the Future: Global Perspectives*, edited by Paul James, Walter F. Veit, and Steve Wright, 109–25. St. Leonards: Allen and Unwin, 1997.
Littler, Craig R., and Gill Palmer. 'Communist and capitalist trade unionism: Comparisons and contrasts'. In *Trade Unions in Communist States*, edited by Alex Pravda and Blair A. Ruble, 253–75. London: Allen and Unwin, 1986.
Lorwin, Lewis L. *The International Labor Movement: History, Policies, Outlook*. New York: Harper and Brothers, 1953.
Macdonald, Duncan, Rachid Zeffane, and Roy Green. 'Managerial ideologies: Do they matter?' Paper presented at the 12th Association of Industrial Relations Academics of Australia and New Zealand, Wellington, New Zealand, 3–5 February 1998.
MacShane, Dennis. *International Labour and the Origins of the Cold War*. Oxford: Clarendon Press, 1992.
McMahon, Peter. 'Technology and globalization: An overview'. *Prometheus* 19, no. 3 (2001): 211–22.
Melchior, Arne. 'A global race for free trade agreements'. 1–28. Oslo: The Norwegian Institute of International Affairs, 2003.
Moody, Kim. *Workers in a Lean World: Unions in the International Economy*. London: Verso, 1997.
Munck, Ronaldo. *Globalisation and Labour: The New 'Great Transformation'*. London: Zed Books, 2002.
Munck, Ronnie. *The New International Labour Studies*. London: Zed Books, 1988.
Murillo, M. Victoria. 'From populism to neoliberalism: Labor unions and market reforms in Latin America'. *World Politics* 52 (2000): 135–74.
Murphy, Craig N. *International Organization and Industrial Change: Global Governance Since 1850*. Cambridge: Polity Press, 1994.
Novella, Agostino. 'WFTU: 5th World Trade Union Congress'. Paper presented at the 5th World Trade Union Congress, Moscow, 4–16 December 1961.
Nye, Joseph. 'The strength of international regionalism'. In *Transnational Industrial Relations: Proceedings of a Symposium Held at Geneva by the International Institute for Labour Studies*, edited by Hans Günter, 51–64. London: MacMillan, 1972.
O'Brien, Robert. 'Workers and world order: The tentative transformation of the international union movement'. *Review of International Studies* 26 (2000): 533–55.
O'Brien, Robert, Anne Marie Goetz, Jan Aart Scholte, and Marc Williams. *Contesting Global Governance: Multilateral Economic Institutions and Global Social Movements*. Cambridge: Cambridge University Press, 2000.
Oldenbroek, J.H. 'Communism and the ILO's work: Statement by J.H. Oldenbroek, ICFTU General Secretary, at the 38th International Labour Conference'. *Free Labour World* 62, no. August (1955): 34–6.
Osakwe, Chris. *The Participation of the Soviet Union in Universal International Organizations*. Leiden: A.W. Sijthoff, 1972.
Pasture, Patrick. 'Conclusion: Reflections on the fate of ideologies and trade unions'. In *The Lost Perspective? Trade Unions Between Ideology and Social Action in the New Europe*, edited by Patrick Pasture, Johan Verberckmoes and Hans De Witte, 377–404. Brookfield: Avebury, 1996.
——. 'Feminine intrusions in a culture of masculinity'. In *The Lost Perspective? Trade Unions Between Ideology and Social Action in the New Europe*, edited by

Patrick Pasture, Johan Verberckmoes, and Hans De Witte, 218–38. Brookfield: Avebury, 1996.
Peterson, Martin. *International Interest Organization and the Transformation of Postwar Society*. Stockholm: Almqvist and Wiksell International, 1980.
Petras, James and Dennis Engbarth. 'Third World industrialization and trade union struggles'. In *Trade Unions and the New Industrialization of the Third World*, edited by Roger Southall, 81–116. London: Zed, 1988.
Pravda, Alex. 'Trade unions in East European communist systems: Toward corporatism?' *International Political Science Review* 4, no. 2 (1983): 241–60.
Pravda, Alex, and Blair A. Ruble. 'Communist trade unions: Varieties of dualism'. In *Trade Unions in Communist States*, edited by Alex Pravda and Blair A. Ruble, 1–22. London: Allen and Unwin, 1986.
Press, Mike. 'The people's movement'. In *Solidarity for Survival: The Don Thomson Reader on Trade Union Internationalism*, edited by Mike Press and Don Thomson, 26–50. Nottingham: Bertrand Russell House, 1989.
Ranald, Patricia. 'Korean unions resisting the International Monetary Fund'. In *Protest and Globalisation*, edited by James Goodman, 185–202. Sydney: Pluto, 2002.
Rechenbach, Jeff, and Larry Cohen. 'Union Global Alliances at Multinational Corporations: A case study of the American alliance'. In *Unions in a Globalized Environment: Changing Borders, Organizational Boundaries, and Social Roles*, edited by Bruce Nissen, 76–99. New York: M.E. Sharpe, 2002.
Regini, Marino. 'The conditions for political exchange: How concertation emerged and collapsed in Italy and Great Britain'. In *Order and Conflict in Contemporary Capitalism*, edited by John H. Goldthorpe, 124–42. Oxford: Clarendon Press, 1984.
——. 'The past and future of social studies of labour movements'. In *The Future of Labour Movements*, edited by Marino Regini, 1–16. London: Sage, 1992.
——, ed. *The Future of Labour Movements*. London: Sage, 1992.
Reinalda, Bob. 'The ITF in the context of international trade unionism'. In *The International Transport-workers Federation 1914–1945*, edited by Bob Reinalda, 11–24. Amsterdam: Stichting Beheer IISG, 1997.
Reutter, Werner. 'Trade unions and politics in Eastern and Central Europe: Tripartism without corporatism'. In *The Lost Perspective? Trade Unions Between Ideology and Social Action in the New Europe*, edited by Patrick Pasture, Johan Verberckmoes and Hans De Witte, 137–58. Brookfield: Avebury, 1996.
Richter, Heinz. *British Intervention in Greece: From Varkiza to Civil War*. London: Merlin Press, 1986.
Ruble, Blair A. *Soviet Trade Unions: Their Development in the 1970s*. Cambridge: Cambridge University Press, 1981.
Rupert, Mark E. *Producing Hegemony: The Politics of Mass Production and American Global Power*. Cambridge: Cambridge University Press, 1995.
SALB-Editorial. 'COSATU, the ICFTU and dictatorships in Asia'. *South African Labour Bulletin* 17, no. 3 (1993): 76–81.
Sanglan, Delphine. 'Child labour: Ratify Convention 182'. *Labor Magazine* 2000/1 (2000/1): 19–20.
Santibanez, Hector and Standing Congress for Latin American Trade Union Unity Executive Secretary. 'The Road to Unity – The Achievement of Common Aims'. *World Trade Union Movement* 1, January (1970): 9–11.

Saville, John. 'Britain: Internationalism and the labour movement between the wars'. In *Internationalism in the Labour Movement: 1830–1940*, edited by Frits Van Holthoon and Marcel Van der Linden, 565–82. Leiden: E.J Brill, 1988.
Scholte, Jan Aart. 'Global capitalism and the state'. *International Affairs* 73, no. 3 (1997): 427–52.
———. 'Globalization: prospects for a paradigm shift'. In *Politics and Globalization: Knowledge, Ethics and Agency*, edited by Martin Shaw, 9–22. London: Routledge, 1999.
Silver, Beverly J. *Forces of Labor: Workers' Movements and Globalization Since 1870.* Cambridge: Cambridge University Press, 2003.
Sims, Beth. *Workers of the World Undermined: American Labor's Role in U.S. Foreign Policy.* Boston: South End Press, 1992.
Slaney, Dave. 'Solidarity and Self-Interest'. *NACLA: Report on the Americas* 22, no. 3 (1988): 28–36, 38–40.
Spalding, Hobart A. 'Solidarity forever?: Latin American unions and the international labor network'. *Latin American Research Review* XXIV, no. 2 (1989): 253–65.
———. 'The two Latin American foreign policies of the U.S. labor movement: The AFL-CIO top brass vs. rank-and-file'. *Science and Society* 56, no. 4 (1992–93): 421–39.
Taylor, Andrew J. *Trade Unions and Politics.* London: MacMillan, 1989.
Thirkell, John, Richard Scase, and Sarah Vickerstaff. 'Models of labour relations: Trends and Prospects'. In *Labour relations and Political Change in Eastern Europe: A Comparative Perspective*, edited by John Thirkell, Richard Scase, and Sarah Vickerstaff, 169–86. London: UCL Press, 1995.
Thorpe, Wayne. 'Syndicalist internationalism before World War II'. In *Revolutionary Syndicalism: An International Perspective*, edited by Marcel Van der Linden and Wayne Thorpe, 237–60. Aldershot: Scolar Press, 1990.
Thrift, Nigel. 'The rise of soft capitalism'. In *An Unruly World? Globalization, Governance and Geography*, edited by Andrew Herod, Gearóid O. Tuathail and Susan M. Roberts, 25–71. London: Routledge, 1998.
Touraine, Alain. 'Unionism as a social movement'. In *Unions in Transition: Entering the Second Century*, edited by Seymour Martin Lipset, 151–73. San Francisco: ICS Press, 1986.
Touraine, Alain, François Dubet, Michel Wieviorka, and Jan Strzelecki. *Solidarity: The Analysis of a Social Movement, Poland 1980–1981.* Cambridge: Cambridge University Press, 1982.
Trinca, Helen, and Anne Davies. *Waterfront: The Battle That Changed Australia.* Milsons Point: Doubleday, 2000.
(TUAC), Trade Union Advisory Committee to the OECD. 'Now is the time to reflate the global economy', 1–2. Paris: Trade Union Advisory Committee to the OECD, 2002.
———. 'Trade and Labour Standards: TUAC Briefing Note for OECD Workshop'. Paris: Trade Union Advisory Committee to the OECD (TUAC), 1996.
———. 'The Trade Union view on International Labour Standards'. Paper presented at the ITGLWF Conference on International Trade, Copenhagen, 5–6 October 1995.
———. 'Transforming the global economy: A stocktaking of trade union action with international and regional institutions', 1–72. Paris: Trade Union Advisory Committee to the OECD, 2000.

Bibliography

UNCTAD. 'World Investment Report 1997: Transnational corporations, market structure and competition policy'. New York: United Nations, 1997.
UNDP. 'UNDP: The Human Development Report'. New York: United Nations, 2002.
Unknown. 'Contacts with communists'. *Free Labour World* 273, March (1973): 2.
———. 'Trade unionism on the air'. *Syndicats*, March (1974): 30.
Upham, Martin. *Trade Unions and Employers' Organizations of the World.* London: Longman, 1993.
Verstraeste, Johan. 'World Confederation of Labour on the threshold of the 1990s'. *World Trade Union Movement* 1 (1989): 9–10.
Wad, Peter. 'The Japanization of the Malaysian Trade Union Movement'. In *Trade Unions and the New Industrialization of the Third World*, edited by Roger Southall, 210–29. London: Zed, 1988.
Walker, RBJ. 'Social movements/world politics.' *Millennium: Journal of International Studies* 23, no. 3 (1994): 669–700.
Waterman, Peter. 'The ICFTU in SA: Admissions, revelations, silences'. *South African Labour Bulletin* 17, no. 3 (1993): 82–4.
———. *International Labour Communication by Computer: The Fifth International?*, Working Paper Series number 129, July 1992. The Hague: ISS, 1992.
———. 'Needed: A new communications model for a new working-class internationalism'. In *For a New Labour Internationalism: A Set of Reprints and Working Papers*, edited by Peter Waterman, 233–55. The Hague: ILERI, 1985.
———. 'The new social unionism: A new union model for a new world order'. In *Labour Worldwide in the Era of Globalization: Alternative Union Models in the New World Order*, edited by Ronaldo Munck and Peter Waterman, 247–64. London: MacMillan, 1999.
———. 'Social movement unionism: A new model for a new world order'. *Review* 16, no. 3 (1993): 245–78.
———. *A Spectre is Haunting Labour Internationalism, The Spectre of Communism* [Web]. Hartford Web Publishing, 2000 [cited 15/8/2001, 2001]. Available from http://hartford-hwp.com/archives/26/035.html.
WCL. *What's the WCL?* [Web]. World Confederation of Labour, 2002 [cited 20 November 2002]. Available from http://www.cmt-wcl.org/1cmt-wcl/cmt-en/01whatis.htm.
(WCL), World Confederation of Labour. 'The policy resolution and the topical resolutions of the WCL'. Paper presented at the 25th Congress of the WCL, Roumania, October 2001.
———. *Social Clauses – Reciprocal Social Commitments (RSCs) as Levers* [Internet]. World Confederation of Labour, 2000 [cited 18 December 2002]. Available from http://www.cmt-wcl.org.
———. *The World Confederation of Labour (WCL).* Brussels, 1977.
———. 'World Confederation of Labour: Activities Report 1998–2001'. Brussels: World Confederation of Labour, 2001.
WCL-Editorial. 'Women – Marching to be respected'. *Labor Magazine* 2000/1 (2000/1).
Weiler, Peter. *British Labour and the Cold War.* Stanford: Stanford University Press, 1988.
Western, Bruce. *Between Class and Market: Postwar Unionization in the Capitalist Democracies.* New Jersey: Princeton University Press, 1997.

WFTU. *In the Thick of the Struggle: 10 Questions and Answers on the Activities and Policies of the WFTU*. Prague: WFTU, 1965.
——. 'Trade unions and the challenges of the 1980s: 10th World Trade Union Congress'. Paper presented at the 10th World Trade Union Congress, Havana, Cuba, 10–15 February 1982.
——. *World Federation of Trade Unions: 1945–1985*. Prague: WFTU, 1985.
WFTU-Dossier. 'The World Federation of Trade Unions and the United Nations Organisation'. *World Trade Union Movement* 11, November (1972): I–XII.
WFTU-Editorial. 'Defenders of the old order'. *World Trade Union Movement* 12 (1981): 1–2.
——. 'Direct broadcast satellites, cable TV and mass participation in television'. *World Trade Union Movement* 9 (1990): 32–3.
——. 'A great moment in the history of the WFTU and of the AATUF'. *World Trade Union Movement* 4, April (1969): 1–6.
——. 'Solidarity for development'. *World Trade Union Movement*, March (1980): 1.
——. 'Transnational corporations and their loot of developing countries'. *World Trade Union Movement*, no. 2 (1983): 31–2.
——. 'The trilateral – its philosophy and objectives'. *World Trade Union Movement* 9, September (1980): 30–1.
——. 'US-led opposition rejects international economic action'. *World Trade Union Movement* 3 (1984): 28–30.
——. 'With the WCL we are ready'. *World Trade Union Movement* 2 (1978): 11–12.
Williamson, Hugh. 'Japanese enterprise unions in transnational companies: prospects for international co-operation'. *Capital and Class* 45 (1991).
Wills, Jane. 'Great expectations: Three years in the life of one EWC'. *European Journal of Industrial Relations* 6, no. 1 (2000): 85–107.
——. 'Taking on the cosmocorps: Experiments in transnational labor organization'. *Economic Geography* 74 (1998): 111–30.
Wilson, Jeanne L. 'The People's Republic of China'. In *Trade Unions in Communist States*, edited by Alex Pravda and Blair A. Ruble, 219–52. London: Allen and Unwin, 1986.
Windmuller, J.P. *The International Trade Union Movement*. London: Kluwer, 1980.
Windmuller, J.P. and S.K. Pursey. 'The international trade union movement'. In *Comparative Labour Law and Industrial Relations in Industrial Market Economies*, edited by R. Blanpain and C. Engels, 83–107. The Hague: Kluwer Law International, 1998.
Wiseman, John. 'Trade union solidarity: The Australian waterfront, 1998'. In *Protest and Globalisation*, edited by James Goodman, 170–84. Sydney: Pluto, 2002.
Wood, Ellen Meiksins, Peter Meiksins, and Michael Yates, eds. *Rising from the Ashes?: Labor in the Age of "global" Capitalism*. New York: Monthly Review Press, 1998.
Woodhouse, C.M. *The Struggle for Greece, 1941–1949*. London: Hart-Gibbon, MacGibbon, 1976.
Zakaria, Ibrahim. 'The unions must coordinate their efforts in the search for a solution to the development crisis (extracts from the introduction to the discussion)'. Paper presented at the 36th Session of the WFTU General Council 1984.

Index

Africa 14, 20, 22, 27, 29, 33, 38–9, 50, 52–5, 58, 70, 75, 78, 83, 88, 90, 117, 124, 133, 147, 151–2
African Trade Union Confederation, ATUC 55
AFRO 29, 147
All-African Trade Union Federation 55
General Union of Workers of Black Africa 55
see also individual countries
African Regional Organization, AFRO 29, 147
see also International Confederation of Free Trade Unions, ICFTU
African Trade Union Confederation, ATUC 55
Agency of International Development 106
All Union Central Council of Trade Unions, AUCCTU 17, 30, 53, 61, 108–9
Profintern 14–17, 28
All-African Trade Union Federation 55
All China Federation of Trade Unions 165n,
All Poland Trade Union Alliance 134
amalgamations/consolidation 28, 32, 46, 76, 107, 123, 124–5, 127, 154, 179n, 180n
ameliorative statism 139, 140
see also corporatism; developmentalism; labour–state nexus
American Federation of Labor 15, 17, 26, 31, 52
American Federation of Labor-Congress of Industrial Organizations, AFL-CIO 38–9, 51, 59, 34, 89, 99, 104, 105, 107, 132, 134, 155

American Institute for Free Labor Development, AIFLD 52, 165, 174n
anarchism 9, 10, 17, 72
Anti Sweatshop Movement 155
anti-colonialism 9, 23, 50, 54, 56, 138
Arrighi, Giovanni 49, 164n
Asia 20–2, 27, 36, 38, 50, 52, 54, 61, 75, 88, 90, 104, 107, 143, 146, 151
Asian and Pacific Regional Organization, APRO 107, 147
Asian Regional Organization, ARO 29, 38
Association of South East Asian Nations, ASEAN 126, 146, 147
see also individual countries
Asia Monitor Resource Centre 152
Asian and Pacific Regional Organization, APRO 107, 147
Asian Development Bank 147
Asian Regional Organization, ARO 29, 38
Association of South East Asian Nations, ASEAN 126, 146, 147
Australia 14, 100, 133, 153, 155
Australian Council of Trade Unions, ACTU 153

bilateral trade agreements 81, 147, 154, 156
Boswell, Terry 181n
Brazil 83, 89, 103, 152
Bretton Woods institutions 22, 67, 71, 145
see also General Agreement on Tariffs and Trade; World Trade Organization; World Bank
Busch, Garry 160n, 161n, 165n, 171n
business unionism 16, 107

Camilleri, Joseph 158n, 167n
Campaign for Labour Rights 155

Canada 100, 132, 133, 155
Canadian Auto Workers 155
Canadian Congress of Labour 32
capital mobility 11, 20, 28, 36
Carew, Anthony 161n, 168n, 169n, 170n, 174n
Caribbean 20, 146
Caribbean Common Market 146
Caribbean Congress of Labour 146
Caribbean Social Charter 146
Carr, Barry 155, 158n, 181n, 188n
casualization 141, 142
Central America 155
Central America Free Trade Agreement 155
Centro de Información Laboral y Asesoría Sindical 152
child labour 111, 136, 137, 151
Chile 52, 89
China 20, 54, 88, 107
civil society 28, 153
class-based internationals 15, 16, 19, 23, 25, 150
 see also Comintern; Industrial Workers of the World; International Workingmen's Association (I and II); Second International
Clean Clothes Campaign 151
Coalition for Justice in the Maquiladoras 155
coercive statist corporatism 47, 104
Cold War 22, 23, 36, 71, 80, 88, 135, 138, 140, 141, 144, 154, 162n, 163n, 165n, 169n, 182n, 183n, 186n
Colonial Labour Advisory Committee 53
colonialism 9, 50, 54, 56, 88, 90, 138
Comintern 14, 16, 17
 see also the Third International
Committee to Support Maquiladoras 155
communication media 8, 21, 33–5, 46, 68–70, 73, 79–80, 82–3, 93, 116, 119, 127, 129, 130–1, 139
 see also internal integrative dimension of change

communism 9, 26, 38, 39, 45, 105, 134
communitarianism 60, 143, 157
company unions 97
 see also business unionism
Confederación de Trabajordores de América Latina 31, 54
Confederación de Trabajordores de Mexico, CTM 132
Confederación de Trabajordores de Venezuela 97
Confédération Générale du Travail, CGT 40, 103
Confederation of Public Sector Trade Unions, RENGO 107
Confederazione Generale Italiana del Lavoro, CGIL 40, 54, 98
conferences 34, 35, 38, 40, 80, 81, 83, 85, 111, 113, 147
Congress of South African Trade Unions, COSATU 133, 152, 168n
conservative worldviews 8, 12, 22, 23, 43–5, 72, 96, 120, 121, 138
 see also statism
corporatism 9, 10, 16, 22, 43–5, 47, 48–50, 56, 59, 60, 65, 95–104, 107–10, 121, 126, 141–3, 154, 156
 statist coercive corporatism 47, 104, 141, 143
 voluntarist bargained corporatism 47–9, 95–6, 98, 99–103, 109, 135
Cox, Robert 59, 165n

decolonization 11, 21, 22, 30, 36, 41, 42, 64
Deutscher Gewerkschaftsbund, DGB 99
developmentalism 8, 9, 12, 19, 22, 23, 24, 42, 43, 44, 45, 46, 60, 63, 64, 65, 72, 89, 90, 91, 92, 93, 94, 112, 115, 121, 123, 126, 129, 131, 138, 139, 144, 146, 148, 150
Drainville, André 17, 159n

Eastern Europe 20, 34, 36, 37, 39, 40, 49, 88, 109, 115, 124, 134, 135, 141, 143, 164n, 173n, 179n, 182n, 183n, 185n, 189n, 190n
 see also individual countries

El Salvador 89, 170n, 171n, 174n
emancipatory civil realm movements
 5, 23, 150, 151, 152, 153, 155
emancipatory worldviews 8, 9, 12,
 22, 23, 42–5, 72, 120–1, 133, 138
 see also anarchism; communism;
  environmentalism; feminism;
  Marxism; socialism
  syndicalism
Europe 16, 20, 31, 81, 90, 108,
 126, 141
European Economic Community, EEC
 32, 58, 62, 87, 114
European Trade Union Confederation,
 ETUC 78, 86–8, 125, 136–7, 146
European Union, EU 125, 126, 146
European Works Councils, EWC 125
Export Processing Zones 69, 97,
 151, 155
external political dimension of
 change 9, 10, 89, 144, 146, 148

Fair Trade Association 155
Fair Wear International 155
feminism 9, 44, 72, 121
Focus on the Global South 152
Food and Agriculture Organization,
 FAO 57, 58, 61, 71, 111,
 113, 114
Fordism 13, 16, 20, 68, 69, 96, 121
 see also managerialism, scientific
  management, Taylorism
Forman, Michael 50
Free Labour World 33, 34, 37, 60,
 82, 151
free trade 31, 41, 58, 69, 72, 91, 92,
 97, 111, 115, 120, 132, 145, 147,
 154, 155, 156
free trade agreements 31, 97, 120,
 132, 147, 154, 155, 156
Free Trade of the Americas 155
Free Trade Zones 69, 97

General Agreement on Tariffs and
 Trade, GATT 22, 57, 71, 111, 113
General Union of Workers of Black
 Africa 55
Gills, Barry 158n
global civil society 4

Global March Against Child
 Labour 151
Global Union Federations 179n,
 see International Trade
 Secretariats, ITS
globalization, agency-focused 3, 4
globalization, structure-focused 3
Gramsci, Antonio 156, 159n
Group of Seven (G-7) 71, 120
Group of Twenty (G-20) 120
Guatemala 52, 89
Gumbrell-McCormick, Rebecca
 169n, 170n, 175n, 182n

Harrod, Jeffrey 158n, 179n
Herod, Andrew 158n, 163n, 175n,
 182n, 183n, 184n
Histadrut 55
Human Resources Management 141
human rights 90, 111, 123, 128, 137,
 139, 151, 153
Human Rights Watch 151

ICFTU Executive Board 58, 59, 81,
 90, 130
ICFTU Online 128, 129
ICFTU World Congress 35, 123,
 136, 151
ideology 8, 11, 12, 13, 29, 22–4, 62,
 72, 79, 96, 100, 111, 112, 120–1,
 129, 132, 140–1, 144
India 88, 133, 165n, 169n,
 170n, 182n
Industrial Workers of the World,
 IWW 16
instrumental statism 154
instrumentalism 8, 9, 10, 12, 22,
 42–5, 49, 72, 109, 115, 120, 121,
 137, 138, 139, 144, 154
integrative dimension of change
 8, 32–46, 79–83, 124, 127,
 131–9, 146
Inter-American Development
 Bank 146
interests and ideas 36–46, 86–93,
 131–9
inter-governmental organizations
 110, 111–14, 119, 120, 123, 126,
 128, 144–7

International Centre for Trade Union
    Rights 152
International Confederation of Arab
    Trade Unions 39, 54, 55, 78
International Confederation of Free
    Trade Unions, ICFTU 34–5,
    38–40, 44–9, 62–3, 66–71, 83–5,
    88–100, 116, 119–23, 131–7,
    141–5, 153–5, *passim*
International Federation of Chemical,
    Energy, Mine and General
    Workers' Unions, ICEM 128
International Federation of Trade
    Unions, IFTU 14, 15, 25,
    26, 28
International Labor Rights Education
    and Research Fund 152
International Labour Organization,
    ILO 13, 57–63, 111–14, 128,
    133, 144, 166
International Metalworkers'
    Federation, IMF 40, 76
International Monetary Fund, IMF
    28, 71, 111, 113, 120, 145,
    147, 153
International Trade Secretariats, ITS
    14, 15, 26–30, 35, 40, 52, 59,
    62–4, 75–7, 82, 87, 113, 114,
    123, 124, 126, 128, 134, 136,
    137, 147, 151
International Union of Food,
    Agricultural, Hotel, Restaurant,
    Catering, Tobacco and Allied
    Workers' Associations, IUF 177n,
    179n, 187n
International Workingmen's
    Association, IWMA (First
    International) 16
International Workingmen's
    Association, IWMA (II, the
    syndicalist international)
    15, 16, 28

James, Paul 159n, 167n
Japan 20, 78, 89, 101, 106, 107,
    123, 143
    see also business unionism;
    company unions; just-in-time;
    RENGO; Toyotism

Jordan, Bill 136
just-in-time 141

Karns, Margaret 119
Keynesianism 9, 22, 23, 36, 42, 47,
    48, 64, 72, 96, 99, 121, 154
knowledge based networks of
    critique 152
Korean Women Workers' Associations
    United 153

labour internationalism 2, 150, 154
Labour Notes 152
LabourStart 187n
labour standards 69, 136, 137,
    145, 155
labour–state nexus 56, 59, 96, 106,
    109, 140, 143, 147
Landsorganisationen i Sverige,
    LO 99, 163n, 170n
Latin America 166n, 168n, 169n,
    170n, 172n, 174n, 175n, 179n
    *see also individual countries and
    confederations*
Laxer, Gordon 143
lean production 141
Lee, Eric 129, 180n, 181n, 187n
liberalism 72

MacShane, Denis 162n
managerialism 16, 167n, 185n
Maquiladoras 97, 155
    see also the Coalition for Justice in
    the Maquiladoras; Committee
    to Support Maquiladoras;
    Mexico; Export Processing
    Zones; North American Free
    Trade Agreement, NAFTA
Maritime Union of Australia 153
Marshall Plan 20, 31, 36, 41, 43
Marxism 44, 76
Meany, George 52
Mehmet, Ozay 43
MERCOSUR 146, 178n
Mercosur Trade Union Commission
    146
Mexican Action Network on Free
    Trade 155
Mexico 29, 48, 97, 103, 132

modernization 9, 16, 20, 24, 40, 41, 42, 43, 49, 64, 91, 154
see also developmentalism
Moody, Kim 161n, 165n, 172n
Multilateral Agreement on Investment, MAI 132, 133
multinational corporations 42, 77, 91, 117, 125, 128, 132, 136, 137, 141, 144
Munck, Ronaldo 158n, 173n, 180n, 188n
Murphy, Craig 160n, 167n

National Endowment for Democracy 106
nationalism 39, 67, 72, 132, 143
neoliberalism 13, 43, 71, 72, 89, 96, 98, 100, 107, 119–21, 129, 134, 135, 137, 138, 141, 142, 144, 146
New International Division of Labour 68
New International Economic Order 111
new social unionism 152, 156n, 188n
see also social movement unionism
Nicaragua 89
non-aligned movement 32, 38, 135
non-governmental organizations, NGOs 71, 150, 151, 159n, 178n
and labour leaders' attitude to 150
see also oppositional civil realm actors
North American Free Trade Agreement, NAFTA 126, 132, 155

O'Brien, Robert 147, 158n, 179n, 182n, 184n
oppositional civil realm actors 5, 23, 150, 151, 152, 153, 155
Organizacion Regional Interamericana de Trabajadores, ORIT 29, 33, 52, 89, 90, 146
Organization for Economic Cooperation and Development, OECD 30, 31, 57, 62, 78, 113, 114, 124, 128, 132, 133, 137, 146
organizational dimension of change 6–24, 25–32, 74–9, 123–7

parliamentarianism 14, 154
Poland 37, 76, 83, 101, 102, 109, 133
Poland's Central Council of Trade Unions 109
post-Fordism 13, 68, 96, 121
Pravda, Alex 101
Press, Mike 174n
privatization 96, 97, 100, 118, 138, 141
Profintern 14–17, 28
see also Red International of Labour Unions

Reagan, Ronald 100, 105
Red International of Labour Unions, or RILU 159n
Regini, Marino 68, 96
regionalism 86, 87, 129, 135, 160n
Reinalda, Bob 168n
relationships (internal communicative) 5, 8, 11, 32, 33, 35, 79, 82, 84, 87, 93, 127, 131, 132, 139, 149
republicanism 16, 100, 138
Resource Centre of the Americas 152
Ruble, Blair 101, 108
Rupert, Mark 42, 162n, 164n
Russia 8, 124, 185n

scientific management 20, 43
see also Fordism; managerialism; Taylorism
Second International 16
self determination 16, 50
see also republicanism, anti colonialism
Sims, Beth 105, 164n
Social Alert 151
social clause 133, 136–7, 146
and free trade agreements 133, 136–7, 146, 175n, 181n, 182n
social democracy 9, 16, 47, 48, 49, 96, 97, 98, 100, 105, 142, 154, 170n, 172n
social movement unionism 152, 153, 188n
see also new social unionism

social movements 2, 109, 151, 152, 153, 155, 156, 158n
socialism 9, 15, 22–3, 40–1, 44–5, 52, 62, 72, 76, 82, 115, 124, 128, 161n, 164n
  see also emancipatory worldviews
Solidarność 76, 102, 109, 175n
South Africa 14, 78, 83, 133, 152, 167n, 168n, 170n, 175n, 176n, 182n
  and apartheid 42, 91, 111, 112, 151, 152
  COSATU 133, 152, 168
South Korea 89, 103, 152, 153, 173n, 188n
Southern African Development Community 147
Spain 15, 16, 17, 44, 180n
Spalding, Hobart 164n, 165n, 174n, 175n
statehood 16, 23, 51
statism 10, 16, 23–4, 44, 45, 47–50, 55, 56, 72, 80, 95, 101–3, 107–9, 121, 123, 126, 138, 139, 140, 141, 143–5, 150, 154, 158n, 163n
statist coercive corporatism 47, 104, 141, 143
Stevis, Dimitri 181n
structural imperatives, outlined 3, 4, 11, 12, 19–24, 28, 32, 36, 65–73, 86, 101, 117–26, 144, 149, 158n
structure of ideology 12, 20, 22, 72, 120, 121, 126
structure of organization 11, 20, 21, 36, 70, 71, 87, 119, 121, 125, 126, 148, 150
structure of production 11, 20, 36, 56, 68, 70, 79, 99, 117, 118, 121, 126
symbolic representation 8
syndicalism 9, 15, 16, 17, 28, 44, 45, 52, 76, 138, 159n

Taylorism 43
  see also Fordism; managerialism; scientific management
technology 21, 24, 33, 35, 43, 68, 118, 119, 121, 128, 129, 177n, 180n

The Voice of Free Trade Unions 34, 83, 169n
Third International 14, 16, 17
  see also Comintern
Third World 23, 40, 41, 43, 69, 77, 81, 83, 91, 103, 105, 118, 120, 133, 135, 136
Third World Network 152
Thomson, Don 174n
Touraine, Alain 2, 158n, 171n
Toyotism 68, 141
Trade Union Advisory Committee, TUAC 30, 31, 57, 62, 78, 124, 128, 133, 137, 146
Trade Union Internationals, TUI 30, 75, 158n
Trades Union Congress, TUC 15, 17, 26, 38, 39, 53, 163n
Transnationals Information Exchange 52
Trilateral Commission 71, 113, 120

Union Aid Abroad-APHEDA 153
Union Network International, UNI 179n, 187n
United Nations 12, 22, 35, 57–63, 71, 91, 111–14, 120, 157
United Nations Development Programme, UNDP 177n
United Nations General Assembly 111
United Nations, Educational, Scientific and Cultural Organization, UNESCO 57, 61, 71, 111, 113
United States of America 15, 17, 26, 38, 39, 45, 51, 52, 53, 59, 60, 61, 70, 90, 105, 106, 113, 151, 161, 164
USSR 13, 14, 17, 22, 30, 37, 40, 42, 50, 54, 60, 61, 67, 70, 102, 107, 108, 109, 117, 124, 185n

Venezuela 38, 97, 98, 172n, 185n
Vietnam War 164n
violence directed at unionists 111, 142, 159n, 183n
voluntarist bargained corporatism 47–9, 95–6, 98, 99–103, 109, 135

Waterman, Peter 83, 158n, 162n, 165n, 168n, 169n, 170n, 180n, 182n, 188n
welfare state 12, 13, 17, 22, 24, 36, 48, 70, 96
World Bank 22, 71, 113, 120, 145, 147
World Company Councils 77
World Confederation of Labour, WCL 43, 78, 81, 82, 87, 88, 113, 124, 136, 146, 151, 166n, 169n, 176n, 178n, 179n, 183n, 186n, 187n
World Federation of Trade Unions, WFTU (post-1949 incarnation) 13, 28, 31, 33, 35, 53, 60, 64, 74, 75, 80, 83, 107, 112, 124, 126, 133, 144
World Federation of Trade Unions, WFTU (pre-1949 incarnation) 13, 25, 36, 40, 160n
World Health Organization, WHO 57, 61
World Organization Against Torture 151
World Trade Organization, WTO 118, 120, 126, 128, 133, 137, 145, 147, 157, 181n
worldwide web 115, 124, 127, 129, 130